THE GALLIC MUSE

Watteau: Mezzetino (*circa* 1715)

THE GALLIC MUSE

Laurence Davies

SOUTH BRUNSWICK

NEW YORK: A. S. BARNES AND COMPANY

THE GALLIC MUSE. © Laurence Davies, 1967. First American edition published 1969 by A. S. Barnes and Company, Inc., Cranbury, New Jersey 08512

Library of Congress Catalogue Card No.: 68–27201

6931
Printed in the United States of America

Voici des fruits, des fleurs, des feuilles et des branches,
Et puis voici mon cœur qui ne bat que pour vous. . . .

Verlaine: *Romances sans paroles.*

CONTENTS

ILLUSTRATIONS

Watteau: Mezzetino (circa 1715), frontispiece
Metropolitan Museum of Art, New York

Portrait of Claude Debussy by Marcel Baschet, facing p. 64
with acknowledgment to M. Paul Baschet

Portrait of Maurice Ravel by Ouvré, facing p. 128
'La Revue Musicale', Paris

Francis Poulenc, facing p. 160
Librairie Plon, Paris

ACKNOWLEDGMENTS

My debts in writing this book will in all probability be familiar to students of the literature relating to French music. I have attempted to list the principal sources upon which I have relied in my bibliography, and diligent readers will have no difficulty in inferring from the range of my quotations which of these I have had to fall back on most heavily.

For help and advice incurred in the writing itself I must acknowledge some rather special obligations. My appraisal of French keyboard music, for instance, was greatly assisted by the correspondence I received on that subject from Mlle Evelyne Crochet, possibly the finest contemporary exponent of Fauré's piano works. I was also fortunate in securing the advice of Mr Patrick Piggott, head of B.B.C. Music Programmes for the Midland Region, who was responsible for giving the English premières of one or two of the works I describe. Mr Terence Beckles, a veteran supporter of Poulenc's music, made several interesting suggestions to me on that subject, and incidentally inspired me with his idiomatic playing of the composer's works. I should perhaps add that my own teacher, the late Mark Hambourg, deserves some credit for having equipped me with sufficient technique at the piano to struggle through many French scores I should otherwise have had no opportunity of hearing.

Messrs Durand, of the Place Madeleine, Paris, very kindly supplied me with information about scores published by them: especially those of Poulenc which the composer saw fit to revise after publication. Similarly United Music Publishers, of Montague Street, London, went to an immense amount of trouble to import scores for me where these were not available in British libraries. I am grateful to the Gramophone Exchange for having obtained pressings of several French gramophone records. The London firm of Discurio Ltd was also helpful in this respect. The librarian and staff of the University College of South Wales and Monmouthshire, Cardiff, have placed me in their debt for having ordered various books and scores on my behalf. Messrs Galignani, of the rue de Rivoli, Paris, and Hachette & Co., of Regent Street, London, have performed a similar service.

I have relied on the assistance of my wife in reading and commenting on the manuscript, and her suggestions have resulted in one or two modifications of expression. Any errors or omissions that may remain are naturally my sole responsibility.

The illustrations used in this book call for special acknowledgment, and I must proclaim my obligation to M. Paul Baschet for permission to reproduce the painting of Debussy by Marcel Baschet; to the Librairie Plon, Paris, for the photograph of Poulenc; to the editor of the *Revue Musicale*, Paris, for the use of the Ouvré portrait of Ravel; and to the Metropolitan Museum of Art, New York, for allowing me to show the Watteau frontispiece.

To the staff of Messrs J. M. Dent & Sons I owe a considerable debt of gratitude, both for editorial advice and assistance with production. In particular I should like to thank Mrs Murielle Paterson, whose courtesy and patience were exceptional.

PREFACE

In a work of this nature there are bound to be certain perplexities
which it must be the duty of the author to clear up at the outset.
These relate to the aim and scope of the enterprise, but may also
concern the method it exhibits. Without some information on
these practical matters, the general reader will doubtless find it
difficult to visualize the range of topics he may expect to see
discussed; while the critic may labour under a misapprehension
regarding the degree of originality or indebtedness of the enterprise.

The aim of this book is to present a series of linked essays on
French composers of the past hundred years, giving some account
of the music they wrote. The object is thus partly biographical and
partly critical. There is a common theme to the essays, and this is to
be interpreted as the development of French music throughout the
period in question. Some effort has been expended on relating
each composer to the others in the gallery, a task which proposed
itself in the realm of personal relationships as well as musical
influences. There is an element of continuity in the productions of
these musicians, as I hope to show, so that one of my purposes
has been to point to the existence of a tradition. This is not
necessarily to say that I have clung to the view that each composer
represented had a direct impact on his immediate successor, as
much as that they responded to a common cultural disposition.
It will become evident that their unity of spirit was what led
to the adoption of the same or similar musical genres. Of these
favoured genres, the two which stand out, and with which I shall
therefore be most concerned, are the art-song, or mélodie, and the
informal piano work. They are two fields in which it is arguable
that the French have especially excelled; though I do not wish
to imply that other forms of music have not gained widespread
importance within the Gallic mould. Upon these remaining forms
—and the opera, the ballet, the symphonic poem and the chamber

divertimento all suggest themselves for inclusion—I have naturally felt quite free to comment. My introduction in fact goes some way towards explaining in more detail what is meant by the French musical tradition, and why it is that certain forms have had such a special appeal.

In stating that my purpose has been both musical and biographical, I should not want it thought that I had deliberately attempted a search for new facts upon which to base a documentary reappraisal of the entire period; on the contrary, my interest has been a good deal more psychological than documentary, and I have above all tried to offer a series of portraits of the men and their music. As with most portraitists, this has meant that I have been more anxious to get a good likeness than I have to add to the historical or technical knowledge which has accumulated around my sitters. As Rollo Myers has rightly said, in his introduction to *The Life and Works of Maurice Ravel*, 'the main task of the musical biographer is to expound the connection between the inner life of the artist, with all its secret tensions, aspirations and deceptions, and its outward projection revealed in his works'. This lucid statement of aim, suitably scaled down to comply with the demands of the essay form, could well serve to epitomize the standpoint from which I approached the writing of this book.

For the facts of each composer's life, then, I have relied on the available sources, both French and English, to guide me. Quite frequently, however, I have discovered discrepancies or contradictions of which the general public may be unaware, and it has more than once occurred to me that these sources are not particularly well known. There even seems to be a certain amount of ignorance about works which have not been translated from the one language into the other. I do feel, therefore, that my efforts at collation—especially where they may have been fortunate enough to aspire to brevity and readability—will serve a worth-while purpose. Indeed it seems to me that there is a clear need for a compact study of the lives and music of modern French composers, many of whom are still suffering from neglect in Britain, if not any longer in their own country. The reader who looks up Duparc or Poulenc, for instance, in a standard history of music for English and American students, such as Paul Henry Lang's otherwise excellent

Music in Western Civilisation—which incidentally runs to over a thousand pages—will find no mention of either name in the index. If this is viewed as a surprising omission, I can only plead that I am not responsible for it, and add that it is time we stopped taking established composers so much for granted and asked ourselves instead how much we really know concerning them and their works.

In the matter of musical commentary, I have again held to the position that the general reader must be first served, and that he is more likely to want to learn something of a composer's style and preoccupations, the development of his musical outlook and so on, than he is to demand constant technical stimulation. There are occasions when I have resorted to technical parlance, and I certainly expect my reader to absorb some of the points I make with the aid of a score, but I have none the less felt inclined to dispense with musical examples, partly because their value out of context seems somewhat questionable and also on account of my wish to preserve the essay format. If I must be judged on the strength of this book I would obviously wish it to be as an essayist and not as a musicologist.

I can offer my reader one further incentive. In choosing the six composers who comprise my portrayal I gave a fair amount of thought to the problem of balance. That is I endeavoured, as far as this was possible within the restrictions imposed by the other ideals mentioned, to select my subjects so that they would constitute a sufficiently diverse assembly. Their profiles were intended to suggest contrast. The reader who makes his way through this book chronologically—and there is no good reason why he should not dip more at random if it pleases him—may accordingly expect to encounter a fresh guise in each chapter.

Finally, those of my readers who are keen on other arts as well as music will discover much cross reference between one art and another. This is the result of a deliberate policy of mine, undertaken in the hope of adding to the reader's illumination. French poetry in particular seemed to me an indispensable attendant study to my consideration of the growth of the mélodie, and I therefore did not hesitate to discourse on poets like Baudelaire, Verlaine, Apollinaire and Eluard, where I felt they had impinged on the imaginations of my subjects. I believe whole-heartedly that too much musical criticism in the past has been concerned with what Mr Desmond Shawe-Taylor has called 'musicological fact-grubbing', and not enough attention has been given to placing music within the prevailing aesthetic mood of the period under scrutiny. Fortunately there is every reason to suppose that this long-standing sin is in the process of being expiated, as the splendid biography of Debussy by Mr Edward Lockspeiser amply goes to show. The title chosen for my own book is meant to stand as an indication of its liberal presumptions.

L. D.

Vienna 1965

INTRODUCTION

THE novelist Stendhal, who was enough of a music lover to have written a life of Rossini, was also prone to deliver oracular asides about the state of that gentle art in the various countries he had visited. Using the licence of his calling to indulge in one of those magnificently insupportable generalizations for which his race is so celebrated, he once argued:

The Germans, who make doctrines out of everything, deal with music learnedly; the Italians, being voluptuous, seek in it lively, though fleeting, sensations; the French, more vain than perceptive, manage to speak of it wittily; and the English pay for it. . . .

Without allowing ourselves to be inveigled into upholding these amusing national stereotypes, let us for the moment simply admit that they present us with at least two awkward questions, which we shall have to try to solve before proceeding any further with our study. One of these relates to whether or not it is really permissible to talk about a nation's artistic heritage as if it embodied certain psychological characteristics more properly attributable to persons or groups within that nation. The second question, which rather presupposes that we shall give some sort of qualified affirmative to the first, is whether or not the French have a specific musical ideal to which their composers naturally subscribe.

To begin with the former problem, few persons who have kept abreast of the recent revolution in the social sciences would nowadays wish to disguise their scepticism about the notion of national character. Rejecting the idea that there is a basis for biological variation between nations, we should prefer to argue, somewhat more cautiously, that it is possible for nations as well as institutions to propose for their peoples some accepted norm of conduct, which may then be fortified by means of laws, rewards and punishments, the establishment of fixed patterns of training and education and the like. This is the process psychologists describe as secondary reinforcement. It constitutes a commonplace of all sophisticated communities. Less generally appreciated perhaps is the corollary that such regularization of behaviour must originate in the conceptions of an élite, and can only be attributed to the mass of the people in so far as they continue to help to entrench it. Artists usually represent an élite, and the cultural diffusion by which their work comes to be entrenched must be related, in any analysis, to the efforts made by teachers, journalists and other professed propagandists who, notwithstanding their own gifts, have most to do with communication. It is out of some such series of configurations that national and other traditions are born. Lest these remarks should already have come to sound too platitudinous, let us move on to where they take us in the matter of aesthetics, since we are not in any case concerned with their social ramifications.

Any art must begin by some act of choice on the part of the artist—that much is axiomatic. Once he has created his art form, however, it comes to fulfil a double function: that of aesthetic object, and also that of model. This second function may not always appear significant to the artist himself, though it usually is to the élite of which he is a member. Models do not invariably provoke imitation—they may well stimulate reaction—but when they do, they are the means by which a tradition is helped in motion; or rather, since it is important for us to make fine distinctions between the use of these terms, a style is perpetuated. The distinction between a style and a tradition is not easy to make clear. The mere act of copying—always providing it is not done with the expressed object of creating a parody or deliberate pastiche—will not in itself guarantee that a tradition will come into being. Such an act only ensures the fixing of a style. To establish a tradition it is necessary for an artist to add something to his copy, or else subtract something from the style invented by his predecessor. A succession of such additions and subtractions may be necessary before there can be a tradition worthy of the name. That this is not the whole story, however, becomes obvious when we reflect on the fact that cultural transmission, like rumour, tends to produce its own unintentional distortions, regardless of the wishes of its perpetrators. Moreover once a tradition is actually in existence, there will inevitably be certain contributors who will conceive it as their duty to dismantle the structure, hoping by so doing to achieve greater purity or singleness of aim. The processes by which traditions rise and fall are thus more complicated than they might appear. Suzanne Langer summarizes the conditions of their existence by saying:

> The introduction of a major device is what gives rise to a tradition in art. A tradition is usually something longer lived than a style; styles may come and go within its history.

Our reason for having laboured these points is that the *avant-garde* of every epoch generally dismisses them and makes a considerable fetish of originality, claiming also that an artist needs to express his own feelings and no one else's. Indeed that art is largely concerned with the expression or communication of feelings. These are propositions which it is possible to deny as well as affirm, and some if not all of them would have been denied by certain great artists of the past. Leonardo would not have considered it so important to be original, neither would Piero della Francesca have thought feeling more important than geometry. Likewise the assumption that the artist must be some kind of social prophet or seer is a relatively recent philosophy. Gray's bard on Plinlimmon is possibly the prototype of the artist as oracle, and he does not go back much further than the beginnings of the Romantic movement. My contention is that we are often misled by contemporary critics who (perhaps out of their need for explaining diversities) work to disabuse us of the idea that artists can pursue similar ends and even adopt similar means to them. These same critics are also very wary—perhaps with better justification—of attempts to impute a tradition in any branch of the arts. Ever since Dr Leavis canonized certain contributors to English literature as together comprising 'the great tradition'—and was later discovered to have included in his list of four names one Pole, one American and a lady of allegedly Welsh descent—there has been an understandable reluctance to engage in this sort of talent-spotting competition. Moreover there is a danger, when following such legislative methods, that personal taste will overrule the need for more objective judgment; and perhaps even a temptation to invent traditions which never actually existed.

Some traditions, however, do exist. This much has been established beyond any doubt in the case of the Italian painters, as Berenson's work on the Florentine and Venetian schools has shown. Similarly there can be few musicologists still willing to doubt the extra-ordinary phenomenon which Mr Norman Suckling has described, a shade ironically, as 'the Beethoven succession'. That Brahms and Mahler, to speak only of two popular composers, were both inspired and inhibited by their awareness of what this phrase meant, is patently clear from their letters and conversations. It will be a part of our purpose in this book to renounce the applicability of the phrase to the various French composers considered. Meantime it is necessary to underline what a tradition, especially in music, can amount to. It is not invariably something that arises out of a group of artists living at roughly successive intervals in the same country. Schumann, for example, lived in Germany directly following the death of Beethoven. Yet one could scarcely charge him with having been either stimulated or bedevilled by this event. He looked more piously in the direction of Bach. Then again it is plausible to argue that if two artists are closely united by means of temperament, preferred *genre*, scale of production or other affinity, they should be regarded as contributors to a common tradition. This is possibly to extend the meaning of the term tradition further than it ought to go. The *Oxford Dictionary* defines the word as 'opinion or belief or custom handed down'; and it is the handing down part that seems vital here. Whether or not artists do commune, either in consequence of direct discipleship, or else by voluntary or involuntary submission to influence, is the key to the dilemma. If they do not, it hardly seems as if the bringing of them together in critical conjunction does more than substitute a new taxonomic system for the older method of chronology. Such a system might have certain insights to offer, but it ought not to be viewed as synonymous with the system of identifying traditions.

Perhaps the arch-villain in the matter of postulating affinities is the French art critic André Malraux, who put forward a revolutionary system of classification in his book, *Les Voix du Silence*, published in 1951. This controversial work advanced the concept of an imaginary museum—which is the author's symbol for our hyperanalytic culture—in which all artistic styles can be viewed in conjunction with one another, irrespective of differences in time and place. This is the situation in which we actually find ourselves today, claims

Malraux, since the invention of new techniques of art reproduction, the proliferation of the gramophone record and the extension of literacy made possible through the paperback book, all combine to enable twentieth-century man to act out the role of spectator in an enormous museum of history. He can do what has never been possible before: subtract any artist from his environment, and by means of an imaginative transplantation see how he appears in company with a different circle. It is as if the critic had been suddenly gifted with the powers of a sort of Olympian landscape gardener, pulling up a root here and putting in a stick there; hoping that the whole quality of his plants will take on a different appearance in consequence of the change of arrangement. Malraux himself has not hesitated to compare the torments of Van Gogh to the intensity of the Romanesque cathedral builders, Cubist sculpture to that of the pre-Columbians, even representatives of different arts one to another, as when he notes the parallel between Michelangelo and Baudelaire. At its worst, this kind of criticism results in what Mr William Righter terms 'ellipsis', or illusory contraction of the time element; and this can lead to a rhetorical view of art, in which names are invoked and aligned at random in order to support a thesis. Nor can such criticism logically account for the masterpiece, which belongs with the bulk of its perpetrator's work, yet remains essentially different from it. At its best, perhaps, the method can assist us to detect resemblances and grasp recurrences which might otherwise have evaded our attention, absorbed as we customarily are in the outward decencies of scholarship.

In this study of French composers I have felt no need of recourse to Malraux's spurious correspondences, any more than it has been part of my intention to assert a Leavisite canon. I did not conceive of my subjects as either exemplifying a particular typology, or as constituting the stepping-stones to some high palace of art, at which only the elect might be permitted to disembark. Several of the composers I have chosen would probably be accorded the adjective 'great' in a history textbook, but I have no wish to imply that all merit this appellation. Erik Satie, for instance, has been a very influential composer, but even his admirers would not claim more for him. The achievement of his teacher Roussel is incomparably more substantial. Similarly only a brave man would advance the claim of Duparc to be considered a great composer, since his uniquely small output makes it almost impossible to judge what he was capable of. As a pupil of the ubiquitous César Franck he revealed scarcely anything of his master's fecundity. The sense in which I should like to claim the right to describe my subjects as belonging to a tradition—and indeed forming a tradition among themselves—can be stated differently.

As in the examples from Italian and German art, the music of these French composers does possess a national and cultural bias. All of them, for instance, tended to reject the expansive spiritual goals which we associate with the Romantics, preferring to exalt those qualities which had been apparent for a number of centuries in France, in writing and painting as well as music, and which included clarity, succinctness, taste and pleasurableness. It is a significant fact that not a single one of the composers chosen wrote a symphony, yet all were very prominent musicians and all certainly possessed the skill to have done so. Aside from an abortive work by Fauré—which he deliberately suppressed—there is not even any record of them attempting this medium. For the most part they were simply not interested in portentous musical issues. Another source of unification was their common interest in song. Of the six composers, Fauré, Duparc, Debussy and Poulenc were first and foremost song-writers. That is to say, whatever degree of success may be attributed to them in other forms, it is very difficult to refute the proposition that their finest work belongs to this genre. Indeed, they are all four among the world's greatest song-writers, and it would not be intrinsically ridiculous to state that together they comprise as formidable a group as the more publicized masters of the Lieder tradition—Schubert, Schumann, Brahms and Wolf. If it is still thought that this represents a tenuous link, let it be understood that the French group not only all wrote songs, but in many cases they constituted settings of the same poets, and even the same poems. Verlaine was set by both Fauré and Debussy, Baudelaire by Duparc and Debussy, de Lisle by Fauré and Duparc. The other interest shared by the majority of the composers selected was the piano. Debussy and Ravel are widely acknowledged to have been among the greatest exponents of this instrument, worth a place beside Chopin and Liszt. It will be one of my claims that Fauré too belongs with them, and is one of the supreme keyboard composers of any time. Satie and Poulenc, though neither reaches quite this level of greatness, both wrote large quantities of piano music, were themselves practising pianists, and thought of their respective roles very much in terms of the French *penchant* for the keyboard, which goes back to the *clavecinistes*.

Still further connections may be adduced. If we think back for a moment to what has been said about the conditions giving rise to a tradition, we can see at once the relevance of the arguments we advanced about innovators and models. Fauré had few models on which to base his conception of the *mélodie*, but through his action in composing a large body of song he did himself act as a model for Duparc, some of whose early songs have a texture distinctly reminiscent of the older man's work. Indeed even the relatively late *Phidylé* opens very much in the manner of Fauré. If we wished to retreat further into history than our scope strictly permits, we could trace the small but significant debts which both of these composers owe to Gounod. At a later stage in the tradition it is possible to regard Debussy as the innovator, demanding new standards of fidelity to the text and a more rigorous choice of poets, with Poulenc following suit at a respectable distance. Again both Mr Martin Cooper and Mr Edward Lockspeiser have profitably juxtaposed the achievements for piano of Debussy and Ravel. The mutual influences are so enmeshed that it becomes tedious to try to unravel them. From our own standpoint, justifying the particular cluster of composers whom we have segregated, it is worth adding the information that Ravel, notwithstanding his ironical avowals of unfamiliarity, was actually Fauré's pupil, while Debussy's piano style is allegedly indebted to Satie, who in turn provided Poulenc with the inspiration that led him to write the *Mouvements perpétuels*. Without examining these claims in detail (at least one of them remains slightly questionable), we can safely declare that it would be possible to go on expounding the various lines of interaction until the entire set-up began to take on an intimidating, labyrinthine appearance. To do this, however, would be to anticipate the essays which follow.

Perhaps it would be more valuable to remind the reader that, in addition to their musical interrelations, these composers enjoyed a very substantial measure of personal contact with each other. Fauré and Duparc met frequently at meetings of the Société Nationale, in which they both took an exceedingly active interest. Fauré's pupil Ravel struck up a friendship with Satie, to whom he always proclaimed a standing obligation as a composer. Both of these men were on good terms with Debussy, who nevertheless spurned them towards the end of his life—Satie through an unconscious snub for which he was sincerely repentant, and Ravel as a result of the manufactured envy with which the Debussyistes sought to inspire him. Later on Poulenc came to be acquainted with Ravel, whose advice he asked in relation to his career; and Satie, who came to act as a kind of bon oncle to the young man. These three actually constituted a sort of triple alliance against the intrusion of supercharged Romanticism. To sum up, it would be difficult to unearth any other group of composers of the period (which is really very much the period of the Third Republic and after) among whom the demands of art and friendship existed in such profuse measure.

Now that we have clarified in part what is meant by the tradition in music, and commented on the principles underlying our selection of composers, ought we not to turn the picture around again and make some final observations on the question of France and the so-called Gallic sensibility? Dr Christophe Campos, in his brilliantly opinionated study, The View of France, has recently lambasted Britons for continuing to take part in the very un-British sport of attributing overall or glaring qualities—usually facetious or immoral—to the countrymen of President de Gaulle. One can appreciate that some of this activity has had a recent uplift as a result of the débâcle in which the Common Market negotiations ended. Dr Campos does well to remind us, however, of the long and not very edifying stream of Francophile literature to have flowed from this island over the past century. It ranges from Arnold's moralizing and not very patriotic sallies—aimed at shaming us into erecting an arbiter of taste to rival the Academy across the Channel—to the cosier Gallomania afflicting the Bloomsbury writers, especially Clive Bell and Lytton Strachey, who were disinclined to believe any suggestion that articles of cultural value might have emanated from other countries than France. The gradual replacement of Murger's ideal of the Bohemian by the more up-to-date concept of l'homme sensuel moyen, and ultimately by existentialist man—that semi-political philanderer among the arts—seems to have had no more marked effect on things than to have redirected all pilgrimages from the Café de la Paix to the Deux Magots. Even from across the wider sea we were regaled with Henry James's vaunted dream of the Galerie d'Apollon in the Louvre, and this too added to the faintly corrupt fascination of the capital, which became the venue in which it was agreed that American innocence could be most affectingly dismembered. All this makes it very tempting for us to fall back on the outworn stereotypes of previous and passing generations, decking out our own view of France with the clichés of the common man or the more glamorous attributions of the littérateur. Such temptations must be resisted. They would merely succeed in adding to our confusion.

Upholding the need for caution, it still would not do for us to relapse into pusillanimity. This is a trap into which Dr Campos himself comes near to being pitched. In his urge to condemn speculative writing, he seems to be asking us to believe that there are no differences between the denizens of our two countries: a proposition which anyone who has had the mixed fortune to order a cup of tea at Boulogne railway station will feel at liberty to contradict. Similarities there may be, but differences are also discernible. At the level of art and philosophy, it is only reasonable to infer that such differences will appear magnified, since they will in all probability be the subject of those prejudices and rationalizations of which the academic, even more than the popular, mind is the master. To subscribe to such expectations should not be regarded as lending oneself to any racial doctrine or theory. It is not even to advertise one's commitment to the belief that traditions are invincible, and represent incarnations of the national conscience or repositories of the national soul. Such glib allegations may be left to the politicians to express. All that our generalizations need to embody are statements about the artistic ideals of a nation's leading practitioners, at a time when communications help to make them widely accessible. If they entice us beyond this rule then we shall have refused to heed our own prescriptions.

One last word on the state of music in France at the onset of our period—which begins in 1865 and ends in 1965—might seem desirable. Much of the historical ethos will became clear as we proceed to the treatment of the individual composers chosen. There are none the less certain items of background information which it will be valuable to possess at once. Amongst these none is more important than the fact of France's musical enslavement to the respective dictates of César Franck and Wagner. The former composer, who stands just outside the scope of our study, benignly threatens the individuality of all those musicians contained within it. He is like a great headmaster, whose portrait looks down upon his pupils, for ever seeming to chide them, exhort them or bully them. A Belgian who took up residence in Paris, he evolved a style of great earnestness and purity, heavy in scholarship and profuse in inspiration. His actual pupils included Chausson and Duparc, both of whom found the task of emulation almost too crushing to contemplate. They and their generation nevertheless attempted this task, and it is an incidental part of this book's purpose to mark the stages in their acceptance and rejection of the Franckist aesthetic.

The extraordinary Wagnerophobia which swept France in the decades following the concert of his works held at the Théâtre des Italiens in 1860 is harder to account for. Nietzsche once said: 'The more that French music learns to adapt itself to the actual needs of the *âme moderne*, the more it will Wagnerize.' As usual his prophecy came true right down to the last detail. The conductors Lamoureux and Colonne became among the first to launch the crusade which was to lead, after years of wrangling, to the admission of *Lohengrin* into that 'sanctum sanctorum' of French music, the Paris Opéra. In the meantime the malignant enchanter wove his spells, and one by one the progressive musicians of the Republic rejected the Second Empire floridities of Gounod and Ambroise Thomas, to cleave instead to the wizardry of the Bayreuth master. At first a healthy reaction, it soon hardened into a cult. Saint-Saëns, with his customary literary skill, put a finger on the crucial distinction: 'La Wagneromanie est un ridicule excusable; la Wagnerophobie est un maladie.'

In the sixties and seventies there were to be few young disciples, but in the later decades there were hardly any musicians in the capital who did not contract a mild case of the *maladie*, to say nothing of those less hardy souls who succumbed to it. Among the composers eligible to have encountered this influence, only Fauré was thoroughly immune to it. Erik Satie is perhaps also to be credited with having successfully resisted it. Duparc, on the contrary, was heavily exposed to it, as he was to the Franckist epidemic. So was Debussy a little later, though Satie helped to turn him away from it in time. Wagnerism in fact left its mark on most of the composers of the fin-de-siècle, though it does not follow from this that all their careers were imperilled.

The period we are about to study—through the lives and work of some of its principal figures—is therefore one which tended to face up, squarely or otherwise, to the two great currents we have described. Always more prone to accept foreign influences than Britain, France has not been as insular in its artistic attitudes as many commentators have tried to make out. Otherwise how can we account for the vogue for Italianate music which it displayed in the seventeenth and eighteenth centuries; the passion for imitating Schumann and Mendelssohn in the nineteenth; and the manner in which it became enamoured of the Russians in the early years of this century?

When we reach the turn of the century a fresh spectrum of influences becomes apparent. Ravel, Satie and Poulenc were none of them satisfied to take refuge beneath that vast Franckist and Wagnerian penumbra which had protected their predecessors. Instead they turned to a variety of extramusical sources. Among these the literary and pictorial arts vie with one another for pre-eminence. Cubism and Surrealism, for instance, may be said to have exercised an effect on the climate in which the last two composers were nurtured, whilst in the case of the whole group there seems a distinct impact from both technology and the popular arts. All three composers responded to the demands of the ballet—which for each of them meant Diaghilev, and all that his superb brand of showmanship stood for. Perhaps more significantly still, all three lived to become acquainted with the cinema, deriving from its mobile processes the new techniques with which to refurbish the musical tradition bequeathed to them by their older colleagues. None of these powerful influences is in need of being invoked as a catchpenny explanation of the music of modern French composers, but without them such music would have been literally unthinkable.

Chapter 1   # GABRIEL FAURÉ
Orpheus of French Song

THERE is a portrait, reproduced in the memoirs of the French pianist, Marguerite Long, of a pensive old man, his chalky hair untidily disposed over a bold forehead, with sensitive hands cupped under the chin—utterly absorbed in contemplation. The painter of the portrait is identified as John Singer Sargent, august embalmer of Victorian notabilities, and the date is given as 1898. At first sight one might have assumed the sitter to be some revered political dignitary—Félix Faure perhaps—worn out by the attacks of the Dreyfusards. The character and pose certainly suggest a man of rank, intelligent and refined, yet harassed by the cares of office. As it happens these speculations prove to have been just, but the man is not the President of the Third Republic. It is his namesake, Gabriel Fauré, composer and teacher, chief organist of the Madeleine and Director of the Paris Conservatoire.

When, some years later, the state funeral of this eminent musician took place, and government officials dutifully assembled at the great church in the centre of Paris, one of the more ceremonious delegates was overheard to remark: 'Qui était-il, ce Gabriel Fauré?' —as if to convince himself of the importance of the person in whose honour they were gathered. Listeners outside France may be forgiven for feeling somewhat like that unfortunate functionary when the subject of Fauré is introduced. They are aware of his high status in official circles, but remain blissfully uninhibited in their ignorance as to the reason. To explain this recurring situation in the terms usually reserved for neglected geniuses would not be strictly accurate. For there is something about Fauré's personality which compels indifference, if not downright hostility. How otherwise can we account for the judgment of Ravel—himself the most distinguished of Fauré's pupils, and not a man given to making enemies—

who paid final tribute to his old master by commenting: 'Je suis injuste à l'égard de la musique de Fauré, en somme je la connais mal.'

Inevitably Fauré's conservatism forces his admirers to tread a hesitant path amid the clamorous advocates of twentieth-century music. Not only does his stance seem old-fashioned, for he did after all live to encounter Satie and Roussel, but his music itself remains so redolent of the *salon*, so merged with the faded splendours of *la belle époque*, that we cannot serenely admit to a taste for it without convicting ourselves of ponderousness. All the same it is music, like that of Elgar in our own country, which obstinately refuses to be stigmatized—an attestation which must continue to exasperate their common detractors. André Hodeir, writing in praise of that musical enclave developing around Pierre Boulez, admits with puzzlement his inability to debunk what he describes as 'the Fauré myth'— which we may rather more charitably take to mean the composer's lasting reputation among orthodox musicians. And indeed the homage paid to Fauré's genius by critics of the perspicacity of Charles Koechlin and Emile Vuillermoz has been such as to undo much of the proselytizing comment of the *avant-garde*, who have tended to see in him only a pallid elegance and charm.

The truth seems to be that Fauré was one of those rare musicians in whom the urge to experiment existed alongside a relentless capacity for assimilating traditional knowledge. His ease of manner has accordingly been mistaken for mere facility, a fate which has also overtaken his lesser contemporary and friend Saint-Saëns. Uncommon enough at any time, the scholar artist—which is the real amalgam he exemplifies—is scarcely credible in an age in which everyone is divided into rebels and ancestors. Perhaps only Paul Valéry, as Mr Norman Suckling has duly noted, occupies an analogous position; and his denigration has proceeded on similar lines to those marked out by the adversaries of Fauré. Both artists have been accused of pandering to established canons of taste, and both have been found guilty of a surfeit of learning. Even if such conclusions were sufficient to convict, which they are assuredly not, there remains little evidence to suggest that they are true. The unrebelliousness which we observe in Fauré stems not so much from conformity as from that characteristically French sense of reasonableness and moderation. Iconoclasm was not in his nature, and he was far too intelligent to confuse art with revolution.

Nevertheless, when we turn to the facts of Fauré's life it is easy to see how his present reputation has been acquired. A church musician by training and inclination, his path to fortune, like that of Bruckner, was paved with diplomas and awards. Born in quite ordinary surroundings at Pamiers, near the Pyrenees, in 1845, he attended the Ecole Niedermeyer, where he won first prizes for piano, organ, harmony and composition.[1] He was accordingly soon occupying a post at Rennes in Brittany; and after a brief period of military service during the Franco-Prussian War, he made his home in the capital, hoping to emulate the great choirmasters and organists among whom he had received his education. Even as a student he had what many would regard as a chillingly precise sense of ambition. M. Koechlin tells the story of the young Fauré, confiding in his friend Eugène Gigout, during one of their Sunday morning walks on the hill of Montmartre: 'I shall have the Madeleine.' And indeed in 1877 he was appointed Maître de Chapelle at that massive Napoleonic temple. Such accuracy of perception scarcely serves to endear him to us.

Our sympathies are much more likely to be aroused by the tribulations which he suffered once he had exchanged his academic designs for a more artistic goal. Thenceforward his successes were not so easily won. His first Violin Sonata, a thoroughly mature work, which some critics have suggested as the probable model for the 'little sonata of Vinteuil' in Proust's monumental novel, was refused by the French publishers to whom Fauré had submitted it, and he had to be content with its being issued by the German firm of Breitkopf & Härtel in 1876. Fortunately the Société Nationale—that sturdy forum for the dissemination of modern music—had been founded in 1871, and Fauré reaped many benefits from its protection. Still recognition came at a painfully slow rate. As a provincial in the city of the Muses he was forced to cultivate polite friendships in the hope of advancing his cause. Some of these connections, including the association with the Viardot family of singers, with

---

[1] The régime at this minor conservatory in the Pigalle district was grim, judged by modern standards. All eighteen piano students were made to practise in the same room, while the din from a neighbouring coach-house added to the confusion. Strangely enough, Fauré always praised the discipline it helped to instil in him.

whom Turgenev also enjoyed cordial relations, provided Fauré with a venue for the performance of his early songs. The year 1865 marked the beginning of the composer's unspectacular ascent as a writer of *mélodies*. It was at these musical soirées that he was to incur the appellation, *indolent charmeur*, a reproach enhanced by his once having surreptitiously taken his place at the organ for morning service while still wearing evening dress.

A part of the difficulty in exonerating Fauré lies of course with this partiality of his for the forms and textures of the *salon*. As a song composer in the age of the *romance*, he had the utmost difficulty in convincing discriminating musicians of his seriousness. His first couple of dozen compositions were all vocal in character, and there is no doubt that the influence of Gounod can be detected even in the comparatively late *Chanson du pêcheur*, which was a setting of Gautier's well-known poem. In the absence of a French tradition of song comparable to the German Lied, it was inevitable that Fauré's earliest attempts at vocal writing should have been in the strophic form and lacking the concision of the great masters. He had little to go on apart from his melodic gifts. Nowadays we tend to look on Berlioz as the precursor of the art-song in France—his cycle *Les Nuits d'Eté* had appeared in 1841—but the term *mélodie*, which at first referred to the more Schubertian type of song from across the Rhine, had at that time only a limited usage; and Berlioz, being no pianist, was himself obliged to orchestrate the earlier versions of his songs in order to court popularity. By comparison Fauré was more dedicated to the smaller forces, and he had a correspondingly harder time ahead of him.

The intelligence which he brought to this task may be inferred, not only from the inimitable song cycles to be weighed against his own name—among which *La Bonne Chanson* and the *Cinq Mélodies de Venise* stand out—but from the rapid apotheosis which French song attained at the hands of Duparc and Debussy, neither of whom could be said to have belonged to a much later generation than Fauré himself. The decision to devote himself to the voice was nevertheless detrimental to Fauré's contemporary reputation, both at home and abroad, since this was the period when instrumental music was being revived by the French and German admirers of Beethoven. Between them the Brahmins and the Franckists held sway over most musical domains, and Fauré was not to find a place in either camp, any more than he was later to be seduced by the blandishments of the Wagnerites. It is not surprising that he was once heard to remark that twenty years usually elapsed before his compositions were given their due.

During these formative years Fauré became engaged to Marianne Viardot, daughter of the celebrated Pauline, and it remains problematic how far his intended relatives may at this time have prevailed upon him to consider a career as an operatic composer. Opera, as opposed to song, continued to flourish in France, with the aid of some arch and fulsome talents. Meyerbeer and Halévy had been all the rage during the Second Empire, and the bourgeoisie were shrill in their demands for a successor. Far from being an operatic composer *manqué*, however, Fauré did not possess the necessary volatility. As the bulk of his work testifies, he had an aversion to any form of display. Only very occasionally, as in his magnificent setting of Verlaine's *Prison*, does he reveal emotions which the public would recognize as dramatic. Those critics who saw Fauré's songs as an earnest of dramatic aspirations to follow were accordingly misguided in their interpretation of his qualities. There is documentary evidence that Fauré himself experienced some relief when the termination of his engagement afforded him the opportunity of concentrating on music as an art quite separate from the theatre. Even if his songs were to suffer the same drawing-room immolation as Tosti's sickly ballads, at least he was saved from the chasm of an altogether misplaced career. A certain stoicism of character enabled him to suffer wrongful appraisal of his work in silence, and in the meantime his technique was unfolding to some purpose. The chance to settle down came later, when he was thirty-eight, and met Marie Frémiet, daughter of a famous French sculptor. They were not madly in love, but she made Fauré a loyal wife and devoted companion.

In view of the impetus given to French organ music by César Franck, and of the nature of Fauré's training, it is more than a little surprising that he did not develop a *penchant* for this instrument, alongside his obvious relish for the voice. Oddly enough there is no evidence that he wrote anything but a few officially inspired voluntaries for it. The piano, on the other hand, captivated him. At

unremittingly applied to Fauré's songs, has also been levelled at his piano music—by no less a person in fact than Debussy. In his acidulous little book, *Monsieur Croche—anti-dilettante*, the composer of the *Images* has many snide comments to make on the piano writing of his contemporaries, his more venomous remarks being reserved for Beethoven. About Fauré's music, which he knew, like Ravel, only imperfectly, he adopts a slightly equivocal pose. After attending a concert at which the Ballade was played by Mme Hasselmans, whose shoulder-strap kept needing adjustment after every agitated passage in the music, Debussy wrote the following ironic footnote:

Somehow an association of ideas was established in my mind between the charm of the aforementioned gesture and the music of Fauré. It is a fact, however, that the play of the graceful, fleeting lines described by Fauré's music may be compared to the gesture of a beautiful woman without either suffering from the comparison.

Such a backhanded compliment does more to vindicate Debussy's skill as a journalist than his percipience as a critic.

Those who continue to share this patronizing view of Fauré's keyboard works should at least do him the honour of re-examining them, now that the modern movement has run its course. For what other composer of his generation has left us such an exemplary body of well-written music for the instrument, so consistent in quality and plentiful in invention? [1] Not Franck, certainly, since his reputation continues to rest on a handful of works, fine though some of these may be. Even less supportable are the claims of the genuinely prolific Saint-Saëns, who incidentally taught Fauré at the Ecole Niedermeyer, and ever afterwards referred to his young pupil as his faithful 'chat', since sleekness and lubricity vitiate his work to a more obvious degree than that of any other French composer of the time—a fact which helped to earn him the comically just rebuke that what he really wrote was 'la mauvaise musique, bien écrite'.

It is unfortunately undeniable that some of Fauré's earliest piano pieces—the three *Romances sans paroles* and the first few nocturnes and barcarolles—do exude a stifling, Mendelssohnian triteness, evident in their over-symmetry of phrasing and deliberate

[1] Yet Kathleen Dale, in her influential book on *Nineteenth-century Piano Music*, published in 1953, does not even mention his name.

8

prettiness of melody. Once he had thrown off the shackles of Romanticism, however, Fauré began to reveal himself for what he really was—a much less shallow and more conscience-driven artist. The change is vividly apprehended by comparing any of these juvenile essays with such a vintage piece as the Sixth Barcarolle, where we encounter the same sense of poise and feeling for the shape of a phrase, even the same illusion of aqueous motion, put at the service of far more cunningly syncopated rhythms. Moreover the harmonies of the middle section (bars 54–66) show what audacities he had become capable of achieving as a result of his habit of suspending the unexpected note in each half-bar. The sequential phrasing of this passage is likewise very characteristic of the mature artist. One of the significant differences between Fauré and the Franckists who surrounded him lay in this capacity of his for modulating, not through the obvious chromatic rise and fall of the melody, but by abstracting and tying over a note common to otherwise unrelated chords, or following a long series of melodic sequences to their conclusion. The E flat Barcarolle offers several transparent examples of these devices, illustrating how natural Fauré could make them sound even when the bass support was thick and dissonant. That no other composer of the period possessed such cool skill in transitional writing is a fact that ought to go without saying. Similar felicities lie in wait for the researcher who examines the remaining piano works of the middle years. The so-called 'Venetian' Barcarolle—number nine in the series—and the Seventh Nocturne, with its elaborate chains of suspensions, again spring readily to mind.

Doubtless Fauré felt that he had reached the summit of his ambitions in this sphere when he completed his Theme and Variations, Op. 73, rightly accounted the most classical of his labours. It is a work that reveals the full range of his qualities as a composer, as well as representing a sample of the variation form far superior to the more often played works of contemporaries like Glazounov and Arensky. The theme itself has a nobility almost without parallel among the richly assorted compositions of the period. It can only be compared to those gravely passionate melodies which so transfigure the greater chamber works of Brahms, a composer whom Fauré evidently did not know or care much about. As for the variations, their model was clearly the Schumann of the *Etudes Symphoniques*, though there is an unobtrusive severity about them which seems to place them in an altogether contrasting intellectual climate to that in which Florestan and Eusebius had their being. Not that there is any absence of poetry or striving—the texture of Variations VII and IX amply disproves that suggestion. But the fancies are never allowed to proliferate, and the music always preserves its dignified tread. Entirely typical is the finale, which has the sobriety of a Bach chorale, so unencumbered is it by the slightest hint of rhetoric. The work remains a monument to the integrity of a devoted artist who refused to be swayed by the popular search for what Stravinsky has termed 'mere *brio*'. One cannot imagine it ever serving to conclude—as even the admirable Handel Variations of Brahms are frequently made to conclude—a fashionable public recital.

Not all of the composer's output is pitched at a corresponding level of seriousness. The impromptus and valses unquestionably inhabit a more facile world. They aspire to some of the same frenetic brilliance as the *salon* pieces of the eccentric M. Durand, the publisher, who allowed himself to become so enraptured with the vision of the executant, his fingers flying and arms akimbo. Fauré's display manner, if one may thus describe it, is naturally a good deal more decorous. Yet the style never managed to suit him, and it is not really surprising that in time he came to abandon it altogether. It was Chabrier who stole the laurels at this special brand of Gallic exuberance, and even his key-breaking exploits have long ago passed, along with those of his contemporaries Diémer and Pugno, into the limbo of pianistic mythology. It is unlikely that Fauré ever derived much stimulus from such antics.

Unlike the great masters of the Romantic movement from whom he gained his sense of direction, Fauré was not a top-flight performer at the keyboard. A solitary recording of him playing his First Barcarolle shows that, on the contrary, he had a somewhat heavy touch, and his pedalling was indistinct. He thus shared with Ravel the distinction of having written wholly idiomatic music for the instrument, while having only a moderate sympathy with its popular image. Throughout Fauré's life, he retained the conception of himself as a chamber music participant rather than a virtuoso, and it was in this humble spirit that he appeared to others.

In the last resort, the explanation attaching to this disesteem into which his piano music has fallen may be sought in Fauré's disinclination to consider the demands of either the virtuoso or the moderate performer. The former is only likely to warm to *bravura* effects of a kind foreign to Fauré's musical outlook, whilst the latter does not find it easy to cope with the sustained complexity of texture, and excursions into distant keys, which so regularly mark these compositions. To glance at a typical Fauré piano score is to behold a wealth of accidentals, apparently designed to bring trepidation to the hearts of all but the most seasoned of sight-readers. Moreover, there is a notable absence of those concessions to amateurism that we customarily find in *salon* composers, such as the repeat of material in ternary form. Conversely, it could scarcely be maintained that Fauré's works are unplayable by the non-professional, as, for instance, is alleged with some justification about the *études* of Scriabin or Debussy. The writing, on the contrary, lies well under the hands, poses no acrobatics, and, provided one can summon up the necessary stamina, is splendidly gratifying.

Despite Fauré's continued devotion to song and piano music, it ought not to surprise us too much to discover that his best known compositions are to be found elsewhere. The various pieces of incidental music associated with his name are scarcely in the Fauré canon, and generally relate to the final period in the composer's life, when he was sufficiently confident of his talents to turn at last to the stage. By that time the fever of Wagnerism had swept Europe, and the chaste music which Fauré wrote for Maeterlinck's *Pelléas et Mélisande*—so utterly different from Debussy's more evocative score—could not have been more contrary to the vogue. The suite compiled from this enterprise, along with the music composed for the nostalgic entertainments of René Fauchois, none the less deserve their present glimmer of popularity. They are interesting, not only to the extent that they reveal Fauré's familiarity with the old French dance forms, but also on account of their superlative quality as light music.

How easily might Fauré have rivalled Grieg or Sibelius in this humble sphere! Beneath his façade of seriousness there lay a versatility which might well have been the envy of any of the great frolicsome entertainers who wrote for the Opéra-Comique. As

Romain Rolland has rightly discerned, the period was more prodigal in popular than serious talents, and it comes as something of a shock to realize that Fauré could, had he wished, have become one of their number. The notorious charm was in fact capable of assuming more earthbound forms than many had supposed.

Favourites like the *Pavane* and the voluble *La Fileuse* were actually among the by-products of his genius. Nor was he anxious to secure a place on the roster of comfortable buffoons. Many of his highly prized compositions in the lighter vein were paradoxically embedded in more serious works. Even the best known among them are better esteemed for their purely musical qualities than for any spurious *bonne-bouche* attributes we may foist upon them. The finely wrought prelude to *Pénélope* acts as a pointed instance. So do the supple antique dances which Fauré dignified by the name *Masques et bergamasques*. These sprightly movements recall, with a touch of old age's melancholy, the enchanted world of Watteau, with its leafy parks, opulently attired lovers and refined pastoral amusements. They can likewise be thought of as embodying the final and choreographic revisitation of the composer's Verlaine troupe, gathered together once more for a last, autumnal *fête champêtre*.

Far removed from such diversions is the beautiful Requiem which Fauré wrote on the death of his parents in 1887. This tender work exhibits all the composer's gift for understatement. The reluctant are inclined to view it as undramatic alongside Verdi's more robust masterpiece. Those who admire its Hellenic calm, on the contrary, will wish to accord it a very high place among Fauré's works. Its appeal has always seemed strongest to those who, like the composer himself, are slightly repelled by the ferments of Christian eschatology. Curiously enough, both Requiems—as indeed the mighty Glagolitic Mass of Janáček, which is their only modern contender—were the product of agnosticism. In Verdi's case, the public has been quick to seize upon the fire-breathing ethics underlying his inspiration. The tradition from which Fauré's work sprang is much less fashionable, and may be traced to that gentle scepticism introduced into French intellectual life in the latter half of the nineteenth century by Renan; its ramifications can be detected in the work of one or two of the Parnassian poets with whom Fauré collaborated. Our own mentality seeks greater extremes of faithlessness and adoration. To allege, as one unkind critic did, that Fauré's In Paradisum should have been retitled In Elysium, is only to remind ourselves of what a gap there is in sensibility between his age and ours.

Fauré's appointment as Director of the Paris Conservatoire was an unexpected triumph for the tradition of bien-chanté and classical lyricism which he sought to uphold. His management of his academic duties, so arduous at a time when many gifted pupils were gravitating to the d'Indy camp at the newly established Schola Cantorum, could hardly have been more skilful. Altogether, his tenure was not an easy one. The appointment itself had been bitterly controversial. The obvious man to have succeeded to the directorship was Massenet, whom Fauré had replaced as Professor of Composition, but he threw a fit of pique on learning of the governors' refusal to make the post a lifetime sinecure. Once he was out of the running, Dubois was brought forward as a rather compromise second choice. Even then several factors conspired to lessen Fauré's chances. He had not been trained at the Conservatoire, and he had never won the Prix de Rome—two crippling handicaps in that hothouse environment. Worse still, there were some enemies on the faculty. Ambroise Thomas, in particular, had cast malicious doubts on his competence, even threatening to resign if Fauré were ever nominated for preferment. It was therefore mildly surprising to all when the minister announced Fauré's name in 1905.

Acrimony showed itself in his very first tasks. Ever since the century's beginning, musical impressionism had been vainly endeavouring to get a foothold in official circles. Older musicians regarded this form of modernism as a dread disease, to be expunged at all costs. On the other hand, progressives outside the academies had already begun to seethe with anger over the shabby treatment meted out to Ravel, who had just been snubbed by the Prix de Rome jury. The whole case quickly became the focus of a heated dispute. Unlike Debussy, whose disenchantment with musical honours had been fairly complete, even before he was declared a winner of this embattled award, Ravel persevered in his attempts to improve on the second place allotted him. By the time Fauré came to occupy his new position, feelings were running perilously high. It is much to the older man's credit that he was able to pacify both sides in this squabble. Not only did he bring order to an indignant and reactionary Faculty, but he even gained the respect of the unruly *arrivistes* who constituted the opposition. Much of Fauré's handling of musical politics reflects this sense of tact and generosity of spirit. As a teacher he could show a like sympathy for diverse attitudes. No other famous composer has bequeathed such a galaxy of pupils.[1] They included not only Ravel himself, but Roger Ducasse, Florent Schmitt, Gabriel Grovlez, Georges Enesco, Nadia Boulanger, Koechlin, Ladmirault, Aubert and many others of lesser stature. What is surprising is that so many of these were themselves to become distinguished teachers, attracting their own range of disciples. Above all, Fauré deserves credit for having introduced the method of teaching by example. Unlike his predecessors, he did not dogmatize, nor did he expound a system of aesthetics to add to the edification of his students. Instead he played music at the piano, surrounded by a cluster of hearers, periodically interrupting himself to venture an illuminating comment. Roland-Manuel was quite right in claiming that Fauré actually established the musical equivalent of Mallarmé's *salon*, a centre where the unfettered mind could continue to be free.

Once launched on his new career, Fauré found it increasingly difficult to devote as much time as he would have liked to composition. Within a few years of beginning his administration he had come to the end of the most fruitful period in his life as a composer. The winter of his genius still lay ahead, and this was to produce an extraordinary collection of works, among them the last Piano Quintet, the Cello Sonatas, the song cycle *L'Horizon chimérique*, based on poems written by a young airman killed in the First World War, and the final group of nocturnes and barcarolles for piano. This may seem a sizeable enough production for a man no longer in the prime of life, but there is the question of the character of the music to be considered. These votive offerings are in fact classed among the most fathomless works in the history of music. Aimed at a complete purity of style, they have frequently been dismissed as so glacial in feeling as to repel all but the more curious listener. There

[1] The single exception among Conservatoire professors might be César Franck, who held an organ class at that staid institution from 1872 until his death in 1890. His pupils included Vincent d'Indy, Ernest Chausson, Charles Bordes, Camille Benoît and Pierre de Bréville.

is unfortunately enough truth in this viewpoint to lend pause to any further encomium. Gone is the blandness of the early period, and vanished are the radiant, surging melodies of La Bonne Chanson. Everything is now spare and stripped of emotion, the texture of the music shorn of accent and contrast. Melodies proceed by a painful crepuscular movement, whilst the rhythms sink almost to a standstill. Like Beethoven before him, Fauré was going deaf. Something of the sensuousness, a part of that pristine immediacy which distinguishes music from the other arts, was actually beginning to desert him. Tones were heard a third higher or lower than their real pitch. Moreover people were beginning to talk behind his back— most cruelly about his unsuitability to grasp and continue his official duties. At this time he stood alone at the edge of life, feeling neither relief nor anticipation, expressing no fear yet finding the prospect of approaching dissolution terrible enough to bear. Forced to resign the directorship, and accorded only a nominal government pension, Fauré eked out his remaining summers near the Mediterranean, the true birthplace of his Muse, returning only to die in the capital. France had lost her Orpheus and only the songs remained.

What was the essence of Fauré's attitude to the art of song? To discover the answer we must examine the three volumes of melodies in the Hamelle collection, since these contain the great bulk of his output. Over sixty songs are to be found in these invaluable editions. They span his entire career, and illustrate his development with unmistakable clarity. The first recueil, which contains the uncharacteristic Hugo settings, also houses at least two songs which helped to make the composer famous. One is his version of Leconte de Lisle's Lydia; and the other is the justly popular Après un rêve, based on a translation of some Tuscan verses by Bussine. These songs have immense freshness of melodic appeal and do not suffer from the excessive reserve which can occasionally be imputed to his later productions. Above all they are eminently singable. The de Lisle song was actually a foretaste of greater riches to follow, since this erudite poet, leader of the Parnassians, was to inspire both Fauré and Duparc to their highest flights of imagination. His classical restraint and recondite charm found their counterparts in Fauré's own interests. The composer had in any case come to regard Hugo as no longer viable, the overblown rhetoric becoming less and less adaptable to his gifts.

It has often been implied that, whereas some other French composers were acutely conscious of literary merit, Fauré had no serious knowledge of poetry, and was indifferent to the exact shape of the verses he set. Certainly he did not possess the innate good taste of Debussy, or the sophisticated knowledge of prosody of a Poulenc. Rather he had a feeling for the mood of a poem, and did not worry overmuch if each syllable did not coincide with a required progression of the melody. In general he had no use for declamatory verse, since it drove him in the direction of stridency, a quality alien to his temperament. The climax of *Après un rêve* comes closer to being inflated than anything which can be found in his subsequent works. On the other hand, he cared for writing which simply possessed descriptive interest, especially if this were craftily emptied of too much romanticized emotion. He was happiest with poetry which contained elements of colour and exhibited an individual range of conceit, but which sought to eschew the grand gesture. The *scena* which certain poems set out to specify was something he found uncongenial—unlike Schubert, who showed, in The Erl-King and many another song, how well he could manage such things.

Perhaps in the early part of his career Fauré did not show as much initiative as he might have done in searching out the poet of his fancy. The unassertiveness he required was not something to be lightly picked up, and may even have been very hard to come by at a time when the Romantic poets, to whom the label 'pleurards' had not yet been affixed, were still greatly admired. Modern musicians have sometimes been too ready to condemn Fauré for having resorted to such essentially minor poets as Samain and Armand Silvestre. Poulenc, in particular, has gone as far as to impugn Fauré's whole stature as a song-writer on this account. The fact is that he did arrive at the right poets in the end, but took rather a long time to do so. The fault was not so much his as the age's. The kind of tearful egoists whose work was vaunted in the eighteen-sixties wrote verse that was much too sonorous for Fauré's buoyant music. The search went on for a poet of lighter specific gravity. Baudelaire was held up as a possibility, but he was too agonized a writer. What Fauré really wanted was someone akin to the Latin poets.

He had always been an intense lover of the classics, as his friend and interpreter Alfred Cortot has testified, and the qualities he looked for in poetry embraced a combination of learning and good taste.

These qualities can be found in ample measure in de Lisle, five of whose poems were set by Fauré with excellent results. There seemed to be just the right amount of personal detail in his poetry, without it ever slipping over into blatant displays of self-commiseration. He was the very opposite of portentous. Moreover he shared Fauré's taste for the classical poets, and had actually made several translations of Horace. The second book of melodies, containing the songs which Fauré wrote in the years between 1880 and 1890, continues his collaboration with de Lisle. Among this collection the matchless *Les Roses d'Ispahan* stands out, showing as it does Fauré's bewitching mastery of cross-rhythms, a feature of his style which can also be observed in the piano works. In this song the orientalism of the poem is perfectly captured in the delicate *melismata* of the vocal line:

> The moss roses of Persia, the jasmine, and the orange blossoms have a perfume less sweet than the breath of Leilah. Her voice sounds lovelier than the rippling of waters or the singing of birds. . . .

No one who has ever heard the incomparable Maggie Teyte sing this mellifluous lyric will easily forget its impact. It remains a fascinating *trouvaille* for those interested in the history of that peculiarly French infatuation with the East, which was to include works like de Bréville's vivid suite *Stamboul* for piano, and Roussel's *Padmâvatî*. The whole tradition may be said to have reached its apogee in Ravel's languorous setting of Tristan Klingsor's poems in the cycle, *Shéhérazade*. The final fruit of the de Lisle collaboration is to be found in the third volume of Fauré's melodies, and consists of the song *Le Parfum impérissable*, which many take to be the finest of all the composer's lyrical effusions. It was certainly his own favourite.

Armand Silvestre was another poet admired by Fauré. A much more superficial writer than de Lisle, he nevertheless embodied some of the deliberately unheroic qualities the composer was seeking. Foremost among the Silvestre settings is *Aurore*, which appears in the second Hamelle volume, and this song harks back to a certain extent to the regular forms of Fauré's apprenticeship. Notwithstanding its conservatism in this respect, its superiority over earlier examples of the *romance* which he wrote, up to and including Op. 8, is unquestioned. The modulations are more interesting and assured, and the weightlessness and sheer refinement of melody infinitely more accomplished. Fauré was to return to his partnership with Silvestre in later years, nearer the time of his success with *Le Don silencieux*. As a whole, though, their collaboration must be accounted only moderately rewarding. No poet had yet been able to give Fauré the full stimulus needed in order to write a succession of masterpieces. He had to wait until 1887 before he discovered the instigator of his maturity in Verlaine.

Psychologists may have an explanation for the bewildering ease with which these two apparently dissimilar spirits achieved their close degree of rapport. If so, we are still in the dark as to what it is. For the high sense of duty and quiet moral dignity of Fauré must seem to contrast bluntly with the debauched peregrinations of *pauvre Lélian*. What on earth did they have in common? We cannot hope to do more than hint at some of the answers. It would be difficult to deny that they possessed a common sense of rhythm as well as a common feeling for the nuances of life, and both distrusted a high-flown histrionic attitude to art. Fauré would readily have concurred in Verlaine's famous injunction to 'take eloquence and wring its neck', which was the moral he advanced in *Art poétique*. Otherwise both were attracted to the eighteenth-century world of the *fêtes galantes*, with its mixed shadows, *rose et grise*. Moreover they possessed a common ability to touch off the rococo gestures necessary to its re-creation. One feels that Fauré lacked the *voyeur's* interest in that sexual anonymity conferred by the velvet domino, and other trappings of the carnival—a mystery which exercised the greatest fascination for the sensual Verlaine. But they had a mutual love of the rituals of spring and summer, with their rush of happy thoughts and enveloping sense of natural communion. Further than this it is difficult to penetrate. Vladimir Jankélévitch, in his pioneer study *Gabriel Fauré et ses mélodies*, has rightly argued that Verlaine lacked the sense of *pudeur*, or civilized reserve, with which Fauré found himself so generously endowed. Nor, despite his successful setting of the poem with that name, can we easily credit Fauré with the acute 'spleen' of his collaborator. Their divergences would make an extremely interesting study, worth a monograph in itself. The bond which united them is harder to make clear, and is perhaps impossible to put into words.

Meanwhile, there can be no doubt that Fauré's setting of the poet's *Clair de lune* marked a huge step forward in his development. It is one of his best rococo songs, though it has a rival in the late *Arpège*. Both songs are remarkable for the use they make of the piano. In *Clair de lune*, the pattern of song plus accompaniment is for the first time completely dispensed with. Instead we have the piano in possession of a crisp and lilting tune of its own, virtually capable of standing alone as a *menuet*. Like Schumann before him, Fauré was coming to regard the art of song-writing as a subtle conjoining of two melodic forces, with total freedom of movement between them. Variety of texture and extension of compass were only two of the beneficial consequences of this new development. More important than either of these even was the enlargement of the repertory of emotions. This was decisive for the future of French song. It freed the form from the otherwise threatening presence of the *romance*, with its ostentatious promotion of the voice and tendency to denigrate the text. Had Fauré not moved when he did to clinch these gains, it would scarcely have been possible for the Debussy of the *Chansons de Bilitis* or the Ravel of the *Histoires naturelles* to have appeared on the scene. Hence Fauré forged the art of the *mélodie* as a form comparable to, though quite independent of, the German Lied.

It may be of some interest to pause at this crucial juncture and ask ourselves how Fauré measures up to other composers who have written songs in a different national idiom. To rate him along-side Schubert would in some ways be absurd. He had not Schubert's heavenly gift of melody—no one else possessed that. And, again unlike the early masters of the Lied, Fauré from the beginning gave greater importance to the piano than was customary. In this respect, if in no other, he is more like Schumann or Hugo Wolf. Even more than either of these composers, however, Fauré's mature work presents the accompaniment—it is sacrilegious thus to describe it—as a vital arterial system breathing life into the song. Naturally such piano parts are difficult to play; indeed they all too seldom avoid the iridescent figuration that so defeats the performer in the piano works themselves. What is so remarkable, however, is that they do not engulf the music, relegating the voice to an inferior role, as sometimes happens with Schumann. Provided the accompanist is a capable one, they enrich rather than impoverish the vocal line. The sinuosity of this line ensures that the voice is able to surmount all changes of register, while the self-discipline shown in refusing to develop accompanying figures beyond the point where they crystallize into melodic fragments of their own forms a part of the composer's genius. Time and time again we encounter fragments of melody similar in shape to the material comprising the nocturnes. La Bonne Chanson is especially rich in such fragments. Pianists listening to this work must find it tempting to speculate on what Fauré might have done with the various germinal strands it contains had he been intent on writing another set of piano pieces. Most pianist-composers would have yielded to the temptations implicit in such a situation, and in so doing would have acted to the detriment of the text.

Any comparison of French song with the German Lieder must be undertaken with extreme caution. Much as they may have features in common, the two genres are in reality quite distinct. James Husst Hall, in his brilliant book, The Art Song, catalogues many of their differences with great thoroughness. Several factors helping to distinguish these complex traditions emerge from his survey, one of these being that the sentiments they provoke are opposed. Also, technique is far from being the same in the two types of song. German song is usually frank in mood and overt in expression, while the French mélodie tends to be more sophisticated, revelling in artifice and paradox. It is easy to infer that the former takes its origin from folk song, whereas the latter relies more heavily on the operatic model. Of all French song-writers, however, Fauré is the least given to displays of irony (he is almost never satirical), and it would be quite misleading to attribute to him the kind of psychological dexterity better withheld to describe his successors. Allowing for the fact that the emotions dealt with by French song are generally of the more attenuated kind, Fauré's treatment of these emotions is straightforward enough. There is nothing deliberately recherché about his work, and his attitudes are not complicated by decadent posturing. Sincerity and not dissimulation is the keynote of his writing.

Of the cycles written on poems by Verlaine, the first in order of composition is the more neglected of the two. This delightful work has been overshadowed by its successor. The title given to it is plainly evocative. It is the most Verlaine-sounding of all his works: *Cinq Poèmes de Venise*. This cycle was written in 1890, and actually begun on a visit to the city, so that it is not wholly a product of that *vie intérieure* to which the composer had recourse elsewhere.[1] Emile Vuillermoz nevertheless concludes that the work is more evocative of Versailles than of the City of the Doges. Chronologically, of course, the Italian comedy took precedence over the French, and Watteau, whose painting of Mezzetino and Columbino helped to furnish both the poet and the musician with their source of inspiration, depicts visiting as well as native troupes of actors. Indeed the Goncourt brothers, in their biography of the painter, make it quite clear that it was with the Italian comedians that he struck up his sympathetic friendship. Their disordered flight, when Mme de Maintenon banished them from Paris, caused him much chagrin and incidentally lent a touch of realism to the players' own histrionic pathos. After their departure France became once again the 'muffled realm' it had been before, though the presence of the players had contributed a new dimension to public taste, one which was never altogether suppressed and which sprang marvellously to life in arts other than drama. It hardly matters, therefore, whether the habitat in which these gracious dupes were portrayed lay to the north or south of Europe. What is significant is that they acted as the perfect embodiment of those qualities of elegance and insouciance which French poets and musicians have so faithfully striven to illuminate.

The Venetian songs, because of the variety of mood they reflect, constitute a genuine cycle. *En Sourdine*, in which the nightingales echo the despair of the lovers, is hushed and passionate, while *C'est l'extase* reaches a similar pitch of intensity. *Green*—which Debussy set so unforgettably—is characterized more by freshness and avoids the voluptuous *sous-bois* atmosphere of the others. *A Clymène* gives Fauré an opportunity to make use of his favourite barcarolle rhythm. Of the complete set, *Mandoline* offers the highest

---

[1] According to Mr Desmond Shawe-Taylor, Fauré was the guest of the Princesse de Polignac at the time, and though she did her best to provide solitude for the composer, he surprised everyone by doing his composing at a table on the Piazza San Marco.

degree of sophistication. As M. Vuillermoz comments in his description of the song:

> Les petits arpèges souriants de Mandoline nous invitent à ne pas prendre trop au sérieux les élégantes marionettes dont l'ont peuplé les peintres et les poètes.

Altogether the album exudes a tender fragrance quite distinct from the driving forces of seasonal change which permeate La Bonne Chanson.

This later cycle, which was written in the following year, is widely regarded as Fauré's masterpiece, as indeed it might be thought to have been Verlaine's. It contains only nine songs out of the twenty-one poems to be found in the book, and these celebrate the joys of betrothal in a completely ingenuous manner. There is nothing of despair in their tone, only a vivid outpouring of happiness in the contemplation of the beloved and in the powerful torrents of nature. The original verses were written to commemorate the poet's engagement to Mathilde Mauté, and they embody all his hopes for a reformed life, without the guilt and misery of his former existence; hopes which were dashed by his own quarrelsome and insidious nature. The song cycle itself has several interesting connections. It was dedicated to Emma Bardac, who gave the first performance of it, and who was later to become the wife of Debussy, himself a piano pupil of Mathilde Mauté's mother. The cycle has often been referred to as the French Dichterliebe, but this is unfair to both composers. Fauré's work actually exhibits a unique combination of religious and pagan attitudes. In its portrayal of the fiancée, likened to a saint in her aureole and Carlovingian lady in her tower, it regresses to the glory of France's Gothic past, with its impulse towards courtly love and spiritual devotion. On the other hand, the 'golden note of horn heard in the distant woods' brings with it a vernal eruption which, by the time the final song is reached, achieves an almost biological vigour and propulsion. It is not for nothing that M. Jankélévitch has compared this work to Stravinsky's Le Sacre du Printemps.

The cycle requires singing of a very high order, by a baritone with a moderate range. The bulk of the songs are in quick tempo, and the soaring and arching qualities of the accompaniments demand a partner of unshakeable confidence. The first song shows Fauré's neat, step-wise counterpoint, and gradually builds up from a gentle *allegretto*. The next—*Puisque l'aube grandit*—begins the extraordinary rhapsodical movement which persists, with interludes, to the end of the work. Supporting *La Lune blanche*, the third song, is some very Schumanesque piano writing in triple time, and the voice's breathtaking ascent at the *dolcissimo* words, 'c'est l'heure exquise', makes a finely judged climax. Agitation threatens to envelop the fifth song, *J'ai presque peur en vérité*, but fears are gradually allowed to melt and subside, the mood of forbearance which supervenes at the phrase '. . . que je vous aime' being marvellously realized. In *Avant que tu ne t'en ailles*, the piano part speeds the voice on its way in a dotted rhythm which vividly evokes the 'thousand twittering quail in the thyme', and succeeds in making this song one of the best in the cycle. Conversely, the voice almost steals in during the *molto più lento* of the next song, leading to a denouement for which Fauré had to coax his imagination over several weeks. The lovely *N'est-ce pas* proceeds to show what Fauré can do by means of simple intervals for the voice, but it is in the last song of all that the composer triumphs. *L'Hiver a cessé* is perhaps the greatest of all spring songs—it is a veritable supplication of joy, overflowing with energy and motion. It makes an inspired conclusion to this testament of acceptance. Seen against the background of his other work, *La Bonne Chanson* expresses Fauré's optimism and belief in the power of innocence; it stands at the opposite extreme from his Venetian settings, which emphasize the sadness of love, and the precious moments of escape from life's entanglements; it asserts the freshness of early morning, where they retreat into the shadows of night. In the history of French song it makes a magnificent contrast to the desolate Baudelaire settings of Duparc and Debussy.

The final songs, belonging to Fauré's old age, do not repeat the affirmation of *La Bonne Chanson*, though in *La Chanson d'Eve*, dating from 1907 to 1910, on poems of van Lerberghe, he renews his preoccupation with the dawn of life, investing this theme with symbolic elements only partially religious. A further book by this Belgian poet, whose work belongs with the products of the fin-de-siècle period, was set to music by Fauré between 1915 and 1918. This was *Le Jardin clos*. Both of these ventures reveal the composer's later manner, which is generally held to be desiccated and devoid of passion, giving rise to what M. Vuillermoz describes as 'une zone aride' in the territory accorded to his genius.[1] Unemotional these later cycles certainly are, though the style of writing they exhibit cannot be so easily disregarded. To the musician, if not to the hedonist, these works show clearly the harvest Fauré reaped as a result of his lifelong study of the classics, and especially the strict contrapuntal composers of the sixteenth century. In his old age he was to strive for something of their formal serenity and humble craftsmanship. There is more chromaticism in Fauré's melodic line than this admission might suggest, but the manner in which his parts converge tends to be increasingly austere and undemonstrative. Only in the tenth and last song in the former cycle—O mort, poussière d'étoiles, in which Eve expresses her longing for death—do we get an inkling of Fauré's own pathetic resignation, now that he had almost reached the end of his journey.

In L'Horizon chimérique, the seventy-seven year old composer embarked on his ultimate voyage across unknown seas towards that indistinct horizon which was to be his final glimpse of infinity. This cycle, set to verses of the young and recently dead Jean de la Ville de Mirmont, inevitably recalls those imaginary voyages of Duparc and Chausson, to whom the reveries of the study gradually became a vicarious substitute for the exotic travels they never undertook. Its restrained pantheism yields up a calm beauty not to be found anywhere else in Fauré's large output of song, and the third in the cycle, the apostrophe to Diana, is surely one of his most touchingly rapturous compositions.

The last decades of Fauré's life were also taken up with a succession of chamber works which have added enormously to his stature as a composer. Foremost among these is the second Violin Sonata, Op. 108, which he dedicated to the Queen of Belgium, who was herself a violinist of moderate attainments and who had expressed some admiration for his work. The sonata has aroused mixed comment. Some, like Edward Lockspeiser, have claimed that it lacks the freshness and melodic appeal of its predecessor. Others,

[1] Perhaps the deepest felt of these later cycles is the short series entitled Mirages which the singer Gérard Souzay has aptly compared to the famous series of water-lily paintings by Monet. The final song—Danseuse—is particularly poignant.

among whom Professor Wilfred Mellers may be numbered, are impressed by the strength and effulgence of the work, particularly its last movement, which recaptures something of the mysterious *élan vital* of the final song in *La Bonne Chanson*. About the Second Piano Quintet there are fewer disagreements. This work has affiliations with Fauré's opera *Pénélope*—also a relatively late composition—and its first movement has been described by Koechlin as the finest in the whole corpus of Fauré's chamber music. Even Poulenc, who deplored the lack of that quality he termed *aigu* in Fauré's work, has been known to praise it. In addition, there are the two cello sonatas, of which the second may once again be taken to illustrate Fauré's fluent gifts, especially for inventing step-wise melody. This flowering of the composer's talent for *ensemble* should not excuse his critics from exploring the earlier chamber works, in particular the piano quartets, which are full of grace and brilliance for the solo instrument. Fauré conceives the role of the piano in these works as almost like that of a harp, and the writing contains delicious examples of his famous *vaporeux* manner. As Edward Lockspeiser has truly stated:

The chamber music of Fauré, consisting of a body of works comparable in range to the chamber works of Schumann and Brahms, was written . . . over a long period. In all these chamber works Fauré was unaffected by his contemporaries (apart from Saint-Saëns), whether they were older men such as Franck or younger men discovering new worlds of their own such as Debussy and Ravel.

Regrettably little of this body of works has yet come to occupy a firm place in the repertory, such as that accorded the Franck Piano Quintet, or the two string quartets of the impressionist masters. M. Tortelier has recently given both cello sonatas repeated hearings, and this portent may easily constitute the signal for a new advance.

Meantime is it possible to pronounce some kind of valedictory upon Fauré and his music? Was he really the last in a long line of composer-savants—a 'classic of modern times', such as Mr Norman Suckling has described? Or does he begin to assume the retrospective aspect of a pioneer, one of those unacknowledged discoverers upon whose shoulders the *avant-garde* continually seeks to hoist itself into position? Perhaps after all he is neither of these things, but simply a late Romantic composer who brought to fruition tendencies apparent in French music from the early days of the Empire, and implicit in those magically youthful songs of a summer night by Berlioz? Justice compels us to choose among these alternatives, yet it is also justice which prevents us from being satisfied with our choice.

A classic, in a sense, he certainly was, though if we consider his position vis-à-vis the Beethoven succession we can see at once that it was Fauré's championship of Palestrina and the Gregorian school that enabled France to escape so easily those suffocating inhibitions which attended the later development of symphonic music in Germany and England. Along with Saint-Saëns, who deserves the credit for reviving the Baroque masters and for reawakening interest in Rameau, Fauré stood for a vitally important national and musical principle—the right to resist those weighty Teutonic goals prescribed for music by pedants and idolaters in neighbouring countries, and pursue instead the traditional French ideals of taste, clarity and economy.

To perceive in Fauré, on the other hand, a harbinger of the age of Stravinsky, is not as far-fetched as it might appear. His influence, through his numerous pupils, has been far more formative on the present generation of musicians than many of them would care to admit. Nadia Boulanger, in particular, has been instrumental in communicating the principles she learnt at Fauré's feet to both her own countrymen and also the expatriate Americans, like Aaron Copland and Virgil Thomson. British composers have since been known to take up residence at the 'boulangerie', and it would scarcely be an exaggeration to state that both Walton and Britten have benefited indirectly from the importations resulting from their stay; so too an important circle of writers and critics, who in their turn have helped to spread knowledge of Fauré and his school. All of these circumstances converge to cast doubt on the assumption that his voice is no longer capable of reaching out to us from the past.

As anyone reading Fauré's biography cannot help observing, he had in some ways a very modern attitude to the art of composition. There was nothing of the romantic soul-searching about this attitude. One young lady was to discover this rude fact when she asked the composer where he had derived the inspiration for that most ethereal of his works for piano, the beautiful Sixth Nocturne. 'In the Simplon tunnel,' replied the aged Fauré, with utmost seriousness. Such is hardly the response of a Romantic composer. He had, moreover, a surprising degree of tolerance of the new music. One can scarcely help applauding his comments on Debussy's *Cinq Poèmes de Baudelaire*, which had appeared while he was still at the height of his powers. These torrid works not only combine the Wagnerian and Impressionist styles—and may thus be said to stand at a sharp angle to Fauré's particular sympathies—but they also embody an erotic element calculated to have shocked most respectable musicians of the nineteenth century. They could by no stretch of imagination be regarded as helping to exemplify Fauré's ideal of French song. Yet the older composer, once he had heard them, did not hesitate to declare that they comprised a work of genius—going on to add, with a characteristic dry wit, that he continued nevertheless to prefer his own songs! And this event, it should be remembered, took place at a time when fashionable opinion was just about to deride *La Bonne Chanson*, and rally around the composer of *L'Après-midi d'un faune*. It is difficult to think of any earlier composer, except perhaps Schumann, who was as generous in his praise of those about to supplant him.

Compared with the formidable d'Indy, who had the reputation of pressing hard on the talents entrusted to his keeping at the Schola Cantorum, Fauré must be seen as an apostle of freedom. Marguerite Long, his favourite interpreter of the piano works, even tells how Fauré's directorship was equated in certain quarters with that other and more infamous Directory in France's history:

Sous son influence, un esprit nouveau souffle qui transforme la vieille maison. On l'appelle 'Robespierre' tant les réformes qu'il impose la bouleversent.

Scarcely the sort of comparison likely to be invoked to describe a conservative!

Equally unexpected is the opinion by which the Professor of Composition at the Geneva Conservatory sought to resume Fauré's achievements in this sphere. Commenting that his directorship had resulted in a seismic movement, which had the effect of rousing other institutions from their torpor, he added the information that teachers all over Europe had been inclined to look to his example when introducing their own reforms. Fauré, he suggested, was the test case in whose person modern music stood its academic trial. Whatever form our final verdict on Fauré takes, it therefore seems unlikely that he will continue much longer to be labelled an unqualified reactionary.

In the last few decades Fauré's own compatriots have been busy attempting to make amends for their and the world's short-sightedness. As early as 1937, Mme Germaine de Jouvenel had founded the Association des Amis de Gabriel Fauré. This organization gradually became responsible for making known the full range of the composer's chamber music and the full stature of his inspiration. Competitions for executants wishing to perform his works were held, and these included both vocal and instrumental prizes. One of the first winners of the piano prize was Jean Doyen. A further creditable outcome of the association's endeavours was the biographical study of M. Jankélévitch, to which we have several times had recourse. Since that time there have been others who have come forward on Fauré's behalf, one notable and unexpected tribute coming from the extrovert Richard Strauss, whose own music seems to have so little in common with that of the French composer. In the years following the Second World War, performances of his work became obligatory in most European capitals, even in Moscow, where the Ballade was vociferously acclaimed in 1955, with Mme Long herself as the veteran soloist. Her performance marked the termination of fifty years during which she had maintained her advocacy of the composer in both classroom and concert hall.[1] In the new climate brought into being by these events, criticism cannot any longer be delayed for lack of evidence.

The world of Gabriel Fauré may not be precisely of our own time and place, but it remains a benevolent and civilizing world, which we can ill afford not to enter. It harbours, in greater proportion than any other since the Enlightenment, those gifts of measure, style and intelligibility which have long been the patrimony of Frenchmen.

[1] As I write these words, news comes from Paris of the death of Mme Long, in her ninety-third year. She was the last pianist to have had personal contact with the Fauré tradition.

Chapter 2

HENRI DUPARC
An Aesthetic Tragedy

AFTER the normality of Fauré, the case of his friend and rival Henri Duparc assumes something of the pathos of genius unfulfilled. For, despite an even longer life than the Director of the Conservatoire, this second great contributor to French song revealed a creative span of cruelly short duration. The complete opposite of his more academic forerunner, Duparc was one of those artists whose talents are burnt out in rapid fashion, and to whom the act of composition is as agonized as it is short-lived. Like his Austrian contemporary Hugo Wolf he represents a case of musical possession on the grand scale, in which formal skill and knowledge were made to dance to the capriciousness of inspiration. And, also like the composer of the *Italienisches Liederbuch*, he suffered the torments of nervous prostration. What makes Duparc unique among musical case histories is the seemingly inexplicable way in which the tap of his genius was, so to speak, suddenly turned off when in full flow; and the poignant manner in which he endeavoured, for almost fifty years that followed, to repossess his lost gifts.

Born in 1848—a fact whose revolutionary implications he himself pointed out in one of his letters to Alexis Rouart—Duparc was in origins a Parisian, another point in which he differed from the provincial Fauré. Although he was ultimately to become a lawyer by profession, he enrolled early at the college at Vaugirard, where his piano teacher was none other than the *Pater seraphicus* of French music, César Franck. The college was a Jesuit foundation, not especially intended to train young persons for a musical career, and there is no evidence that Henri was disposed to take his piano lessons any more seriously than his other studies. When the teacher was Franck, however, it remains hard not to suspect that an influence—baleful or otherwise—was at work. At all events the effect of the older man's personality was such that music became a growing obsession with his pupil. Having, on his own testimony, no aptitude for the piano, young Duparc responded better to the theoretical aspects of music, and he was early set to the task of reading scores by Bach, Gluck, Beethoven and others. By the time he had outgrown adolescence he was already something of a composer himself, and had a few tentative works, either for piano solo or piano in combination with another instrument, to his credit. The next step was to seek publication, and this mark of professionalism was achieved in 1868, when his set of six piano pieces—*Feuilles volantes*—was issued by the firm of Flaxland. These, as their titles imply, owe much to Schumann, and though they do reveal a mature grasp of pianistic idiom— something which was to serve the composer well when he came to devise accompaniments to the songs—they do not otherwise call for analysis. The sentiments they evoke are facile and romantic. A series of songs which Duparc embarked upon at the same time come into a different category. Altogether there were five songs written during this year, only two of which—*Chanson triste* and *Soupir*—the composer decided to retain. Even these were not acclaimed at that time, but had to wait until 1910, when Duparc's stature was more widely recognized. In the meantime it was assumed that he had destroyed the others. At least this was the assumption up until 1945, when one of the supposedly rejected group, *Le Galop*, was rediscovered. It was published a few years later by the house of Durand. When in 1949 Dr Sydney Northcote came to write his admirable book on Duparc's songs, he was not unnaturally forced to conclude that further discoveries were unlikely. Writing of the significance of the year 1868 in Duparc's career he had this to say:

> To it belong, also, five songs: *Sérénade* (Gabriel Marc), Romance de Mignon (after Goethe), *Galop* (Sully-Prudhomme), *Chanson triste* (Lahor) and *Soupir* (Sully-Prudhomme). But of all of the year's work the composer suppressed all but the last two songs. There is reason to suppose that *Galop* might also have been spared if the manuscript of a second version of the song had not been lost.

Since the writing of Dr Northcote's book certain new finds have nevertheless come to light. It is now possible to see the manuscripts of the two outstanding songs, previously considered missing, at the Bibliothèque Nationale in Paris. These melodies—*Sérénade* and

Romance de Mignon—assist further in building up our portrait of the composer's style. The score of *Sérénade* is actually reproduced in full in what has now become recognized as the standard work on French song—Frits Noske's masterly *La Mélodie française de Berlioz à Duparc*, written while the author was Professor of the History of Music at Amsterdam, and published in 1954. The importance attaching to these discoveries may not be immediately obvious, but we must remember that, without them, Duparc's entire output is limited to fourteen songs. In such a slender production each new addition must alter our perspective, if only very slightly.

Accordingly we now have in our possession a total of sixteen melodies, all written somewhere between 1868 and 1885, when the composer's nervous affliction caused his creative gift to be extinguished. Before examining each of these in the detail they merit, we would do well to remind ourselves of the other salient facts in Duparc's life, and also to note briefly the few remaining compositions, outside the field of song, which occupied him. At the point at which the 1868 songs were completed, Duparc's interests became greatly enlarged in a number of different directions. In the first place, he made a trip to Munich, in the company of Vincent d'Indy, where the two young men heard *Das Rheingold* and *Tristan und Isolde*, the newly written music dramas of Richard Wagner. The Wagnerian influence, successfully resisted by Fauré some years later, was one to which Duparc immediately fell prey. This does not, as we shall see, imply that evil consequences were to ensue in his case. It is merely that we must reckon with Wagner as a potent factor in the development of Duparc, as indeed in that of Debussy. Where the composer of *Pelléas* was able to outgrow his experiences of Wagner's music, Duparc's much shorter career, creatively speaking, gave him little opportunity to break completely free. Listening to Duparc's songs, with the hindsight of over a century of Wagnerism, we can observe numerous signs of preoccupation with this influence. Professor Mellers speaks, without any intention to slight, of the 'Wagnerian amplitude' of many of the songs in the Rouart-Lerolle collection, and indeed one can scarcely avoid noting the great length of the harmonic periods and the unusually protracted phrase rhythms, both features of style we have nowadays come to associate with Bayreuth. Chromaticism and the use of enharmonic modulation are additional traits to be found in both composers. Dr Northcote devotes much space to repudiating the suggestion that it was only Wagner who appealed to the French composer in this way. His analysis points instead to the no less discernible influence of Liszt, some of whose orchestral technique was certainly appropriated by Duparc, when he came to write his symphonic poem, *Lénore*, and whose influence has been underestimated.

What now seems indisputable is the fact that Duparc was able, through a series of friendships which he developed in the years leading up to the Franco-Prussian War, to make his way to the centre of a group of keenly sensitive and progressive musicians, intent on hearing as much of the new music as possible, and indeed in contributing to it themselves. He became secretary, as well as one of the founders, of the Société Nationale, and on the cessation of hostilities we find him consistently being deferred to as something of an authority on the promotion of musical activities in the capital. This aptitude for organizing, and sensitivity to civic duty, can be traced in Duparc's extramusical career, first as a lawyer and ultimately as mayor of a provincial town. It contrasts somewhat oddly with his reputation as a neurasthenic. At this stage, however, it was certainly true that Duparc worked hard at the society's activities, which he took exceptionally seriously; as may be inferred from his decision to renounce even his place on the committee once it became obvious that his composing days were at an end. Through his work the society's aims became tangible and recognizable throughout France. His colleagues in this sterling work were the brilliant Alexis de Castillon, whose own compositions are at last beginning to get some of the acclaim they deserve, and of course the great teachers of the period, Franck, Saint-Saëns and Fauré. The ties of friendship created as a result of this common pursuit were remarkable, and survived many a subsequent rupture in musical circles. Even at the end of Fauré's reign as director, when factionalism had reached its height, and the S.M.I. (Société Musicale Indépendante) had been formed to rival the older society, it is surprising how the loyalties engendered by the members of the group towards one another continued to surface. Perhaps it is not too partisan to credit Duparc himself with having done a good deal to bolster these sentiments. He was a man who throughout his long life was devoutly loved by his friends, of whom he made a great many. Whether it was his courage in the face of illness—shown movingly in the letters he wrote to his fellow musicians—or simply his naturally gregarious temperament which made him the recipient of such affection, it is now hard to assess. We owe it to his memory to stress this aspect of his character, whatever were the motives underlying it.

In our post-Freudian age it is always a temptation to classify people according to their psychological disabilities. Duparc, on account of the drying up of his gifts, and the gradual withdrawal from active life which helped poison his later years, might easily present himself to the twentieth-century imagination as a sinister recluse. Nothing could be further from the truth. A photograph taken of the composer in early middle age shows him, in practice, to have been a large, comfortable-looking man, dressed as a bit of a dandy, with smoothly immaculate skin and a wavy set of *boulevardier* moustaches. He looks all the world like one of the boon companions of Boni de Castellane, that turn-of-the-century Sun King about whom Miss Cornelia Otis Skinner has written so amusingly. We are not told whether he, like many Parisians of his period, lingered in the company of the *grandes horizontales* at Maxim's or the Café de la Paix, but there is no doubt that he was what Dr Johnson would describe as a 'clubbable' man, happy in the company of his fellow mortals and amenable to the distractions of the *flâneur*.

Deferring for a while the opportunity to explore these ramifications of Duparc's personality, let us instead take a closer look at some of the compositions which belong to this burgeoning period in the artist's life. In addition to the 1868 songs, the composer was to write a new song for each of the succeeding years up to and including 1871. At least one of these three is acknowledged to be a masterpiece. The first, written in 1869, relates directly to the war and is entitled *Au pays où se fait la guerre*. The text is taken from a poem in Gautier's *La Comédie de la Mort*, and it depicts the anguish felt by a young girl whose lover has been called away to the front. The second, written in 1870, is the well-known *L'Invitation au voyage*, a setting of Baudelaire's famous exhortation to Marie Daubrun, inviting her to accompany him on an imaginary journey to Holland, land of tulip-laden fields, canals and misty suns. The song realizes exceptionally clearly those sensations, *luxe, calme et volupté*, by which the poet sought to transcend his Parisian existence. Both it and the poem are superbly atmospheric creations. Finally, in 1871, came the highly charged *La Vague et la cloche*, on verses by François Coppée, which shows Duparc at his most intensely dramatic.

Taking each of these melodies individually, beginning with the reclaimed *Sérénade*, we find some of the same characteristics that we encountered in the initial songs of Fauré. Frits Noske, for example, stresses the probability that the point of departure for both writers was Gounod. He argues in respect of *Sérénade*:

La suavité de la ligne vocale, la division des temps forts, les syncopés fluides, l'harmonie marquée par l'emploi des accords de médiante, tout cela décèle nettement l'influence de l'auteur de *Vénise*.

Like Gounod's own song of that title, it is in 6–8 time, and the rhythm remains uncompromisingly clear throughout. The accents fall regularly on the first beat, even when the syllables concerned are isolated pronouns ('*Je me fanerais*', etc.). In this connection it is interesting to make plain the difference between French, as a language for singing, and the other principal tongues. French song tends to avoid any really strong accentuation not already suggested by the rhythm. This usually means that the declamatory aspects of singing are conveyed more through tonal contrasts, changes of register and the like. It is certainly unidiomatic singing which seeks to impose on a French *mélodie* the same sort of emphatic stresses as are inflicted on the Italian aria.

Paul Valéry has many illuminating things to say on the special qualities which go to make up French speech—it is a subject upon which he has no peer among living commentators—and it is worth while quoting some of his more salutary suggestions:

Three characteristics clearly distinguish French from other Western languages: French, well spoken, hardly sings at all. It is a discourse in a narrow register, a more level speech than others. Next, the consonants in French are remarkably soft—no harsh or guttural forms. There is no French consonant that any European cannot pronounce. Finally, French vowels are numerous and very finely shaded, forming a rare and precious collection of delicate tones, offering to poets worthy of the name values they can play upon to compensate for the temperate register and the

generally moderate accentuation in their language. The variety of the é
and è; the rich diphthongs, such as feuille, paille, pleure, toise, tien, etc.; the
mute e which is sometimes sounded, or again hardly heard at all, before
fading altogether, allowing many subtle effects of perceptible silence, and
either ending or prolonging many words in a kind of shadow left behind
by an accented syllable: these are the means, whose efficacy can be shown by
endless examples.

All exponents of French song would do well to consider carefully
these profound observations. They help to explain, not only many
of the nuances of song-writers such as Fauré and Duparc, but also
the characteristic vocal effects by which artists of the calibre of
Bernac and Souzay have enhanced their reputation. We shall have a
good deal to say a little later about Duparc's own strictures to the
performer: it is sufficient at this point simply to affirm the fact that
he wrote all his songs in deference to the principles which we have
described. A voice which was inclined to bellow nauseated him, as
did any attempt to add spurious 'expression' to a song by means of
histrionic emphasis. What he liked best was what he called the
'violin voice'—which was another way of describing those qualities
of springiness or elasticity necessary to overcoming obstacles with
a sense of ease. As for 'expression', this was considered a problem
for the song-writer rather than the singer. All in all, he would have
agreed with d'Indy that vocal declamation should approximate to
the speaking patterns.

Other important Duparc trade marks which appear in Sérénade
include the characteristic use of an arpeggiated accompaniment. In
this case the arpeggio figure, which remains unchanged throughout
the entire composition, consists of a run up of three notes in the
bass, to be played with the left hand, followed by a broken chord
in the right hand. The manner in which the chord is broken is quite
significant. It consists of a single note for the thumb and a triad
played together in the upper part. Thus the whole figure has the
spread-out quality of an arpeggio proper, as well as the solidity of a
chordal accompaniment. The originator of this unusual type of
pianistic device is generally held to have been César Franck, who
certainly uses it to telling effect in his Prélude, Chorale and Fugue. In this
work the extended arpeggios are completed by crossing the left
hand over the right, and they are crowned not by a single top note,

but by the chord of the third. This ingenious idea helped to give Franck's piano music some of that sonorous power for which it is rightly famous. However, Franck's chorale was not written until 1884–5, and we must therefore regard this kind of experimentation as quite new at the time Duparc uses it in his song *Sérénade*. Accordingly whether Franck's young pupil was in some degree responsible for inspiring his master reverts to being an open question. In all probability, the piano lessons which Duparc received at Vaugirard, and which he somewhat sheepishly disclaimed as a source of practical benefit to him as a pianist, had a lasting impact on him as a composer. In this sense he was doubtless able to apprehend some of the various forms of piano writing taking shape in his master's head. These forms were to have quite a marked effect on the evolution of piano style. They can be clearly discerned in the compositions of many other Franck disciples who wrote more extensively for the instrument than did Duparc; in particular in the works of Duparc's friend Pierre de Bréville, and later on in the variations of de la Presle.

Romance de Mignon, the second of the newly discovered 1868 songs, was based on an adaptation of one of Goethe's poems made by the little-known Victor Wilder. It is rather a mediocre poem and it did not inspire Duparc to a distinguished setting. Here the writing is Wagnerian and in contrast with *Sérénade* it has a slow repeated chord accompaniment, located in the treble, rather in the manner of the prelude to Act I of *Lohengrin*. It is a strophic song, which should lead us to inquire what attitude Duparc took up towards the matter of stanza repetition. In general he is not as impatient to get away from the strophic idea as Fauré and Debussy were. The traces of strophic form can easily be detected even in such an inspired song as *L'Invitation au voyage*, where the variation in the texture of the accompaniment, plainly apparent in the second verse, is scarcely a radical departure. Occasionally Duparc will choose a poem which allows him to repeat a verse exactly—like *Testament*, in which the first and last verses are identical; but he never commits the venal sin against which Tennyson inveighed when he protested about his words being set to music not once but twice or even thrice, while the composer paused for a metaphorical breather. In *Romance de Mignon* there is some anticipation of the rhythm during the repeat, and a few chromatic notes are added to the melodic line. Otherwise its forms are simple enough and the mood of the song is nostalgic and uncomplicated. Whether the composer was right to suppress this and *Sérénade* is hard to say.

Le Galop also seems to have German rather than French affinities, and Professor Noske sees the song as reminiscent of one of Schubert's dramatic monologues. It certainly possesses some of that driving impetuosity which we impute to the *Lied*, though the chromatic scales which underlie the repeated chord accompaniment give a hint of Franck's influence. Considered in the context of Duparc's complete output, it belongs with those virile and hurtling melodies, like *La Vague et la cloche* and *Le Manoir de Rosamonde*, which stand in sharp distinction to the more quiet and dejected group of which *Lamento* and *Elégie* may be taken as typical. A strong undercurrent of anxiety seems to lurk in all of Duparc's songs, however, and is present even in such a volatile outburst as *Le Galop*. In this and in one or two other instances a purist might question whether Duparc has not come dangerously near to mixing his moods; or, if that is putting it too forcibly, whether he has not occasionally intruded into a poem emotions which the author did not envisage. Even *Chanson triste* has been regarded by certain critics as too light and airy to be an exact realization of the text, though in this particular case one cannot help feeling that the title is not a good indication of the poem's mood. This further song, which was set to verses of the French doctor who took the pen name of Lahor, is possibly the most advanced of the 1868 melodies. Both vocally and in its piano part it poses some complex ideas; though the sentiments aroused by the music are not in any way remarkable. To begin with it requires a very extended range, the notes of the melody covering an octave and a sixth. This is exceptional for French and German song alike; Richard Strauss commonly wrote for a wider compass than any other German composer, and his settings average about an octave and a fourth, which is a clear two tones in excess of what Schubert, Schumann or Wolf would aspire to. French song, even though one might not expect it to do so, on account of the greater recitative it employs, does in fact tend in the direction of a large compass, though not so large as Duparc uses here. Fauré and Chausson are both content with a normal *tessitura*. Debussy is the exception, and his songs, though again they do not seem to suggest it on first hearing, actually go beyond those of Strauss in amplitude. This song of Duparc's is therefore not unique in French music, but it does enter a territory which, at the time it was written, had not been explored. Later on Duparc had to put in some alternative notes for the benefit of moderate performers.

The last of this set, *Soupir*, is without doubt the best. It is not heavily weighted, despite its grief-stricken tones, and the tentative but piercing notes of the piano immediately evoke the right atmosphere. In fact the voice and piano blend beautifully in this song, each going its gentle way as if lost in reverie, yet they do not seem to collide. It is dedicated to Duparc's mother, and it is probable that Sully-Prudhomme's verses in this case touched off some very personal feeling in the composer. The poet, who was a scientist by training, was incidentally struck down by a paralysis somewhat resembling Duparc's own malady, and is another instance of a life circumscribed by the sick-room. He did, however, continue to work at his poetry until his death in 1907. His verse was much admired by Anatole France, and the text of *Le Galop* was also written by him. *Soupir* is a good example of a song in which the voice steals in quietly, fairly high up on the stave, with magical effect. Both Fauré and Duparc were fond of such openings, and they could be said to represent a feature more commonly found in the French *mélodie* than in the *Lied*. Debussy again offers many instances of the same predilection. Harmonic subtleties become evident in *Soupir*, especially the use of suspensions to add piquancy and colour. Duparc's favourite dominant minor ninth chords are also tried out. The alternation between major and minor tonalities gives a certain ambiguity to the song, and the way in which the voice seems to 'run down', by means of diminishing phrase rhythms, is responsible for the feeling epitomized in the title. The long-drawn-out '. . . toujours' at the very end is particularly effective, with the low tonic resolution gently assisting the sound to merge into silence. James Husst Hall claims to detect the Franck influence in the chromatic drifting of bars 29–35. Possibly the mood of the song is also Franckist, since the whole setting conveys that peculiar feeling of 'serene agitation' which critics have paradoxically attributed to the composer of *Les Béatitudes*. Martin Cooper, however, describes it as more in the *Tristan* manner. In his valuable book *French Music from the Death of Berlioz to the Death of Fauré* (1951) Cooper makes a point of paramount importance when he notes that Duparc's use of chromatics never extends to the typical Franckist sliding bass line. On the contrary, Duparc's basses are steady and provide a solid foundation over which passing harmonies can bring a sense of inflection. The harmony does not change at a very rapid pace in Duparc, and in this trait he imitates Wagner. Cooper goes on to argue that, whereas the static harmony created in this way might be thought a disadvantage in an operatic or symphonic composer, in the song composer it is not so. Writing of this habit he says:

This is possible in song-writing, where the danger of monotony is small owing to the smallness of the form. It is not possible in larger works, but Duparc either did not write or else destroyed his larger works, and for him it was a solution.

From this it is only a step to the position that Duparc is least successful in his longer songs, like *La Vie antérieure* and *La Vague et la cloche*. Such a view is not necessarily a logical corollary of the first. There are many critics who, quite to the contrary, describe these two songs as Duparc's best. A more convincing line of argument has been advanced by those, once more including Cooper, who detect a certain tendency on Duparc's part to pad out his texture with the sort of semi-orchestral material which has no place in the compact world of the song. This, however, is another, though related, question. We shall attempt to make some assessment of this claim when discussing the equally controversial question of whether Duparc's orchestrations of the accompaniments to some of his songs deserve to supplant the piano versions.

Meantime what are we to make of the three songs written between 1869 and 1871? *La Vague et la cloche* is something of a monster among songs, both in its length and its gruesome content. Dr Northcote makes no bones about disliking the poem, and he cannot have been the only one to experience a vertiginous sensation of a most unpleasant kind after reading it. It reminds one of a short story by Edgar Allan Poe. The following specimen will give an indication of the style and subject matter:

'Once, laid low by drink, I dreamed I floated lightless through the

39

waves and turmoil of the nightbound sea, a gloomy oarsman despairing of a landfall. The ocean spat its slime upon my brow, the wind froze me with horror to the marrow. . . . '

All of a sudden the dream changes and the poet imagines himself to be alone in an ancient belfry, terrifyingly astride a rocking bell. In the final stanza the crazy swinging of the bell, embodying no ascertainable purpose, is compared to man's life on earth—a compound of useless toil and endless din. The whole poem is an example of grotesque symbolism. The poet, François Coppée, was at one time archivist to the Comédie Française, and was elected a member of the Academy. As may readily be inferred, his talents were of a more dramatic and personal order than those of the typical Parnassian poet. His appeal for Duparc remains obscure. It is possible that the composer's sojourn with Liszt at Weimar left him with something of the great man's taste for the diabolical. If so, there is no other evidence of it in the songs written during this period, or indeed any other period of Duparc's career.

The setting itself is tremendously full-blooded and offers limitless opportunities to the singer with a powerful lower register. The impetus of the song derives to a large extent from the rhythmic figure in the bass of the piano part. This can be heard throughout the setting, providing an insidious and menacing background to the singer's vivid declamation. Later in the song, when the bell-ride is evoked, the clanging fifths of the piano enact the hideous row. For those who like such macabre sensations, the song must be regarded as a *tour de force*. There is nothing quite like it in the entire literature of the voice. Schumann's piano piece entitled *In der Nacht* (from the *Fantasiestücke*, Op. 11) comes closest to it in atmosphere, though it is far from realizing the full pitch of morbid elation to which Duparc's song gives rise.

By comparison the war-time lament—*Au pays où se fait la guerre*—is more typical of the recitative and aria accorded to operatic heroines. That is, it has some declamatory qualities, but is also romantic in feeling. An old French rondeau in form, the song is not so often heard as many other Duparc settings, perhaps because the sentiments evoked are considered to have period associations of the less fashionable kind. Despite this, the acclaim in which the song has been held by critics is greater than that attaching to its companions, except for the Baudelaire and de Lisle settings. Perhaps it is on account of the song's independence from obvious influences. The melody is modal and conspicuously avoids the factitious *salon* qualities which neither Fauré nor Duparc was always above resorting to. It grows in intensity from verse to verse until it reaches a peroration quite powerful enough for the opera house. This is a characteristic we find in other Duparc songs—the unexpected final strophe in *Lamento* comes quickly to mind—as he seemed to enjoy, in common with many of his operatic colleagues, the climactic impulse which seeks to finish a song in a blaze of glory. In this inclination he was at the opposite remove from Fauré. Perhaps the most outstanding example of climax in Duparc comes at the end of *Phidylé*, where the piano's efforts at imitating a full Wagnerian orchestra are pathetically insufficient.

Few would deny that, among these earlier songs, *L'Invitation au Voyage* stands in deepest affection with the composer's admirers. It is by any standards one of the most marvellous songs ever written. Philip Hope-Wallace speaks for a devoted circle when he says:

. . . when I hear the climax of the second verse of *L'Invitation au voyage*, where the singer describes the great barges crowding the Dutch canals, I momentarily think it the crown of all lyrical effusions, specially at that marvellous deep plunge from the left hand in the piano part!

There are so many unsolved problems relating to this song, however, that it is difficult to know just where to begin. Commentators seem hopelessly divided over whether it really needs orchestral support to do it justice. Clearly the shimmering broken chord effects, over a double pedal—both tonic and dominant—with which the song opens, are a gift to the sensitive accompanist and cry out for retention on the keyboard. The same could be said of their replacement by high-pitched arpeggios in the second verse, though these could be managed as well by a harp. The reservations concerning the use of the piano come in when the left-hand plunge described by Mr Hope-Wallace makes its appearance. At this juncture the eruption of a full orchestra seems called for. As with the famous case of Moussorgsky's *Pictures at an Exhibition*, there are times when one is convinced that the piano is the best instrument for the work, and other times when the rightness of the orchestral version seems unquestionable. Professor Mellers has, as usual, put his finger on the precise dilemma in saying:

> The piano parts are beautifully written and a delight to play: but they are all orchestral in the sense that they suggest the 'pianistic' orchestration of the nineteenth century. Floating arpeggios approximate to a haze of strings, pedal notes to sustained horns.

That Duparc was himself fully aware of the difficulties his accompaniments posed is proved by the fact that some of the songs —notably La Vague et la cloche and La Vie antérieure—were actually composed for orchestra, and were only later transcribed for single instrument. Duparc was an amazingly skilful orchestrator, as one might expect from a disciple of Wagner and Liszt, and the question is not whether his own orchestrations are adequate, but whether they outshine his equally skilful piano arrangements. Here we begin to receive a hint of some of the conflicts which were at the back of Duparc's consciousness. He was an indefatigable reviser of his scores, and to state that he was a perfectionist gives no idea of the torments of indecision he experienced whenever he was faced with this sort of conundrum. In some ways his trouble as a composer stemmed from the fact that he was too clever by half. Plagued with doubts, he would return again and again to a score he had considered complete, with results which would not invariably seem an improvement. There is one tragic letter in which he begs his friend de Bréville to give him his candid opinion about the orchestration of Testament, a project which Duparc describes as having imposed a 'cruel martyrdom' upon him. Nagged by the suspicion that his confidants would keep the truth from him, out of a desire not to hurt his feelings, the composer would make attempt after attempt, each one coming to seem less conclusive than the last. This hysterical element in Duparc's make-up is highly significant, as is the destructive impulse which led him to cast off scores with which he had become restive. These unfortunate afflictions were not to become apparent till a later stage, however, and we must consider first the remaining features which combine to give the Baudelaire song its enigmatic interest.

Another difficulty the song poses is in the matter of register. It is written, like most of Duparc's output, though in contrast to the songs of Fauré, for high voice. Duparc himself tended to be inflexible in the matter of transposition. The words of the song make it clear that the singer is a man, so one must conclude that the low baritone voice, generally accepted as the most suitable for French song, is in this case inadmissible. This fact has not prevented baritones from attempting the song, and it has now become a trifle invidious to suggest that some of the radiance it possesses may have been lost in the act of transposition. An even more flagrant case of failing to carry out the composer's intentions is encountered in Phidylé, which is as often as not sung by a woman, despite the contrary indications contained in the words. Possibly the songs of Duparc depend much more than those of any other composer on being sung in the keys in which they were originally written. Gifted female singers have of course been known to bring special beauties of tone to their interpretations of certain of the songs; perhaps most notably in the case of Victoria de los Angeles's performances of Phidylé. One wonders whether the composer, if he had been allowed to hear them, might not have relented a little. As it is, Soupir, L'Invitation au voyage, Extase, Le Manoir de Rosamonde, Sérénade Florentine and Phidylé are all demonstrably intended for the male voice. Moreover it is only La Vague et la cloche which specifies a low voice—indeed this song would be utterly inconceivable sung by anyone other than a bass or baritone. Many of the remaining songs are ambiguous as to the personae who inhabit them, and could equally feasibly be managed by men or women.

What is so unusual to us, looking back on a song like L'Invitation au voyage, is the astonishing maturity it exhibits. Its bold melodic contours seem hardly likely to have occurred to a relative beginner in song-writing. We can only conclude that Duparc sprang fully formed into the musical arena, an asseveration which could not be made with regard to any other French song-writer of the first rank, unless we make an exception for Poulenc. Most remarkable is Duparc's flair for handling very long melodic phrases—and here he contrasts significantly with the early Poulenc, who tended to be embarrassingly short-winded in his melodic thinking. However many turns there are to the melody in a Duparc song, we always feel that the climax comes in the right place, and is neither too soon nor too late. This is surely one of the greatest gifts a song-writer can possess, being even more important than the ability to invent tuneful material. The impact of Duparc's songs is always striking, however depressing some of them may be, and they have no difficulty in carrying an audience, something that could not invariably be said on behalf of the melodies of Debussy or Fauré, both of whom are now and then handicapped by a failure to project the music sufficiently. They reserve their appeal for those whose dramatic instincts are less overt. Duparc has something of the power to move masses, and would perhaps do so if only his songs were better known. He shares this capability with Mahler, whose *Lieder* also generate near-cosmic emotions.

The ensuing stages in the composer's career are not easy to account for. His next song, *Elégie*, was not written until 1874, after which there was a further gap of four years before the writing of *Extase*. The former is a setting of Thomas Moore's lament on the death of Robert Emmet, and is a remarkably restrained expression of grief. Both songs indicate the depth of Duparc's undeviating commitment to Wagner. It is more than probable that this commitment was now beginning to steer the composer in the inevitable direction of the opera house. Dr Northcote argues very plausibly that the hiatus in Duparc's production can be explained by his protracted search for a suitable libretto through which to embark on this new career. Documentary evidence relating to the composer's life during this period is extremely slight, and we can only assume that if this search really did take place it did not yield any results. His tastes in drama were impeccable, and it has also been suggested that he spent much time pondering on the possibility of setting *King Lear* or another Shakespearian story. It is certain that he once toyed with the ideal of writing music based on Molière's *Amphitryon*. Neither of these projects ever came to fruition, perhaps because of the same over-fastidious attitudes we have remarked earlier. That he was well up to writing an opera no one can seriously doubt. His orchestral writing, for example, shows a good deal more professionalism than that of Fauré, who foisted his more tedious chores on to his pupils, as he is reputed to have done with *Pénélope*. Evidently the plethora of details characterizing opera as a form must have come to plague him when it got to the planning stage. In the following decade he did write a quantity of music for an opera entitled *Roussalka*, and he claimed in one letter that this project had been on his mind for over twenty years. It is not clear whether he himself had written the libretto for this work or was using a translation of the Pushkin tale. There is some evidence that he possessed literary talent (and indeed even talent for painting), so that it is quite possible that he decided to work to his own inspiration. At least one act of the opera was alleged to have been completed during the eighteen-eighties, and there might well have been more. *Roussalka*, however, never saw the light of day. In a fit of self-criticism, and out of despair at his encroaching blindness, Duparc consigned the manuscript to the fire. It is entirely characteristic of the man that, not content with this appalling act, he rewrote most of it from memory, only to do exactly the same again. The second conflagration was the last, and there were no further promptings of regret.

Despite this pathological attitude, it would be misleading to imply that all Duparc's work for larger forces met with a destructive fate. In 1874 the composer had written his symphonic poem *Lénore*, which, gratifyingly for those days, received a number of performances within its first few years of life. The Société Nationale performed it in 1875 for the first time, after frantic and copious revisions had been made to the score. De Bréville admired the work enormously, as did many other discerning musicians of the time. As a concert piece it is very much of the *genre* of *Mazeppa* and *Hunnenschlacht*, and fits well into that tradition which culminates in the ebullient Strauss works. Duparc was of course not the only French composer to have attempted the symphonic poem. Franck— if he can be regarded as French—had already written *Les Eolides* in 1876, and Berlioz had set something of a precedent with his 'Witches' Sabbath' movement in the *Symphonie Fantastique*. Later composers were to build on this tradition, most notable of whom were Dukas (another artist who was smitten by the destructive impulse) and of course Debussy himself. In its propensity for attracting colourful, though not necessarily profound, music it could be said to suit the French genius very well. About *Lénore* Grove is highly complimentary, stating that it represents 'one of the best models of its kind'. Less flattering is the assessment of it made recently by Lionel Salter, who has described it as 'excessively contrived' and goes as far as to denounce it in the following terms:

. . . the debt to his teacher may be seen not only in the dedication to Franck but in its whole idiom, which is almost a Franckian parody, with subjects crawling about chromatically and phrases constantly breaking off for a breather.

The same writer compares the work unfavourably with another symphonic poem written by one of Franck's pupils, the neglected *Viviane* by Chausson, which is a re-enactment of the Merlin episode in the Arthurian legend. This work is thought by some to be superior to the same composer's much better known *Poème* for violin and orchestra. Both *Lénore* and *Viviane* have been revived recently at the Strasbourg Festival under Marcel Levine. Dating from the same time as *Lénore* is another orchestral fragment belonging to Duparc. This is the piece known as *Aux Etoiles*, originally part of a triptych entitled *Poème nocturne*. It too secured a performance under the auspices of the Société Nationale, though its two companions were to be among the subsequent victims of the composer's private incinerator. A valse, also for orchestra, completes the list of music by which Duparc may hope to be perpetuated in the concert hall.

By the time he came to write the next of his songs he had assumed an unwanted role—that of French apologist for Wagner. The attacks on that unsettling composer had been so virulent in preceding years that Duparc, who was by no means a lackey of Bayreuth, felt that something positive should be done to repel them. His own contribution was to write *Extase*, which many have compared to the last of the Wesendonk *Lieder* which Wagner wrote in preparation for *Tristan*. It is easily the most Wagnerian of all Duparc's songs, for the good reason that it was conceived as a tribute to that composer. There is no need to read into it anything more than this acknowledgment from an unextravagant admirer. The more extravagant admirers, of whom there were to be a depressingly large number over the succeeding decade, were eventually put to rout by Debussy, whose 'Golliwog's Cake-Walk', from the *Children's Corner Suite*, cocked a typical snook at the love music from Wagner's opera. Duparc himself remained unshaken by these upheavals. He had too many turmoils of his own.

Extase is, for all its indebtedness, a heartrendingly beautiful song. Particularly admirable is the way in which the accompaniment, by its unhurried quaver movement, permits the voice to unfold gradually, encouraging a cumulative build-up of emotion. Here again the accents on the first beat are given added firmness by the very low placing of the left-hand octaves in the piano part, tending to express at further remove the 'sweet sleep like death' for which the singer longs. The instructions 'lent et calme' indicate the spirit of the song, which reveals yet again Duparc's talent for counter-melody. As in *Soupir*, both pianist and singer seem to be giving vent to their own independent strivings, each moving serenely onwards without a single false step to jar their communion. As is sometimes the case with Schumann's songs, this *mélodie* is bracketed by a piano prelude and postlude which serve to encase the vocal part like a picture within a frame; and the piano writing is a sheer joy to play. The next song, *Le Manoir de Rosamonde* could not be more different. Though not as bizarre as *La Vague et la cloche*, the words exhibit a grim vein of conceit. The poem is about a love-sick wanderer condemned to scour the countryside in search of his beloved, and the whole is worth quoting as evidence of Duparc's highly metaphysical tastes:

With love's sudden and voracious dog's tooth I am stung. Follow my shed blood, go, and you can follow my trail. Take a fine bred horse, depart, and mark my hard path through the trackless wastes—if the chase does not weary you. And passing where I have passed you will see that, wounded and alone, I have traversed this sad world; and that, far off, I have died, without discovering the abode of Rosamunde.

If this also has Poe-like elements—the combination of necrophiliac and aesthetic motives again suggests his literary presence—it nevertheless remains more of a lyrical and less of a dramatic work than the François Coppée poem. This is a distinction of which Duparc shows himself to be well aware when he makes his setting. Instead of the hectic and phantasmagorical movement of the earlier song we have a nervous agitation, powerfully expressed in the octave accompanying figure, above which the voice declaims in perfect faithfulness to the poem. That is to say, the horrifying images of the opening lines are set to suitably rhetorical music, while the more pathetic mood of the end of the lyric is accorded quieter tones, the whole song being rounded off by a terse series of *pianissimo* chords on the piano. It illustrates very well how a song can achieve forcefulness without overbalancing into bombast. This last quality is one which Duparc studiously endeavoured to avoid— not always, it must be admitted, with complete success. The dominant seventh arpeggios in *La Vie antérieure* (at the point where the singer enters with the words 'mes yeux') are dangerously near to overemphasis, and there are other cases. Like Hugo Wolf he sometimes found it difficult to know when to stop. The manner in which poor Wolf took occasional refuge in grandiosity can be heard, for instance, in the excessive *tremolo* octaves in his song *Wenn du, mein Liebster* from the *Italienisches Liederbuch*. Duparc had a similar tendency to let the climaxes in his weightier songs reach the pounding stage. Both of these composers in fact suffered from manic-depressive symptoms, which may have resulted in their being drawn to depict alternate moods of pessimism and elation. In *Le Manoir de Rosamonde*, however, Duparc was successful in curbing this weakness, and the song is a masterpiece of fidelity.

In 1880 a very short song, *Sérénade florentine*, was to make its way into the composer's output. This is most reminiscent of Fauré, and much more gracious than most of Duparc's songs. The piano has a tinkling, bell-like clarity, and the vocal part undergoes a series of charming undulations. Though the two songs are given quite distinct settings, the words of *Sérénade florentine* and *Extase*—both written by Lahor—suffer from a common archness and prettiness. Neither is a particularly good poem, *Extase* being perhaps slightly preferable. The succeeding song, *Phidylé*, provided Duparc with a far more interesting collaborator—none other than the underrated de Lisle, whose verses were to have such a catalytic effect upon Fauré. The setting of *Phidylé* in 1882 preceded by two years Fauré's version of *Les Roses d'Ispahan*, though of course the early Fauré settings of *Lydia* and *Nell* had occurred in 1865 and 1880 respectively, so there is no question of Duparc's having filched this poet's verses from under the gaze of his contemporary. It is possible, on the contrary, that Duparc's enthusiasm for the poet may have derived from acquaintance with Fauré's settings; though de Lisle's fame was at that time much more widely spread than his present reputation might suggest. In view of the success of Phidylé, one cannot help repeating the belief, already expressed in connection with Fauré, that French song-writers would have done well to have paid more strenuous attention to the work of de Lisle. Not that it has ever been easy to see at the time which of the poets of a given period are likely to possess lasting attributes. Musicians are not literary critics, and even if they were it would be no guarantee of their powers of prophecy. All we can say is that it seems a pity that Duparc did not hitch his fortunes more consistently to the Baudelaire and de Lisle constellation, and Fauré more consistently to that of Verlaine and de Lisle.

Greater consciousness of the value of choosing first-rate poets for setting to music is something which has come about only since Debussy's time. It is noticeable, for instance, that a composer like Poulenc has a far more sophisticated and discriminating attitude to the texts he chooses than most of his predecessors have shown. Debussy had a marvellous instinct in this matter, but one feels that, with the exception of Milhaud and his seed catalogues, contemporary French composers reveal more deliberately cultivated tastes. Notwithstanding this development, it has been argued by some composers and critics that second- and even third-rate poetry lends itself better to musical treatment than work of the greatest literary merit. This is the view that Richard Strauss took in relation to his Lieder, if not his operas, where he persevered, not particularly happily it must be admitted, with the first-rate Hoffmannsthal. Reger too had an aversion to mighty poets, finding Goethe's poems so perfect that nothing more could be added to them. These composers in general agreed with Weber, who once declared his apprehension towards poetry which possessed 'too much music to start with'. By and large the French school has not clung to this defeatist account of the matter, and has not shrunk from the proposition that great music can be wedded to great poetry, provided that the conditions are right. It must be admitted that there are plenty of examples to support their belief. Duparc's output is so small, and his attitudes to literature so little inferable, that it remains problematical where he fits into this scheme of things. He seems to have had more concrete literary skill than most other composers—Berlioz being a notable exception—but this does not appear to have led to a consistently unimpeachable taste in poets.

Phidylé stands at the very summit of Duparc's production. A magnificently voluptuous outpouring, it begins somewhat like a late Fauré song, with an innocent chordal accompaniment, only to rise to unprecedented extremes of passion, calling for resources quite beyond anything even the modern grand piano can provide. The harmony is rich and complex, and seems to mark a real step forward in the composer's technical virtuosity. The sentiments expressed by the song are simple enough—it is a naïve summons to love-making —but the sultry evocation of the countryside in which the lovers reside gives to the song an almost physical aura. The third stanza exudes a Keatsian mood of rapture:

> A warm scent flows along the pathways,
> The red flowers of the corn droop;
> And the birds, skimming the hillside with their wings,
> Seek the shade of the wild rose bushes.

Far from being a simple strophic setting of the poem, Duparc's treatment is climactic to the point of ripening into a deliberately symphonic texture by the time the last verse is reached, creating a circumambience of sound to celebrate the lovers' embraces. Together with *L'Invitation au voyage* the song comprises Duparc's greatest achievement.

The remaining list of melodies need not occupy us very long. In 1883 Duparc paid a deserved tribute to another of his exemplars, this time to Fauré himself. It was embodied in the dedication of his song *Lamento*. The title, it will be remembered, was used by the older composer in respect of the early *Chanson du pêcheur*. Both settings were taken from Gautier, another point of correspondence. The Duparc song is certainly a very mournful composition, the slow chromatic chords of the opening emphasizing by their downward movement the dejected spirits of the poem. In the final strophe, however, the despair gives way to a bitter outburst, providing the composer with an opportunity for one of his grandest perorations. At the words, '. . . Ah! never more will I approach that tomb', the voice suddenly sweeps upward into a higher register with superbly dramatic effect, the change of mood being most skilfully prepared by the running figures of the accompaniment. The other song written in the same year is Testament.[1] This makes use of yet another Fauré poet, the trite Armand Silvestre. In this case any doubts concerning the poet's abilities are put to flight by the impressive character of the song. This was one of the songs Duparc was to orchestrate later on, and its driving anguish and elaborate climaxes would seem to render it particularly amenable to this sort of modification. Dr Northcote describes it as 'one of Duparc's finest songs', and points to the fact that the doubling of the vocal line in the bass marks it out as for the male voice. That the old Franckist influence is still as pervasive as ever may be seen in the proliferation of chromatic passing notes, and in the tendency to fall back on augmented triads.

In the last of all Duparc's melodies, the Baudelairean La Vie antérieure, this temptation to elaborate results in such a thickening of the texture that many have refused to see the song as the masterpiece it might otherwise claim to be. We have already noted the melodramatic use of wide-ranging arpeggios. This habit had been with Duparc right from the commencement of his career, the final bars of Sérénade containing a prominent example of an arpeggio figure extending over four octaves. Such flourishes, on the face of it, seem incompatible with those economical principles upon which French song rests, though it would be folly to subscribe to the view that great composers cannot be allowed the freedom to make their own rules. Perhaps we have been guilty of placing too much stress on the French passion for la clarté. After all, there are several French composers who have succumbed quite disastrously to the sin of over-complexity. Chabrier's delightful Pièces pittoresques are partly spoilt through this vice. So is the Sonatine of Roussel. And Chausson's habit of overloading the inner parts of his compositions was so notorious that even his friend Debussy could not refrain from giving him a gentle chastisement over it. Whatever effect it may have on the tidiness of our classifications, then, it might seem better if we suspended our customary criteria when judging a song like this last one of Duparc's.

The words of Baudelaire's poem are themselves curiously

[1] According to M. Charles Duparc, the composer's son, a water-colour painting of the Swiss Lakes was done by his father in illustration of this song. It evidently serves to underline the impression made on him by Armand Silvestre's poem.

inflated, though this is not to deny that it is a singularly powerful lyric. Its subject matter is the recollection of another life—relating perhaps to the Hindu notion of reincarnation—and the poem begins:

> I have long lived under vast porticoes
> Which the suns of the sea painted with a thousand fires,
> And which their tall columns, straight and majestic in the evenings,
> Made like basalt grottoes.

Professor C. F. MacIntyre regards the poem as having been inspired by one of Gérard de Nerval's oriental soliloquies. In his setting Duparc strikes a note of nostalgia in keeping with the old man's vision of his previous life, and the song begins quietly enough, almost in the manner of a gentle romance. In the third verse, when the writing becomes more declamatory and the images begin to verge on hyperbole, Duparc adopts a more heated style. He does an unusual thing in repeating the phrase 'C'est là'—which Baudelaire emits only once—though, since this is in the nature of a salutation at the beginning of the verse, it is hardly sufficient to convict the composer of tampering with the text. The song itself moves on by means of a recitative-like section to the final strophe, and ends with quiet dignity. Little did Duparc suspect that this final cadence was also to be his own. For it was after this effusion that he was to relapse into silence for nearly fifty years, struck dumb at the pinnacle of his powers.

We shall probably never know the exact nature of the illness which wrought this havoc on the composer. His letters refer only to the embarrassing privations he endured as a consequence of the loss of his gifts.[1] His French biographer Dr Oulmont, has provided us with a number of anecdotes about Duparc, many of which indicate that although he was never able to return to composition after 1885 he was nevertheless very active, in a spasmodic way, up to quite a late stage in his life. At first, on his awareness of the disorder—which his friend de Bréville claimed to have originated in childhood— Duparc retired to the country, near Lake Leman. Subsequently he

---

[1] Twenty hitherto uncollected letters which Duparc wrote to his friend Auguste Sérieyx were published for the first time by the editions du Cervin, Lausanne, in 1961. They shed little further light on the origins of his condition, though the photostats show an aberration of handwriting that leads one to suspect his deterioration was brought about by psychological causes.

went to live at Tarbes, then ultimately at Mont-de-Marsin. He hoped for a while for a cure at one of the Swiss spas, and even towards the end of his life he was to be seen at Lourdes. It did not take him long, however, to discount the possibilities of therapy or medication as solutions to his problem. Doctors were able to do little or nothing for him, and as he entered middle age things became progressively worse. His eyes began to trouble him greatly, making it impossible to carry out revisions to existing scores—these chores having constituted his only remaining musical outlet. Finally, he became afflicted with paralysis, at first partial then almost total. In the last years he was to spend most of the time on a specially prepared couch in a semi-recumbent posture. There was no remission of symptoms, and he died in February 1933 at the age of eighty-five. Fate had seen fit to deny him the recovery of his genius, since on his death no further trophies were hatched. A few scribblings testified to the will's persistence. Otherwise the vault was bare.

In the same year as Duparc's death a young doctor at Bordeaux University submitted a thesis entitled *Psychologie et pathologie d'un artiste: Henri Duparc*, purporting to reach an understanding of the composer's illness. Its conclusions, however, are vague and are unsupported by clinical evidence. Professor Noske, whilst rebuking would-be psychological biographers for their intrusiveness, nevertheless comments on the light that the songs might themselves shed on the nature of Duparc's troubles. He himself gives us several valuable pointers in this direction when he notes:

. . . l'absence totale d'allégresse, son penchant pour des sentiments nostalgiques, l'écriture troublé des accompagnements.

Certainly the principal impression which a hearing of Duparc's songs makes on the unprepared listener is one of desolation and lugubrious emotion. Hardly any of his songs are happy, despite their frequently rhapsodical style. Moreover his commitment to aestheticism did equip him with a vision of heaven—similar to Baudelaire's invoked 'ordre et beauté'—which could in no circumstances be imagined as realizable on earth. Did this knowledge, as Professor Mellers has claimed, disqualify Duparc from leading a life among ordinary mortals?

Tempting as such an explanation may be, it scarcely stands up to close scrutiny. Many other dedicated aesthetes have, when all is said and done, continued to be creators; and it is difficult to see how any alleged contempt for human values could have affected Duparc's musical gift. There is the almost parallel case of Delius, with whom he may be compared. Both composers suffered blindness and paralysis, and in Delius's case at least there was every sign of a Nietzschean loathing for the bulk of humanity. Yet the creative gift did not wither and perish. On the contrary, it blossomed. One cannot help suspecting that the truth about Duparc's illness is to be found elsewhere, especially in view of his general reputation for bonhomie and courageous spirits.

Looked at on purely circumstantial grounds, the outstanding psychological characteristics which Duparc reveals are hysteria and obsessional neurosis. The former can be legitimately adduced in explanation of his paralysis and defective sight, since both of these disabilities are sometimes to be found as part of a conversion syndrome exhibited by hysterical patients. Moreover Duparc's physique—which we can infer from the surviving photographs—is clearly of the pyknic or endomorphic type, which correlates under stress with both hysterical and manic-depressive behaviour. That the act of composition imposed such stresses on the composer can scarcely be doubted. As Lionel Trilling has observed:

Nothing is so characteristic of the artist as his power of shaping his work, of subjugating his raw material, however aberrant it may be from what we call normality. . . .

In Duparc's case this power of 'subjugating his raw material' was badly flawed. His personality was such that he could not write 'finis' to a work of art. No more could he summon the ability to see his tasks steadily and see them as a whole. He was cursed with the kind of imagination that quickly outruns its attendant executive skills. Accordingly he tended to anticipate every difficulty before it arrived, and reacted with the helplessness of a man who knows that a disaster will happen, but also that he is powerless to prevent it from happening. Such a condition lies at the root of hysteria. Duparc's continuing outward amiability is perhaps only another indication of how successful he had been in converting his psychological tensions into physical symptoms. It also shows the degree of repression which his conflicts reached. To say that an artist creates out of the repressed material of the unconscious may be a Freudian truism, but in Duparc's case his repressions weighed so heavily on him that they combined to crush the vitality of his genius. No other musician has experienced quite so abrupt a reversion to impotence.

What of his final stature as a composer? Rewarded by such a minuscule production, Duparc could scarcely have expected a place on the highest slopes of Olympus. Even within the confines of French song his achievements begin to look discouragingly slight alongside those of Fauré and Debussy. Yet he brought a nobility and capaciousness to the *mélodie* which it has neither aspired to nor exceeded since his time. In so doing he established the standards by which the whole canon has come to be judged. If the quantity of his output has thus been insufficient to earn him the title of *chef d'école* of French song, its quality has been such that no one else can rob him of that distinction. Francis Poulenc, surely an unrivalled witness of the tradition we are describing, has summed up the reasons why Duparc will continue to occupy a position of significance within that tradition:

Les mélodies de Duparc sont très belles. C'est le seul musicien qui a pu transposer Baudelaire musicalement. Duparc me fait toujours penser au peintre Bazille qui, avec tout juste quelques tableaux, occupe une place de choix dans la peinture française. Avec douze mélodies, Duparc est un grand musicien.

Only a Mozart could wish for a better epitaph.

Chapter 3

CLAUDE DEBUSSY

Hedonist and Voluptuary

THOSE who only knew him superficially might have thought him a
fantastic, whimsical creature. But, on the contrary, he was very strong-
willed, and he knew his own mind. He was capable of the most faithful
friendships, was very sensitive and emotional, gay and full of verve. He
was quite incapable of dissimulation; his face reflected all his feelings—his
joys and his slightest sorrows. Nor could he keep his troubles to himself.
It was absolutely necessary for him to have a friend to confide in. He was
very extravagant, and could rarely resist any desire or temptation. His
moods were very changeable. He had all the caressing ways of the felines
and, like them, was given to sudden outbursts of temper. He delighted in
all that was refined, delicate, complicated and strange—and that in every
domain.

Such were the words used to describe Debussy by his friend and
fellow Prix de Rome scholar, Xavier Leroux, when writing his tribute
to the composer in the *Revue des Arts Français* in 1918. So apt and
penetrating a character sketch do they comprise that almost all of
the vicissitudes the composer underwent in his public and private
lives might be thought predictable from them, to say nothing of the
hints they vouchsafe about the nature of his art. To trace the life
history of this vulnerable man in a few short pages is rather like
attempting to subsume the vagaries of a mighty river under a single
geographical metaphor. For, unlike Duparc, whose passionate music
belied the uneventfulness of his days, Debussy's case goes far
towards presenting us with the opposite set of circumstances—or,
lest that should seem unfair to the variety of his inspiration, the
upheavals of his personal life in no way help to prepare us for the
pellucid calm and reticent accents displayed in his work. A natural
hedonist and voluptuary, Debussy possessed few of the defences by
which his comrade Ravel was able to rebut the advances of the
public. Not equipped with as much temperamental independence,

he was a constant prey to those intent on invading his privacy, while his highly sensual instincts constantly sought an outlet in clandestine affairs which were designed to bring him as much pain as lasting happiness. He was not an unintelligent man, but he was none the less a continuous prisoner of his feelings, making him faithful only in the strength and intensity of his passions. That he was able to sublimate these tumultuous emotions to the extent of producing such airy and tenantless musical compositions must be reckoned one of the enduring paradoxes relating to the man.

Belonging to a slightly later generation than Fauré and Duparc, Debussy was not born until 1862, and so comes more closely within the purview of the modern movement, of which he must certainly be regarded as one of the principal founders. Léon Vallas, his earliest important biographer, surrounds the circumstances of his birth with a shroud of mystery. So enigmatic does his account become that we might almost be persuaded that the composer was in reality a pretender to the monarchy, and not just the simple *musicien français* of his own choosing. Hinting darkly at the possibility of illegitimacy, Vallas invokes the very aristocratic names of the godparents, listed in the parish register at Saint-Germain-en-Laye, in the Île-de-France, where the composer was born, to implant the suggestion that the child was actually the fruit of their liaison. The corollary of this view, of course, is that Manuel-Achille Debussy and his wife were only invited to enact their role for the benefit of the boy himself and also for the sake of public decency. Whether there is any truth in these speculations is very hard to determine at this late date. Mr Edward Lockspeiser, in his more recent biography of the composer, accepts without question that there was no conspiracy. The fact remains, however, that the godparents, who consisted of the child's aunt, Octave de la Ferronière, and her lover Achille Arosa, a well-known financier and amateur of the arts, took a particularly strenuous interest in his subsequent upbringing, even going as far as to subsidize his musical career. Debussy himself invariably displayed a curious reluctance to discuss the details of his ancestry, giving the impression that he was somehow ashamed of it. It is by no means clear whether this feeling of his related to the obvious fact that the Debussy family were what we should nowadays describe as working class, or whether there was some other information, possibly of a scandalous nature, to which he alone was privy. Whichever was the case, there does not seem to be any concrete evidence to buttress the claims of the sceptics, and even Vallas himself later withdrew from the position which his remarks predicated, with the assertion that he had not intended any insinuation—a thoroughly puzzling *volte-face* which inclines the observer to renew rather than abandon his previous suspicions. Perhaps the matter is not of such momentous consequence as many critics have insisted.

One of the reasons why it continues to press for solution is that Debussy's early history otherwise appears to present unusual features. Coming from a family of artisans who, on the testimony of Paul Arosa, the son of Debussy's godfather, were 'not respectable', it is not easy to account for the qualities of taste and refinement which appeared in the boy at a very early stage. Handicapped by a severe lack of schooling (evidenced by his mechanical errors in language, which persisted to a quite late phase of his development). Debussy none the less wrote poetry when little more than a child, and harboured ambitions of becoming a painter even before it became obvious that he possessed musical talent. This proliferation of gifts—which may be the reason why he has often been referred to as 'a poet's musician' or 'a painter's musician', but very rarely as a 'musician's musician'—would seem remarkable enough amid a family of minds. In the child of unintelligent and improvident parents, whose other offspring revealed no such interests, they must at the very least be considered fortuitous.

When Debussy was ten years old his precociousness at the piano was observed by Mme Mauté de Fleurville, that same lady whose presence we have recorded before in these pages, whose chief claim to fame is that she was Verlaine's mother-in-law, her daughter having inspired the poems which went to make up *La Bonne Chanson*. Seeing the extent of the boy's talents at the keyboard, she took it on herself to provide him with lessons free of charge. This stepping-stone to success was to have several salutary side effects. Not only was the youngster imbued with a passion for the piano as a result of her coaching, but the fact that she had herself been a pupil of Chopin was of distinct significance for Debussy's development. The Polish composer was actually to remain one of Debussy's few enduring idols among his fellow creators, as he was also to remain one of Poulenc's. In both cases the influence of Chopin is clearly detectable in their respective styles of piano writing. At the end of his life, when Debussy was preparing his authoritative edition of Chopin's works—still one of the best editions to use, and superseded only by the recent Chopin Institute publication based on Paderewski's teaching—he came to regret that he no longer had Mme Mauté at his side to advise him on various points of pedalling and phrasing, matters on which he believed she possessed expert knowledge. Nurtured by this tradition, Debussy turned out to be an exceptionally refined pianist, with a rare capacity for coaxing the more ingratiating sounds from the instrument, rather as the composer of the nocturnes was held to have done. 'Debussy's playing', wrote André Suares, 'was like a spell, the most immaterial and the most varied in tone that was ever heard.' When he was asked about the interpretation of his own tremendously important works for the piano, Debussy is alleged to have replied: 'Above all, play so that I can forget when I listen to you that the piano has hammers.' It is not difficult to discern the source of this pianistic philosophy, which stands in sharp contradistinction to the percussive approach favoured by Bartók, Prokoviev and other modern champions of the instrument. For Debussy, the claims of le plaisir were always as important as any revolutionary prescriptions which might be in the offing.

Despite these early presentiments of success, it would not be true to say that Debussy's path to glory—symbolized by his winning the Grand Prix de Rome in 1884—was a particularly smooth one. Entering the Conservatoire in Lavignac's solfège class in 1873, he was not long before coming up against the demon of academicism, a spectre which was to haunt him throughout the remainder of his career. Far too original, especially in his experimental approach to harmony, Debussy was not the man to knuckle under and practise the same dreary exercises as generations of students before him. Possessing none of Fauré's benign patience, he had not the slightest intention of becoming a professor, and his gifts demanded far more urgent expression. Oddly enough, he did better at solfège than at the piano, where his teacher was the stern and dogmatic Marmontel. Debussy's unusual abilities were recognized by both teachers, but their reactions were not uniform. Lavignac used tact and persuasion to encourage the boy to respond to his studies in a more disciplined manner, while Marmontel fed him a diet of classical composers for whom Debussy had scant respect. Never keen on Beethoven, it was the tepid account of Op. 111 that he gave which lost him the first prize for piano in 1876. Once he had attained his standard in theory of music, he transferred to the master class of Emile Durand, another mediocre composer with rigid ideas. It was in this environment that Debussy gave birth to his first serious compositions. These include a trio for piano, violin and cello, and a number of songs, of which only the rather saccharine *Beau Soir* has achieved any measure of popularity. It is a work of drawing-room presumptions, having a languid accompaniment and rising to a typically declamatory climax. Liszt evidently exercised a mild influence on the youthful composer of these efforts, since there is also a record of a *Rapsodie* in the *bravura* style then so eagerly imitated by aspiring Titans of the keyboard. For the most part Debussy persevered at the conventional tasks alloted to composition students, displaying only a half-hearted interest in the rights and wrongs of pedagogy, and from time to time he took a perverse delight in sprinkling his scores with a liberal allowance of consecutive fifths and octaves.

Yet another lady who exerted an influence on the composer during these impressionable years was none other than Tchaikovsky's patroness, Nadezhda von Meck. This cultivated wife of a rich Russian engineer possessed a European residence at Interlaken, where she entertained with the aid of a trio having a repertory of modern as well as classical works. On the look-out for a pianist for this *ensemble*, she engaged the student whom she later described endearingly as her 'little Bussy'. As Gervase Hughes has implied, it is probable that her affections were not entirely motherly. The arrangement was a happy one, for all that, since Mme von Meck was in a good position to enlarge the young man's musical experience. She took him with her to Russia, and on the homeward journey he enjoyed the privilege of hearing Richter conduct *Tristan und Isolde*, always to remain an imperishable memory and even a factor in shaping his development as a composer. Moscow itself did not prove quite so fructifying an experience, though he did undoubtedly hear some Russian music during the trip. His enthusiasm for Moussorgsky was not apparent at this date, and did not ripen until his appearance at the Exposition Universelle in 1889, when concerts of works by this master and his compatriot Borodin formed part of the fare. As one might expect from the nature of his association, the more immediate influence upon Debussy at this time was that of Tchaikovsky himself. Russia was always a name to conjure with as far as Debussy was concerned, however, and this early visit prepared him all the more judiciously for the ardent interest the group known as 'The Five' was to inspire in him. Aside from certain Slavic-sounding uses of the pentatonic scale, and a marked predilection for the Tchaikovskian habit of permitting the woodwind and other orchestral instruments lengthy solos, Debussy's musical technique does not seem too overtly indebted to the Russians at this point in its evolution. As James Husst Hall has sensibly suggested, it is probable that the most powerful effect they had on the French composer was to strengthen him in his determination to stand on his own feet, convinced of the rightness of his abhorrence of academies and the installed charlatans they had no choice but to protect.

By the time Debussy set off for Rome and the enforced seclusion of the Villa Medici, where the prizewinners were obliged to pursue a three-year sojourn, he was accordingly disillusioned about the values likely to accrue from scholastic hibernation. His cantata, L'Enfant prodigue, which had simply followed the text prescribed by the examiners, had in the outcome proved a most melodious and attractive work, owing more than a little to Bizet and the operatic tradition, but also showing signs of keen originality. The aria of Lia, which forms one of the work's dramatic peaks, is still very much worth reviving. Having pleased the majority of the jury, who were probably canvassed for their support by Debussy's last mentor at the Conservatoire, the sympathetic Guiraud, Debussy was temporarily persona grata with the authorities. What was far more important was that he found himself famous at the age of twenty-two. Life at the Italian villa was the reverse of congenial to him, however, and it says something for his integrity and singleness of purpose that he did not allow his academic triumphs to dissuade him from taking the more unpopular path his genius had marked out for him. His letters home at this period display a resigned and somewhat jaundiced attitude, and are highly characteristic of the composer's pessimistic outlook. He describes the regime at the villa in the most unflattering terms, stating that it successively resembled 'a cosmopolitan hotel, a private college and a compulsory civilian barracks!' Without doubt it was this last association that had caused him to rebel. Any restriction of his freedom was expressly designed to provoke abuse. Still, he remained there for two out of the three stipulated years, occupying a grisly apartment known to the incumbents as 'the Etruscan tomb'. During this time he wrote very little of interest, perhaps the most alluring task he set himself being the projected opera *Salammbo*, based on Flaubert's novel, which never got beyond the planning stage. He returned desultorily to Paris, empty-handed, in 1887. Any reference to the Prix de Rome afterwards made within his hearing became the signal for a rancorous diatribe on the subject.

Once he was outside the clutches of the enemy Debussy resumed his accustomed working habits. Still obliged to produce some evidence of his labours at the villa, he chose a theme of his own for the second cantata he was to write; this was based on Rossetti's poem 'The Blessed Damozel'. The etherealized medievalism of this work appealed to Debussy's rather precious tastes. The Pre-Raphaelite movement was in fact becoming a source of fascination to French composers, as the response it later aroused in Satie goes to show. Debussy's setting of the Rossetti work strives to respect the pure tone of the text, though it does not altogether succeed in conveying its quiet sense of abnegation and devout spirituality. It is very hard for us not to recollect that the same composer was to embark, only four years later in 1892, on his lazily Arcadian portrayal of Mallarmé's faun. The two works could scarcely have reflected more diverse leanings. Using a French translation of the English verses, Debussy appropriated only the first ten stanzas of the Rossetti text. These are distributed alternately between a solo narrator and a female choir. As with the earlier cantata, there is much to admire in the lyrical writing, which prompts us to the observation that, for all the absence of what a purist might describe as melody in the works of Debussy, he was not deficient in the ability to write tunefully and with charm. Like Fauré, he could write excellent music of the more unpretentious kind when he wanted. That he did not wish to pursue this urbane aim should be attributed less to any intellectual arrogance than to his gradual absorption in more sophisticated concepts of pleasure, which he later came to feel resided as much in tonal as in melodic contrasts. The composer's 'melodic period' is all the same of special interest to his admirers, many of whom prefer it to the ponderously static phase associated with the later works.

A fine testimony to Debussy's melodic prodigality is the Petite Suite for piano duet, later transcribed for orchestra by Busser. This little compendium of dance movements stands in much the same relation to its composer's canon as do the Masques et bergamasques to that of Fauré; with the proviso that, whereas Debussy's suite was written at the outset of his ambitions, Fauré's came at the end of a long and distinguished career. Both works continue to be unhackneyed and irresistible. In four movements—En Bateau, Cortège, Menuet and Ballet—the Debussy work is as inventive in its material as it is derivative in its style. The first movement, both by its title and its succulent progression in thirds, over the conventional 6–8 arpeggio pattern, proclaims its debt to Fauré. The Cortège, on the other hand, is pure Bizet, and recalls the mood of the gay L'Arlésienne suites. By comparison, something of Massenet's supple grace lives again in the Menuet, which has a splendidly French-sounding principal theme, given to the bassoon. The finale to the work shows Debussy at his most exuberant, once again its sonorities being much magnified in the orchestral version. The tune in the bass with which the movement begins has a good measure of Chabrier's ebullience and might have been prompted by the second episode in that composer's lively Scherzo-Valse. Not much of Debussy's subsequent music utilizes the quick tempo in evidence in these pulsating numbers, a fact which should make us doubly grateful for them. They seem to constitute a souvenir of his youth.

Somewhere around 1888 Debussy began the first of his notorious amorous liaisons. The recipient of his ardour was a woman of striking appearance but rather commonplace mind named Gabrielle Dupont, better known to the composer's friends as 'Gaby'. The two remained together for more than a decade, establishing a relationship fraught with every kind of temperamental hazard. Debussy's selfishness and devotion to pleasure gradually became resented by the querulous and green-eyed Gaby, to whom jealous scenes and dire threats were all part of the variety of life. Their domestic existence conjures up a bracing vision of slammed doors and packed

Portrait of Claude Debussy by Marcel Baschet

suitcases. And indeed the affair came to a near-tragic end when the composer decided to marry the colourless Rosalie Texier in 1899, leaving his former mistress to stage a dramatic suicide bid by shooting, which fortunately did not quite succeed. Indeed it is almost unthinkable to reflect that this tempestuous survivor from the Bohemian age was still to be found working as an usherette at a Rouen cinema until very nearly the outbreak of the Second World War, having outlived her famous lover by a couple of decades.

It was while Debussy shared his life with this earliest *inamorata* that he wrote many of the songs which go to make up his unique contribution to France's treasury of vocal music. Foremost among his efforts in the genre are the *Cinq poèmes de Baudelaire*, which are like no other songs in the entire history of music, so curious a mixture are they of the Wagnerian and Debussyist styles. Heavily chromatic in their approach to tonality, they yet avert the calculated tonal ambiguity of vintage Debussy, and seek to retain more in the way of a continuous melodic line. Hence they represent the composer at precisely the point where his infatuation with Tristanesque harmonies was beginning to give way to the more static, or deliberately aural, conceptions which were to form the basis of his own style. Selecting five poems from those Baudelaire wrote to Jeanne Duval—that 'Vénus noire' who played much the same role in his life as Gaby was about to act in Debussy's—the young musician gave them a luxurious setting for voice and piano, in which the accompanying instrument is treated with full acknowledgment of its sumptuous tonal properties. Indeed the weight of tone supporting the voice in these songs is alone sufficient to lend them a new richness and glitter. They proceed from where Duparc left off.

The first song, *Le Balcon*, was not the earliest to be composed, though it shows this complication to a greater degree than several of the others. Much of the accompanying texture in fact suggests a Chopin ballade rather than the economical spacing which we customarily associate with this aspect of Debussy's art. The resonant tenths in the bass assist in conveying this impression, as do the rocking sixths that occur in the right hand at certain points, anticipating by many years the same composer's étude 'pour les sixtes' from Book I of the *Douze études*. Other features of *Le Balcon* include the manner in which the cadential phrases of the voice are echoed by the piano in octave chords—a device much employed in the other songs —and the particularly Debussyan habit of using parallel descending common chords on each degree of the chromatic scale. The common chord is often experienced by the listener in a rather exotic sense in Debussy's work. The very extensive use made of it in the prelude from his suite, *Pour le piano*, though it has not gained the composer many plaudits, gives a clear indication of what is meant by this assertion. Deprived of its appointed place in a natural scheme of tonality, the ordinary root position triad possesses an unexpectedly modern sound, and it is through his appreciation of how to secure such novel effects that Debussy deserves our praise as an innovator.

Harmonie du soir, which is the second of the Baudelaire series, is perhaps less interesting. It is also an *andante*, shorter than its predecessor, and endeavours to illustrate the Baudelairean theory of correspondences implied in the title of another of Debussy's pieces, *Les Sons et les parfums tournent dans l'air du soir*. This time the accompaniment is based on an ornamental triplet figure. Out of such tiny cells, perpetually growing beneath the architectural lines etched by the voice, the movement of a Debussy song so often seems to be generated. Rarely making use of a dominating method of propulsion, his songs progress through the slowest tempo from one such cell to its counterpart in the next bar or so, finally comprising a complex molecular structure as logical as anything viewed under a microscope. Indeed form in Debussy's music is explicable only in terms of some such analysis. It is in the third song, *Le Jet d'eau*, that the composer really finds himself. This masterly inspiration is possibly the greatest of all Debussy's songs, a veritable triumph of imagination. Its dissonant seconds have commonly been likened to Borodin, but, utterly paradoxically, they succeed here in yielding a mellifluence no other composer has been able to extract from the interval. The subject of this song is not clearly inferable from the title, which might simply be taken to suggest yet another piece of programme music. Actually the fountain is a symbol which the narrator holds up to remind him of the flow of tears of his beloved, who lies asleep while he listens in penitence and rapture. The section which begins with the words 'La Gerbe d'eau' is especially moving, with its spread-out augmented

66

chords underneath a simple step-wise melody which, on its last appearance, is rendered infinitely poignant by the tiny staccato notes interspersed between the elevations of the theme. Elsewhere, the mobile arpeggios form a shimmering background, not dissimilar to that which distinguishes the composer's setting of Verlaine's *Green*. Particularly memorable is the way in which the piano figures plunge lower as the voice rises to the words '. . . de larges pleurs', near the end of the song. Debussy orchestrated this sublime lyric in 1907, though his disciple André Caplet, feeling that the transcription had not done it full justice, re-orchestrated it some years after the composer's death. Few of Debussy's songs demand such treatment, however, since they do not possess the natural expansiveness one senses in, say, Duparc.

Recueillement does not quite maintain this standard. It is none the less a well-judged song, the high G sharp on the words 'qui marche' achieving just the right balance with the open-spaced chord struck above a pedal E on the piano. This delicate blending of sonorities might well have provided Poulenc with the formula for attaining those melting climaxes which help to account for the success of such songs as *Montparnasse* and *Sanglots*. The Debussy song is otherwise very Wagnerian, and not as fetching as the last of the group, *Le Mort des amants*, in which Baudelaire's concept of easeful death—which the historian Thibaudet envisages 'not as a hope of Paradise, not a purification through afflictions, not as a fall into Hell, but as a passage into Limbo'—is magnificently evoked. This was the first of the series to have been written. It once again demonstrates the powerful lyrical impulse which Debussy was later to abandon—the dark radiance of the music expressed in the phrase '. . . nous échangerons un éclair unique' being almost overwhelming. Some very effective doubling of the vocal line by the piano takes place near the conclusion of the song, on the triplet figure signifying the 'flammes mortes', and the work ends on a succession of soft D flat chords, seeming to echo quietly into space.

Though Baudelaire might have seemed the natural poet through whose work Debussy could expect to fulfil himself, it was actually to Verlaine that he turned once his talents had sufficiently ripened. Having several times unsuccessfully tried to persuade the publisher Hamelle to commission him to do a set of Verlaine songs, Debussy in the end decided to please no one but himself and go ahead with the project. The result was a long series of compositions, including two major song cycles, in which this privately sought partnership was to arrive at fruition. As early as 1880 Debussy had been making settings of individual poems, but the first published cycle was to be the work known collectively as the *Ariettes oubliées*, appearing in 1888 at about the same time as the Baudelaire settings. These comprise six songs altogether, the last two of which are given the added designation of *Aquarelles*, following the practice of the poet himself. Several of the poems chosen, including the famous *Spleen*, were also set by Fauré.

The first in order of composition of the *Ariettes* was the extrovert *Chevaux de bois*, a picturesque evocation of the Flemish countryside during one of those riotous fairs which Verlaine must have witnessed in the company of his fellow poet Rimbaud, when the companions went on their carefree travels together. Edward Lockspeiser has graphically called to mind the poem which inspired the song, describing as it does:

. . . the lifeless wooden horses of a local merry-go-round, ceaselessly revolving as the crude tones of oboes and cornets emerge from the primitive band.

Debussy's account shuns none of the difficulty of incorporating these allusions to other instruments, as well as the cries of the village children as they tumble and cavort with amusement. The voice part has a distinctly folk-like melody to impart, fast and boisterous, while the piano indulges in one of those whirling *ostinato* figures also to be found in the more animated preludes. The whole song is much more of a *tour de force* than most of its composer's vocal products, but there is a beautifully nostalgic peroration, beginning with the exclamation 'Tournez . . .', as the fair begins to die away, permitting Debussy licence for his inimitable *diminuendo* tactics.

The other *Ariettes* are not all as memorable. Possibly the best of them is the delightfully fresh *Green*—yet another song common to both Fauré and Debussy. The harmonic freedom of this setting may be judged from the fact that its G flat tonality is not firmly established until the twentieth bar. Equally audacious is the rhythm, which is ostensibly 6–8, though more than half of the bars correspond to a

4–8 pattern. Both voice and piano have scintillating parts to play in this expansive song, which is one of the two subtitled *aquarelles*. The brilliant cascades of notes in the piano part, lit up by flashes of whole tone colour, give us a glimpse of the composer of the later *Images*. Not included with the *Ariettes*, but as irresistible as the best of them, is the gay and tripping *Mandoline*, which predated Fauré's setting of the same poem by eight years. The agile plucking of the instrument is conveyed through the rapid alternation of chords in a catchy triple rhythm. The playful 'la-la-las' of the voice were added by the composer, a conceit which others setting this delectable poem have not scrupled to appropriate. Among the remaining Verlaine experiments we should not forget the obvious *Clair de lune*, a gift to any sensitive composer intent on ransacking the works of this most musical of poets. When Debussy came to assemble the songs comprising his first series of *Fêtes galantes*, which appeared in 1892, he was to include another setting of this tempting *morceau* at the end. Since this series represents the composer's most ambitious attempt to come to grips with Verlaine's verses, it will repay us to give it our closer attention.

The series—which actually forms one of a pair of works carrying this title, the second not appearing until 1904—consists of three songs, making it a very short work as song cycles go, and these are held together by little more than the author's name and their careful juxtaposition of mood. The first song, *En Sourdine*, can only be translated by the title 'Muted' or 'Veiled', and it opens and closes with the cry of the nightingale. Listeners may wish to compare this refined summons to the more terse cock's crow which Proust's biographer, George Painter, has detected in the first phrase of the composer's string quartet, a work that belongs to much the same period. The song calls for very delicate singing, unemphatic in style and demanding a particularly gentle *sotto voce* for the high *pianissimo* notes at the conclusion. Its atmosphere of stillness shows better than most of his works what Debussy could do in the way of evoking sensation by means of a single sustained tone. *Fantoches* trundles along with comic pathos, the slow trills in the bass helping to give a touch of that sinister suggestiveness that many people claim to discover in Debussy's music. A more popular vocal style tries to break through in the song, which ends with an exhilarating *glissando* on the keyboard. The setting of *Clair de lune* is much more forlorn and genuinely moonstruck than that of Fauré. Once again there is a trace of theatrical revelry in the lower line, but the crestfallen accents of the song hint that this moon is misty and clouded.

The second series of *Fêtes galantes* is the work of a much more mature Debussy, coming some twelve years after the first. Many critics are accordingly inclined to judge it as the better of the two. Certainly it gives the impression of containing more that is essential to the composer's personality. The innocent pedantry of *Les Ingénus* is very much in keeping with that side of his character which Wilfred Mellers describes as hiding behind the 'mask of Harlequin'. The crystalline harmonic changes of the last few bars are particularly touching. By comparison, *Le Faune* is a pale and ghostly reminder of the fleshly creature resurrected in Mallarmé's legend. The interest in this song is contained in the piano writing, surely the most attention-capturing of any that Debussy wrote. Probably the finest of the set is the last, the gentle *Colloque sentimentale*, in which two reincarnated lovers dispassionately recollect their past in an abortive and pallid serenade. The melodic line remains for long stretches almost unaccompanied, and the range of the song covers an octave and a sixth, unprecedented even for Debussy. It has been compared to the best of *Pelléas*.

The story of Debussy's only opera—which occupied him for ten long years—is too full of complications to be expounded here. Standing at the centre of his productions, its place is analogous in importance to that of *Daphnis and Chloë* in the canon of Ravel. Everything of Debussy's genius can be experienced in listening to the work; it is his supreme testament, and could not conceivably have been followed by any other. Indeed the extraordinary fortuitousness by which Debussy was brought to interest himself in this of all plays must be regarded as providential—a rare conjunction which could not but lead to a masterpiece. The moment Debussy began to read this dreamlike and poetic play by the Belgian dramatist, Maurice Maeterlinck, he knew at once that the single vehicle through which he might express his sequestered musicodramatic gifts had been announced. Descending upon the author at his home in Ghent, the composer was astonished that his proposals secured such immediate and liberal assent. Far from offering objections to the operatic metamorphosis which threatened his play, Maeterlinck was actually full of enthusiasm for the idea, even volunteering to assist the composer in carrying out the necessary cuts. Dividing the play into a number of contrasting scenes within each act, Debussy proposed to link these with musical interludes, consistently pursuing the aim of heightening rather than manifestly transmuting the drama.

Nothing is as difficult for the opera-goer nurtured on Verdi's resplendent heroics as to visualize the art as a species of sung play, which was the manner in which Debussy conceived it. Abandoning the popular belief in that credulous brand of *verismo* in which, as W. H. Auden has amusingly suggested, 'the villain, when stabbed, instead of dying, sings', Debussy clung to his conviction that the form should not be construed simply as an excuse for musical chauvinism. Having much more respect for the rights of the dramatist, he came to view his own role as that of providing a discreet accentuation of the emotions suggested by the text. The opera *Pelléas et Mélisande* is accordingly unlike any other to have been written, and upholds a theory of dramaturgy quite opposed to that on which most other musicians have proceeded. Although it is arguable that Debussy's adoption of the *leit-motif* technique owes much to Wagner—as indeed does the very theme of *Pelléas* itself, redolent as it is of the same conflict between love and duty as assails the principals in *Tristan und Isolde*—the Debussyan aesthetic is actually as far removed from Bayreuth as it is from Milan. For whereas Wagner imbues the orchestra with a responsibility for enacting the entire drama in musical terms, making of the opera a kind of magnified symphonic poem, Debussy's tactics consist of permitting the instruments only to hint at or underline the action. Similarly, in the matter of setting the words, the method of *Pelléas* is to avoid any suggestion of forceful declamation, never becoming as artificial as the older recitative and aria convention. Instead Debussy makes do with more of a speech-song approximation, not going as far in this direction as Alban Berg and other moderns, but none the less striving to mirror the contours of the speaking voice.

That this is not so revolutionary a conception as Debussy's contemporaries undertook to believe may be gathered from a study of the very early development of the art—before it had become what

Dr Johnson inimitably described as 'an irrational and exotic entertainment'. The opera of the pre-classicists offers what amounts to a clear adumbration of Debussy's views. The critic Joseph Kerman has pointed this out in his intelligent study *Opera as Drama*, in which he states:

A literary form of drama continuously supported by music; this brings to mind the classicizing experiments of the Florentine *camerata* at the end of the sixteenth century, and indeed, Greek drama itself. Peri, Caccini and, a little later, Monteverdi formed an ideal of musical declamation on the musical translation of the diction of a great actor. And as one tries to define the actual dramatic function of Debussy's declamation, one can put it in the same terms: music fixes the inflection at every point, doing the actor's work. More purely perhaps than anyone else's recitative, Debussy's follows the cadence of the momentary word, as a great actor might be imagined to speak it, without any aspiration to purely musical coherence.

If this sounds a far cry from Mozart's famous exhortation that words must continue to be 'the obedient daughter of music', at least we must admit that it constitutes a less tainted ideal than those being proposed by the orchestral power stations and genteel aviaries which passed for opera houses during the late eighteen-nineties and after. The delicate murmurings and shadowy presentiments of Debussy's score were a perfect illustration of the unassertive part he felt himself called upon to play, and it is hardly surprising that his audience regarded the whole venture as a literary conspiracy, destined to subvert the rights of the singer and the prospects of livelihood of the composer. Even today, when the principles for which it stood are universally respected, the opera is scarcely a favourite with those addicted to the form.

The plot of Maeterlinck's play is simple enough in outline, its subtleties residing in the nuances by which its climax is approached and the heavy symbolism with which it is impregnated. Set in one of those insubstantial countries of the mind, the tale revolves around the relationship of the half-brothers Golaud and Pelléas, who are heirs to the kingdom of Allemonde, at present ruled over by their aged and world-weary grandfather Arkel. Out hunting in the forest one day, Golaud comes upon the maid Mélisande, whose diaphanous beauty overwhelms him, and who offers no resistance when he suggests returning to his grandfather's castle with her as his bride. Once they are married the appearance of the younger brother Pelléas casts an unexpected cloud over the relationship, which then degenerates, on Golaud's part, into suspicion and foreboding. In a crucial scene Mélisande loses her wedding ring in a 'blind man's well', at the same time that Golaud is flung from his horse while out riding. The incidents comprise a portent of what is to follow, the jealous husband returning to murder his innocent half-brother, while Mélisande herself dies in childbirth, watched over by the despairing Arkel, to whom the tragedy has appeared as a typical instance of the fatalism in which he has come to believe.

Of the various tense moments in which the score abounds, it would be invidious to single out any as representing the climax of the work. Particularly memorable is the love scene in which Mélisande artfully allows her hair to descend and align itself with Pelléas's aspiring touch; the accumulation of emotion generated by the expressive preludes for orchestra, especially those preceding the second act; and Mélisande's death scene, in which the prophetic pronouncements of Arkel are reinvoked without dramatic irony and in music of heartrending sadness. That Debussy carried out his intentions in Pelléas with perfect fidelity can no longer be denied. Future objections to the work will be forced back on the assumption, still adhered to in relation to the songs by many detractors, that in so subjugating music to the dictates of literature Debussy belied the summons of his own calling.

It was inevitable that the long, almost purgatorial sessions spent in composing Pelléas should have been broken up, from time to time, by work on other less definitive scores. At practically the exact moment when he decided to embark on his setting of Maeterlinck's play he also made a tentative start on yet another piece with literary associations, the symphonic poem L'Après-midi d'un faune, which had been inspired by Mallarmé's highly tinctured verses. This delicate labour of love again caused Debussy some hard work and much consternation. Originally conceived as part of a triptych, it came in the end to stand on its own, bearing the title of prelude, the planned interlude and finale never materializing. Such failures to execute his initial schemes are a characteristic of Debussy's career, and may be attributed in part to the composer's moodiness, but more usually to his need for accepting commissions in order to make sure of the fee, which he more than once demanded without having any but the vaguest intention of earning. Against this tendency to unscrupulousness must be set the fact that, unlike many *avant-garde* composers, who have felt assured of a *succès de scandale* at the box-office, Debussy knew only too well that his music lacked sensational appeal. It was not bold (or deafening) enough to provoke the sort of indignation which attended the *premières* of some of the Stravinsky ballets a few years later. The composer had few rich connections upon which to fall back—the indulgent Pierre Louÿs being perhaps the only reliable patron he ever had— and his combination of extravagant tastes and reckless misunderstanding of money values served to render him a prey to every device.

L'Après-midi d'un faune is important in the catalogue of Debussy's works for numerous reasons. In the first place it established more convincingly than any other single work the new values, formal, tonal and orchestral, which the composer was anxious to proclaim. The effect of this brief musical eclogue, scored for small orchestra and lasting only ten minutes, was in fact such as to tear the scales from the eyes of the older as well as the younger generation of musicians. This did not happen at once, however, and at the initial performance, attended by Mallarmé, who genuinely admired Debussy's talents, most of the professional critics were unable to see the epoch-making significance of the work. Its apparent formlessness and peculiar instrumentation baffled the audience, which nevertheless did not dislike the piece, reacting to it rather as they would have done towards any harmless but puzzling novelty. The work itself is a very free interpretation of the poem, eschewing deliberate pictorial devices of the Straussian variety, and practising that deliberate thematic deliquescence which we are accustomed to find in the compositions of the Impressionists. Even the beautiful opening motif on the flute breaks up into tiny oscillating fragments, in which the tonality is carefully blurred, while the continuous ebb and flow of the orchestra simulates the movement of some natural phenomenon, such as the play of light in a flickering landscape. There are no trumpets or trombones in the score (unlike the later *La Mer*) and the texture may be deduced from the active role entrusted to the two harps, which go far towards supplying the drugged mood in which the piece languishes. Some heavier scoring is evident nearer its conclusion, however, when the theme appears in unison backed by the full resources of the orchestra. Listening to the work's fluid vibrations today it is hard to believe that it had its first performance as long ago as December 1894. It must have sounded weird enough to ears made pious by the angelic jubilations of 'Father' Franck and his disciples.

The years of Pelléas and L'Après-midi were, as we have already commented, years of domestic disharmony for Debussy. The uncertainties surrounding his personal life were temporarily resolved by his marriage in 1899. Rosalie Texier—or Lily as she became known to the circle in which they moved—was scarcely more equipped to share in the composer's tastes than had been the vacuous young creature whom she had supplanted. It has been alleged that Debussy saw in her something of Mélisande's frail charm. If so, it did not prevent him from giving equal rein to the profane side of his nature, an aspect which found a sinister outlet in his perverted friendship with the sardonic Louÿs. This relationship had been in existence since 1893, and was reinforced by the many highly sensual interests the two men had in common. Both were very much attracted to literature of the more voluptuous kind —in Louÿs's case there seemed to be a rabid connoisseurship of pornography at the root of his tastes—and this united them in the profitable quest for a wide circle of literary acquaintances, which eventually included both Gide and Valéry. Their influence on each other was mutually stimulating since Debussy was instrumental in assisting Louÿs, who at that time was also something of a Wagnerite, to overcome the limitations inherent in his musical outlook. In such circumstances it was natural that Debussy should think of setting to music a few of the verses of his friend. Best known today for his novel, Aphrodite, Louÿs was also esteemed as a poet in the rather specialized circles in which he and Debussy moved, and the Chansons de Bilitis are a good instance of the sort of pagan eroticism he was accustomed to express. In 1897 Debussy decided to set three of these poems to music. The result was one of his finest cycles, embodying the most impious and concupiscent writing in the whole range of French song. Sometimes sung too romantically, they are heard to best advantage when given the blandness of enunciation which their mythological character seeks to assume.

The first of the three is entitled, appropriately enough, *La Flûte de Pan*, and has obvious affinities with the piece Debussy called *Syrinx*, a delicate exercise in which that instrument is awarded unaccompanied status. This song has a similarly naïve and improvisatory character, the common chords of the accompaniment adding a suitably diuturnal feeling. The croaking of the green frogs in the background is rendered by means of complex *appoggiaturas*. In the tender Bilitis and the uxorious Pan we glimpse two figures as characteristic of the Debussyan world as any of the pathetic puppets the composer was to coax into life out of the pages of Verlaine. Their posturings represent the very stuff of his genius. The very animated *La Chevelure*, in which the repeated notes help to generate a more oratorical rhythm, presents a vision of the two lovers united in eternal happiness. There is a wealth of harmonic momentum in the last of the series, the expansive *Le Tombeau des naïades*, which contrasts markedly with its companions by virtue of the solemn processional which imposes itself throughout its length. In this tone-painting Bilitis is shown following the trail of a faun to where it leads among the naiads' tomb. Vallas considers it the best of the set, describing it as 'a magnificent fresco', in which is poured forth the broadest and least adulterated of Debussy's lyrical melodies. Shortly after the first performance of these amatorial works Debussy was enjoined to write some incidental music for a mimed recitation of the same poems. This he was able to supply in the form of the *Six épigraphes antiques*, subsequently published for piano duet. They sound more ascetic than the Bilitis songs and seem to mark a step forward towards that abstract musical aesthetic in which the composer anticipated the trends evident in the second half of the twentieth century.

The special qualities of Debussy's piano writing have already been touched upon. The contribution which he made to this instrument's development really merits a book in itself. Beginning with the too stylized *Arabesques*—nowadays come to fulfil the function long presided over by Chaminade's correct school of pianism—Debussy eventually moved on to a more exploratory and individual idiom, and one which has influenced modern writers for the instrument to a very considerable degree. His idiom is only barely discernible in the next work he wrote, the tender *Suite bergamasque*, since at this time he was plainly still endeavouring to extricate himself from the clutches of Fauré, whose calm transparencies can be observed in bars 24 and after of the Menuet, and in the passage beginning with bar 39 of the Passepied. The four pieces comprising this miniature work in fact constituted a free pastiche on the older French masters, a genre that Debussy did not normally relish as much as Ravel, whose talents were far better adapted to such tinkering. One indication of the mature Debussy in this venture is his unwillingness to resist tone-painting. The Clair de lune, which has by now become wearisome to us, and which later on Debussy introduced into this suite, is the popular one and should not be confused with either of the two vocal settings to which he also gave that title. Its appeal is obvious enough, though the manner in which it is continually blocked off in two-bar phrases accounts for a certain monotony which can easily attach to the piece. Possibly the volatile Passepied has established itself as the best of the group. It certainly sounds more Debussyan than the others, if only on account of the deliciously light coda, exploiting the extreme ends of the keyboard, and the preponderance of his favourite four against three rhythms. An examination of the texture of bars 95–105 will also confirm the identity of the composer, since it clearly foreshadows many similar passages which coruscate so unmistakably in the later works.

In 1896 Debussy wrote yet another pastiche in Pour le piano. This carries the devices of his pianistic manner several stages further along the road to maturity. That it is not exactly deserving of a place among the finest of its composer's keyboard works is perhaps to be attributed to the odd and only partly digested element of orientalism to be found in it. This exoticism appears to consort rather strangely with the avowed intentions of the work. The Prélude too has come in for its share of criticism, and is perhaps the most obvious instance in which Debussy sacrifices his customary exquisite harmonic sense to the demands of virtuosity. The Sarabande, on the contrary, is an extremely fine piece, far better than the second attempt Debussy made at this ancient form in Hommage à Rameau. Its dissonant sevenths and ninths, undeniably effective in their context, have none the less been traced to Satie, who is often alleged to have been the first to use them in this way. The question of priority involved in this innovation has never been satisfactorily cleared up, and is perhaps not as important as many critics have intimated. Debussy's *penchant* for daring improvisations at the piano, involving highly ungrammatical chordal sequences, is well known to have been present in his Conservatoire days, so that it is doubtless a case of great minds having thought alike. It is in the final Toccata of *Pour le piano* that Debussy shows the extent to which he was beginning to outdistance other writers for the piano, Ravel always excepted. This brilliant piece is still very diatonic in view of its composer's reputation for harmonic audacity, but the figuration is infinitely more like that of the *Images* or the *Estampes* than that of the many over-aqueous *salon* pieces of the previous decade.

It was in this last-named set of musical impressions—literally translatable as 'etchings'—that Debussy reached the pinnacle of his powers as a piano composer. Here we experience for the first time that entirely fluid pianism, unshackled by the least need for solid musical declamation. It is aimed at mimicking the natural sounds previously considered extraterritorial to the musician's universe —the hammering of raindrops on the leaves amid Parisian thickets on a showery afternoon, the bell-like vibrations emanating from a Cambodian pagoda, or the muffled cries of the *feria* heard during a night at the Alhambra. These and similar impressions were the means by which Debussy raised up piano music from its withered resting-place between the pages of a musty convention, and exposed it to the alternate glares and shadows of the naturalistic world, creating for the instrument a whole new dictionary of symbols and metaphors which it has taken us half a century to exhaust. Messiaen and Jolivet are among its beneficiaries.

Pagodes, which formed the first of these startling departures, employs Debussy's favourite whole-tone scale, in conjunction with those undisguised intervals of a second upon which we commented in connection with *Le Jet d'eau* from the Baudelaire songs. No doubt the piece was written in imitation of the sounds made by the Eastern *gamelang*, or primitive orchestra, to which Debussy listened with such enchantment on its visit to the French capital many years previously. *Jardins sous la pluie*, on the other hand, calls upon a homegrown folk tune or nursery ditty, which is cunningly submerged in the fast repeated-note patterns used to indicate the rain falling. The inspiration which led Debussy to write *Soirée dans Grenade* seems to have been more purely literary, since at that time he had been no nearer to Spain than a single visit to San Sebastien. His mastery of Spanish rhythms in this restrained and not at all vulgarized piece of *espagnolerie* was none the less so convincing that his friend De Falla did not hesitate to acclaim it as authentic. The three pieces that go to make up this suite are therefore attractively varied, a fact which may account for its frequent appearance in recital programmes.

A work that stands more on its own as a brilliant formulation of the virtuosic problems inherent in Debussy's style of writing is the scintillating *L'Isle joyeuse*. Presuming to recall the nostalgic revels of the Venetian carnival, it represents the composer in one of his most abandoned moods. The soft trills and quasi-*glissando* whole-tone effects make it exceptionally tricky to play. Thematically it expresses that cult of Watteau *à la* Fragonard familar to us from the songs and poems to which we have already devoted so much space. Yet the ardour of this reveller is such as to remove the work to another plane from that on which the ghostly amorists of *Colloque sentimentale* pursued their twilit posturings. There cannot but seem in the piece an ill-fated effort on Debussy's part to tear himself away from the all too insistent harshness of the real world and lose himself instead in a mad whirl of pleasure, culminating in a frenzied denial of tomorrow and all that it promised. Professor Mellers, who estimates this as the greatest of the composer's piano works, gives us a less fatalistic but equally emotional explanation of it:

The title itself, with its reference to Watteau, is strangely fascinating, for whereas all Debussy's music may be said to exist in an island—a world remote from the everyday world—the last thing one could say about the world most typical of the composer's imagination would be that it was joyous. The gaiety, luxuriance and vitality of this piece are unique in Debussy's earlier work, its intricacy of ornament, gorgeousness of harmonic colouring and excitement of rhythm overwhelming; it is the world of Carnival, of Pierrot, become magically alive and actual, almost comparable with the outward-turning Chabrier or the ardent sonority of Albeniz's Iberia.

That Debussy sought to return again and again to this hedonist's paradise is proved by the urgency with which he took refuge in its delicately libertine characters—they are to be found in the mournful strains of the Etude in Sixths and the conceits of the cello sonata, with its revealing subtitle, *Pierrot fâché avec la lune*. Like both Picasso and Cocteau, Debussy discovered beneath the mask of Harlequin a clue to that melancholy rejection of the world so typical of the artist, to whom private dream and public incomprehension are always the ultimate irreconcilables. As in all such fancies, the wisdom which this knowledge brought him acted as more of a solace than a solution. In the meantime the composer had other and less intangible problems on his mind, and it was while in pursuit of these that he found himself abruptly recalled to the mundanities of existence.

The trials from which he was now forced to escape were the old ones which had plagued him before, chief among which was the drudgery of his domestic existence. Alternately attracted and repelled by the members of the opposite sex whom he encountered, Debussy found it almost impossible to achieve a lasting relationship with any of them. Having tired of Lily's provincial ambitions, the composer became drawn to the company of Emma Bardac, an accomplished singer who was at that time married to one of Paris's most eminent bankers. It was she who had given the first performance of *La Bonne Chanson*. Incomparably more cultivated than either of Debussy's previous female companions, she offered him what he had never been able to rely on before—physical charm at the service of an inquiring mind and a distinctive array of artistic gifts. What was possibly even more enticing to the still penurious musician was the comfortable bourgeois setting in which she displayed these attractions. This too had been denied him all his life. After much cogitation he decided, in the summer of 1904, to leave his wife and elope with Mme Bardac.

The consequences of their impetuosity were as painful as those which had attended Debussy's previous escapade, and curiously enough they were to provoke an almost identical reaction. Lily, now the deserted party instead of the victor of the struggle, resorted to the same fashionable act of despair as her predecessor, even completing the parallel by making the same inconclusive mess of the deed. Whatever was the effect upon Debussy himself of the knowledge that two women had been so attached to him as to consider ending their lives for his sake, the impact of such knowledge on the composer's friends was in most cases shocking. Believing that he

had behaved in a revolting manner, they one after another conspired
to cut him dead, wishing to have no more to do with such perfidy.
Put entirely out of countenance by this unexpected development,
Debussy hurriedly took refuge in England, hoping that by the
time he returned the whole episode would have blown over.
Putting up at an hotel in Eastbourne, he and his new mistress
escaped the censures that were hurled at them both. Whether
as a result of the ostracizing of him by his friends, or the mere
flagging of energies due to middle age, this was to be the last
of Debussy's amatory adventures. It was regularized by marriage in
1905—Mme Bardac and the composer having been successful by
that time in obtaining their respective divorces—and the birth of
their daughter Claude-Emma, also known by her pet name of
Chou-Chou, had the further effect of stabilizing once and for all the
composer's muddled existence.

It was while being dogged by these matrimonial difficulties that
Debussy completed what is by common consent regarded as the
finest of his orchestral works, the marine triptych La Mer. More
ambitious in its resources than the early L'Après-midi, and far more
vigorous in conception than the composer's other orchestral trilogy
—the alternately light and tenebrous Nocturnes, dating from the turn
of the century—this majestic seascape marks the highest point to
which Impressionism can aspire. Yet to represent the piece as an
example of musical brushwork would be to ignore the designation 'symphonic sketches', which the composer has attached
to it. Never enamoured of the principle of sonata form, Debussy had
nevertheless come to appreciate that the weakness as well as the
strength of Impressionism lay in its tendency to gravitate towards
formlessness. He accordingly attempted in these uninhabited vistas
—significantly prefaced by a print of the Japanese artist Hokusai's
famous drawing of the great wave—to give a musical shape to each
that would succeed in disarming the purists of their customary
charge of nebulousness. Thus the three movements correspond
more closely to a pattern of sonata, rondo and free fantasia, respectively. The first is an evocation of dawn breaking at sea, notable for the
boldness of its themes and the richness of its polyphonic texture;
the second, the playful Jeux des vagues, is almost the paradigm by
which Debussy's prismatic methods of scoring should be judged.

The finale goes beyond either movement in the lavishness of its orchestration and the intensity of its climaxes, the last of which, with its thrilling brass fanfares on the quadruple B flat, leading down to an F, exceeds even Triton's horn in its dramatic power.

Despite the work's incredible originality, many of the critics did in fact see it as a falling off in standard after the composer's other nature-portrayals. Some were disappointed at not encountering another wash of colour similar to that which Debussy brought into being for the grotto scene in *Pelléas*. Others, more acutely, pointed out that, for the first time, the composer had abandoned his uncompromising reticence, his discreet *pointillisme* of scoring, and reverted to the rhetorical outbursts of his predecessors. The Nemesis which had for long threatened to confront the Impressionist composers had been that their experimental approach to sound would in the end lead them into a cul-de-sac. Debussy was aware of this fate, which beckoned to him as much as to any of his imitators, of whom there were by now a great deal too many. Whether he succeeded in averting it must remain a matter of opinion. This opinion will determine in turn whether *La Mer* can be regarded as the peak or the nadir of the composer's fortunes.

It might be said that Debussy was more sure of his ground when he reverted to the piano, which he did in the two sets of *Images*, published in 1905 and 1907 respectively. These inventive compositions followed the principles already exemplified in the *Estampes*. The major source of difference between them was that in the interval Debussy had absorbed more thoroughly the innovations introduced by his friend Ravel, whose *Jeux d'eau* had appeared in 1901. It would be invidious to claim that Ravel rather than Debussy deserves the full credit for carrying out a more systematic exploitation of the compass of the instrument, and adding to its capacity for opaque pedal effects and deliberate chiaroscuro. All the same, it was the younger man who led the way in the matter of adapting the discoveries of Liszt to the techniques of Impressionism. It might be said that, whereas Debussy was always interested most of all in the musical aims he had set himself, Ravel was by nature more of a technician and had the craftsman's fanatical devotion to the tools of his trade. Without his empirical approach it remains doubtful whether the perceptions of his contemporaries, including Debussy, would have enlarged sufficiently to grasp the possibilities confronting the instrument. Conversely, there can be no doubt that Debussy's own experiments—more concerned with sound effects, perhaps, than with the invention of virtuoso devices—were of equal interest to the future composer of the *Valses nobles et sentimentales* and *Gaspard de la nuit*. The truth is that the two musicians were deeply indebted to one another, and it is a tribute to their joint intelligence that they were able to realize this almost at once. Nevertheless as time went on and factionalisms appeared to beleaguer them, their mutual tolerance became strained, especially on Debussy's side. It was he who first felt disposed to drive the breach between them. Persistently slanderous activity among their respective supporters was perhaps the principal factor in concluding this misalliance. The Debussyistes, in particular, tended to be a vociferous crew, hurling insults at all whom they suspected of detracting from the glory of their idol. Even the composer himself was led in the end to cry out: 'God save me from the Debussyistes!'

Although Debussy had more common sense (in musical matters) than these stipulations might suggest, and was never less than courteous to Ravel, there were indications, especially towards the end of his life, when illness dragged him down in his relations with people, that he was stuffily resentful of the attempts that were made to magnify Ravel's influence on him, and his irascible and moody behaviour often threatened to erupt into open hostility. The *Images* do contain at least one splendid example of skimming piano figuration of the Ravellian kind, however, and it is no contradiction to say that the piece owes just as much to Debussy's own genius. It is the magnificent *Reflets dans l'eau*, in which the calculated blurring of the harmony is contrived by juxtaposing above the tenor notes of the melody a succession of soft, floating chords which seem to suggest, in their smooth timbres, the ever-widening ripples of the water. *Mouvement*—which is the next of the set—is far more a product of the composer's interest in abstract pattern making. It has a forceful, arid rhythm of the kind attributed by M. Cortot to Bartók and Casella. The last of the group is the Rameau pastiche, which is perhaps a shade too opulent to be readily associated either with its creator or its dedicatee, though it has a dignified and solemn tread. The succeeding set of three *Images* is much less popular with pianists, with the exception of the sprightly *Poissons d'or*, suggested to the composer by the designs on a piece of oriental lacquer in his possession. Their notation on three staves may have been responsible for this neglect, since to amateurs, if not professionals, they appear unduly complex and intimidating. The little-heard *Cloches à travers les feuilles* is really a study in pedal effects, and even the popular-sounding *Et la lune descend sur le temple qui fut* is actually much more static in conception than the previous evocation of moonlight, known to every budding student of the instrument. The set as a whole influenced Samazeuilh's *Le Chant de la Mer*, published in 1919.

The twenty-four preludes which Debussy wrote for the piano are in general more accessible, since they are short and do not attempt to exhaust the minuscule perceptions which they invite. Each is a tiny sketch, quick to convey mood, and done with as rapidly as the sights glimpsed from a train window. Indeed they recall no one so much as Monet, with his dissolving canvases in which the scene almost begins to change before one's eyes. Debussy published these ingenious works in two books, as he did the *Images*, the first appearing in 1910 and the second in 1913. Most critics have found the initial book fresher and less contrived. Among the many unforgettable pictures projected in it are the sculptured *Danseuses de Delphes*, beautifully arrested with their flutes and timbrels; the tonally ambiguous *Voiles*, expressing the sails of a boat, cosseted by the wind; *La Sérénade intérrompue*, which reminds us of Roussel's song *Le Bachelier de Salamanque* in its mocking of the romantic throbbing of the guitar; the phantasmagorical *La Cathédrale engloutie*, spoilt by its making of the first climax more thrilling than the second; the quicksilver *Le Danse de Puck*, as irresistible as any Shakespearian song; and not least the jocular *Minstrels*, so dear to the heart of the composer. The complete set is a milestone in piano history.

That there is still much to admire in the second book may be demonstrated by a glance at *Feuilles mortes*, with its unflurried attempt to savour each rich chord; *La Puerta del vino*, perhaps the composer's most virile-sounding piece of Hispanic writing; the calm and monochrome *Bruyère*, evoking the banks of heather growing wild in the woodlands; *Ondine*, which constitutes a far more reserved portrayal than Ravel's; and, most vividly conceived of all, the dashing *Feux d'artifice*, which comprises an explosive account of a fireworks display, evidently undertaken on Bastille Day, since it ends with a half-recognizable reference to the *Marseillaise*.

Debussy's farewell to the instrument he loved best did not actually come for a further two years. Stricken with cancer of the rectum, and reduced to a shadow of his former Puckish self, he at last found time to write the purely 'musician's music' which his critics had for so long accused him of neglecting. The *Douze Etudes* which were to result from this final spurt of creative interest are unlike any other works by the composer. Hardly just a series of technical exercises, they resemble in aim, if not in content, the great studies of Chopin, in which the entire known technique of the instrument is reviewed and epitomized. Deliberately left without any indication of fingering, these studies of Debussy's do not cover much in the way of new ground as far as their titles go, but once one looks at the music itself it becomes obvious that the treatment of each set problem—whether it is the playing of thirds, repeated notes, arpeggios or whatever else—is quite revolutionary. The *Etude* in Sixths, for instance, is not just one of those racy exercises in up-and-down movement for the right hand, so beloved of Moszkowsky and Saint-Saëns. It employs the interval in both hands, and at a slower tempo. Likewise, the *Etude* in Fourths, instead of attempting to disguise the harshness of this unpleasant interval, exults in the clangour of it. It is in the second group of six studies that Debussy permits his lyrical impulse to triumph. In the *Etude pour les agréments* and the very difficult *Etude pour les arpèges composés*, he apotheosizes his art in much the same manner as Ravel had done in *Gaspard* a few years previously; raising it not merely to the summit of the French keyboard tradition but also to that of the entire European tradition of which the French school's contribution is only a part.

In February of 1908, a year before his illness had been diagnosed, Debussy was invited to come to England and conduct a number of concerts of his work. Not normally very devoted to the life of the travelling performer, or for that matter to the vanities attendant upon the conductor's art, he none the less consented to appear. The fact was that Mme Debussy's situation had not turned out to be as financially unassailable as they had supposed. Her estrangement from Bardac meant that she was now cut off from many of the sources of her wealth. The upshot was that Debussy was forced to undertake a number of tours in order to recoup their fortunes. It was particularly hard on him to have to put himself on show in this way, especially at a time when the embarrassments and sufferings his dreadful disease brought with it were becoming more and more apparent. Making a second visit to London in 1909—the first had secured some very favourable reviews—the afflictions became almost more than he could bear, and he had to resort to morphine and cocaine to keep him on his feet. As he wrote to his publisher Durand:

> *Fêtes* was encored and it only depended on me to get an encore for *L'Après-midi*. But I was ready to drop—a very bad posture for conducting anything.

In 1910, however, he was on his way to Vienna and Budapest, and in the following year to Turin. The year 1913 saw him once more in Moscow and afterwards in St Petersburg. It seems more than likely that the effect of these strenuous trips was to shorten his already dwindling span of life.

The compositions of these final years show that he was still endeavouring to work on the most varied possible front. In the field of song, his stark *Villon ballades*, which Edward Lockspeiser has described as possessing 'the terrifying and endurable strength of Gothic sculpture', were succeeded in 1913 by the *Trois poèmes de Mallarmé*, yet another step on the road to abstraction, though not so obviously cast in the Schoenbergian mould as Ravel's extremely modern settings of the same poet. The orchestral sector continued to occupy him through his work on a final set of *Images*, in which the sonorities of the keyboard had at last been exchanged for the more lambent textures of the larger medium. In these, his last purely orchestral works, Debussy makes an overt use of folk material, though in the single panel where one would have expected this borrowing to succeed—the resplendent *Iberia*—he relies entirely on his own inspiration to carry him through. The challenge of Albeniz's work was perhaps enough. In the lively *Gigues*, based on the well known Northumberland Keel Row tune, and in the more enigmatic *Rondes de printemps*, where the core is an old French round, the debts to the existing heritage are patent. The amazing transformations these traditional melodies undergo, however, testify to the composer's still uneroded sense of ingenuity.

By far the largest undertaking he was able to complete at this time was the music for d'Annunzio's play, Le Martyre de Saint Sébastien, first produced in 1911. This rather pretentious miracle play, in which pagan and Christian elements conflict, might have been supposed outside the realm of Debussy's tastes. He was on the contrary extremely taken with it, partly out of his desire to write music resembling the old medieval organum, much as he had tried to do in the Villon settings, and partly by the opportunities it offered to render the pantheistic feelings so well expressed by the text. The entire work is in five acts, and calls for several soprano soloists as well as a speaking narrator. The genre to which it belongs is problematical to a degree, some preferring to regard it as an oratorio, in which form it might be thought to give less offence to religious sensibilities. In the purely dramatic framework in which it was originally performed, it incurred the censure of the Archbishop of Paris, as well as a number of leading Catholic writers, including the conscience-stricken Péguy, so soon to be killed in the war.

Less controversial, and much less of an ordeal for the composer to write, were the two ballets Debussy managed to finish in 1912 and 1913 respectively. These were the advanced and polytonal Jeux, directed by Nijinsky for the Diaghilev Company, and the relatively simple but charming La Boîte à joujoux, which had its origin in a piano score which the composer had promised to write for Chou-Chou. In Jeux, the games specified are 'l'amour' and 'le tennis', making the ballet one of those primly flirtatious affairs in which a couple of young ladies are subjected to prolonged siege from the other side of the net, a succession of lost balls being the occasion for much mildly indecorous rummaging among the shrubbery. The theme is one that looks forward to the nineteen-twenties, and might well have appealed to Poulenc or Milhaud. Neither of these composers could have matched Debussy's nimble orchestration, however, with its daring parallel seconds and rapid alterations of timbre, which Emile Vuillermoz aptly compared to 'backhand volleys' such as those indulged in by the principal characters. Despite the speed with which it was composed, it caused Debussy more than one revision, for he was anxious to avoid any hints of coarseness in the music, which could easily have lapsed into banality. *La Boîte à joujoux*, on the other hand, could afford to be as flippant as the music for a children's pantomime, which was virtually what the work amounted to, its medley of bugle calls, musical-box tunes, and comic-opera parodies, combining to make a delightful jumble of *bonnes-bouches* which somehow retains its charm and freshness through repeated hearings. It occupies a place in Debussy's *œuvre* not unlike that of *L'Enfant et les sortilèges* in Ravel's. Both works show how compulsively attached French composers are to the tender drolleries of their nation's childhood.

By the middle of 1915 it was obvious that Debussy had come to the end of his tether. An operation only helped to postpone the inevitable, and by slow stages the composer was reduced to complete and bedridden privation. Still obsessed with the idea of writing another opera, this time on Edgar Allan Poe's *The Fall of the House of Usher*, the libretto caused him to work feverishly and in an increasingly possessed state. Debussy began to realize that his powers were failing and that he would never live to complete the project. Whether he destroyed what music he wrote for the opera, or whether he was ever able to get down on paper anything beyond the few pages which are to be seen at the Bibliothèque Nationale, we shall probably never know, so secretive were his final wrestlings. At one point he even began to suffer from the delusion that he was actually Roderick Usher himself, improvising his dirges amid the pestilent precincts of that awful Gothic edifice.

When at last the time came for him to call a halt to his productions, he had written only three of a series of chamber works he had also planned, the sibilant sonata for flute, viola and harp being perhaps the finest of these mellow offerings. In March 1918, as the German guns pounded and shells crashed on the suburbs surrounding the capital, France's greatest musician gained release from his agonies, having confided to his faithful Durand:

> Truly my life is too hard, and besides Claude Debussy has no longer any reason for existing if he cannot make music any more. I have no fancies: I was never taught anything but music. . . .

That Debussy's music is held in higher esteem today than ever before or since his death should be sufficient to assure his admirers of the rightness of their prognostications. Regarded no longer as an insipid water-colourist, but as perhaps the only musician of the nine-teenth century who fully understood the direction in which music was to move in the twentieth, he occupies the same place in relation to present-day composers as Wagner occupied for his own genera-tion, a place of unquestioned pre-eminence and probably inestim-able influence. Only a handful of composers in the history of music are singled out for such canonization, and if we wished to seek out the reasons underlying Debussy's magnetic attraction we could not do better than listen to the words of his friend de Bréville, who said of him:

Debussy does not ask of music all that she can give, but only that which she alone can suggest.

In an age when the demands of so-called pure music are everywhere being canvassed, it would be hard to imagine a less incontinent aim.

The present writer remembers, in the summer of 1948, attending a master class by the late Artur Schnabel, the apostle of Beethoven. After a while discussion began to centre upon the status of Debussy, who had recently been made the subject of a flattering comparison with the composer of the 'Eroica' Symphony; the judgment having appeared in Ortega y Gasset's tract The De-Humanization of Art. Schnabel had read this book and was deeply incensed at what he took to have been an insidious attempt at devaluing his idol. 'De . . . bussy!' he exclaimed, in his broad Teutonic-American accent, and threw up his hands in horror. Most of his audience agreed with him that the comparison had been far-fetched. Today, nearly two decades after that event, when we have witnessed the panegyrics of Pierre Boulez and the eloquent testimony of Edward Lockspeiser, it may not be so apparent that Ortega's accolade was undeserved. At any rate it is difficult to think of any other composer to whom it might readily apply.

Chapter 4

ERIK SATIE
The Nightingale and the Tramcar

WHEN Debussy published his *Cinq poèmes de Baudelaire* in 1890, he felt inclined to pay tribute to one of the most eccentric and endearing of his friends. He therefore inscribed on the score the following strange dedication:

> For Erik Satie, gentle medieval musician
> who strayed into this century to give joy
> to his best friend, Claude Debussy.
> 27th Oct., 1892.

To describe the composer of pieces with such arch and uncompromisingly contemporary titles as *Le Piccadilly* and *Je te veux* as a 'medieval musician' might seem to many critics to be stretching things a bit far. And indeed the incorrigible *farceur* who was later to be seen in one of René Clair's films, firing a cannon from the roof of the Théâtre des Champs-Elysées and sticking out his tongue at the gargoyles of Notre Dame, can only be transplanted into the age of Machaut or Dufay by means of an imaginative somersault of the most dizzying kind. Nevertheless such an act of historical gymnastics has to be performed if we wish to comprehend the personality and music of Erik Satie.

Long considered one of the supreme charlatans of art—a sort of musical counterpart to Salvador Dali or the inventor of the computer-poem—Satie has lately secured recognition as the more complex phenomenon that he undoubtedly was. Notwithstanding the artistic hoaxes, scandals and rumpuses alongside which his name has had the knack of appearing, it is now being gradually appreciated that beneath the publicity-seeking *persona* lay a conscience of unimpeachable integrity and a musical sensibility marked by a total absence of dishonesty. We still have some time to make up before reaching the interval of fifty years which Darius Milhaud thought would be needed before we should fully understand how far Satie was the benefactor of us all. The indications are that by that date the composer's reputation will have attained sizeable dimensions. As it is, his position, both as an innovator and as a pivotal figure around whom most of the significant musicians of the modern age in France are seen to have clustered, seems quite unassailable.

One of the most important facts to remember about Satie is that, for all the associations he has with Dada or Surrealism, he did belong to the earliest generation of moderns, the generation in fact of Debussy himself. This is sometimes forgotten by those of his critics who point to the ponderousness of some of his attacks on the musical establishment of his day, and the long periods of artistic bankruptcy from which he was known to suffer. Part of the genius of a man like Satie is that he was among the first to prick the bubble of traditionalism, and like all such primary revellers he was bound to experience a few of the self-doubts and fears of a Satan among the angels. Actually he was born as long ago as 1866, so that we are already in the midst of his centenary, an event at which he would almost surely have doubled up in self-mockery had he been spared to witness it. The very idea of an 'Hommage à Satie' movement emanating from our present foundries of scholarship carries with it more than a hint of Surrealism, and would certainly result in some choice ironies being perpetuated along with encomiums. It would be kinder, and far more in keeping with the spirit of the man himself, to do what Delacroix once recommended to his students when they encountered the work of Ingres in the Louvre—proceed with eyes fixed firmly on the floor, but with the *chapeau* politely removed.

Satie's background, geographically speaking, has some similarities with that of Fauré and Debussy, and consisted of a provincial childhood, succeeded by a boyhood and adolescence spent in the capital. Unlike the other two composers, however, Satie was born in a seaport—that of Honfleur on the Normandy coast. It was there that he grew up and went to school, but, although his father moved to Paris on the death of the boy's mother in 1872, Satie himself did not join his parent in the capital until he was twelve years old.

This maritime background is not without some significance in the composer's career, and might be reckoned as going part of the way towards accounting for his cussedness and the fixed resolve with which he determined to fight his own battles. A more specific source of influence was the character of his uncle, known locally as 'The Sea-Bird', who was not only something of a wag, of the kind his nephew was to typify, but who had a sailor's relish for the subculture of the dockland. He had no inhibitions about hawking young Eric (whose Christian name did not acquire the 'k' until later) around with him on his travels. These privileged glimpses of squalor, with their attendant corollaries on the subject of moral relativity, were no doubt what helped to give Satie his peculiar philosophy of life, of which the first article was voluntary acceptance of poverty. Like Van Gogh, he was all his life to remain a staunch member of the fellowship of the poor, and it was the contrast between the principles implied in his poverty, and the comically bourgeois manner in which he used to dress—complete with bowler hat and galoshes—that caused such amusement among his more emancipated companions.

Once the move to Paris had been effected Satie managed to divest himself of the need for further general education, and entered the Conservatoire to study music, which his father, being an imaginative though not very practical man, regarded as quite a sensible course to adopt. It was his father in fact who was to publish the first things the boy wrote, a few songs that were printed and distributed at the stationer's shop which he owned. The path followed by Satie during his early studentship at the Conservatoire is obscure to us. An early biographer even tells us that he did not actually enter the institution until 1883 or 1884, though this seems unlikely from the evidence that we have of his long and desultory labours under Mathias, who taught him the piano, and Tadou, to whom he went for composition. It is more probable that he attended, as David Drew has suggested, from about 1879 or 1880, but did not put in a very regular appearance for the first year or two. We do know conclusively that he quitted the institution in 1886, by which time it had become apparent to all concerned that academic training was doing little to equip him for the career he aspired to. His return to the academic fold at the age of forty is another story, which we must not anticipate our narrative by relating. Suffice to say that at this stage Satie's musical education looked like ending in a flop.

The ostensible reason for his removal from the Conservatoire being military call-up, Satie spent the next year as a soldier—a spectacle his officers must have come near to disbelieving in, so improbable must it have seemed—and it does not surprise us to learn that he deliberately exposed himself to bronchitis in order to secure his release. Back in civilian life he harboured no thoughts of another profession, and instead took a small room at the foot of the Butte, in the Rue Condorcet, where he began the drab and shambling existence in which he was to persist for the remainder of his uneventful life. To earn a living he hired himself out as second pianist at the Chat Noir, the famous café at which the Montmartre shadow plays were performed, and a favourite haunt of painters like Toulouse-Lautrec and singers like Yvette Guilbert. This was the sort of company in which Satie felt thoroughly at home, and he was not long before moving up to the Place du Tertre, that pleasant little island of greenery at the summit of the hill. His stay at the Chat Noir was rather short-lived for all that, an altercation with the manager causing him to transfer after a few months to another, similar spot, the Auberge du Clou, where he was to meet Debussy.

There is another event, equally significant for the composer's development, upon which it would be worth while to dwell. This was the contact Satie arranged for himself with the amateur theologian Joseph Péladan, at that time well known for his Rosicrucian plays and general mystical leanings. Although the Satie family had been Catholics, Satie himself was baptized an Anglican, presumably on the wishes of his Scottish-born mother, so that religious factors had already played some part in his life prior to coming to Paris. Indeed since his grandparents, under whom he had lived after the death of his mother, had insisted on his returning to the family faith, he could be said to have undergone several religious transformations. None of these affiliations really represented the opinions of the man himself, however, and it was only when he met Péladan, and became acquainted with the mysteries of the Rosicrucian movement, that he realized where his vocation lay in the matter. Attracted partly by the hieratical flavour of the movement, its dependence on the customary trappings of secrecy and initiation, Satie may also have been won over by the Chaldean or astrological elements in its teaching. A more cynical view would be that he declared his allegiance to the society merely in order to be allowed to write the music for its ceremonies, which function he performed from about 1891 onwards. In either case there is no doubt that the first period of Satie's composing career is best interpreted as an attempt to give expression to these vaguely spiritualized convictions.

Before taking a closer look at the Rose Croix music it is necessary to say something about the remarkable compositions for piano which remain the composer's most controversial legacy. These consist of the three sets of pieces—each of which in itself comprises a further triptych—which were given the enigmatic titles of Sarabandes (1887), Gnossiennes (1890) and best known of all, Gymnopédies (1888). The first-named, whose title is perhaps more completely within the understanding of musicians, are a set of slow chordal structures, in which the 3–4 rhythm predominates. Their originality lies in their static use of harmony, which resembles nothing so much as the Cubist habit of aligning blocks of colour one against the other, without any thought for the principles of linear movement. The chords used by Satie are, as we have already observed in our essay on Debussy, highly prescient in their implications. Consisting largely of unresolved ninths, they not only foreshadow the developments in harmony which we associate in a more systematic sense with Debussy and Ravel, but in their unconscious attempt to dismantle the tonal apparatus of music they represent a minor mobilization in the war waged by Schoenberg and his followers. Certain of Satie's critics have attributed these sequences, not to Debussy's own unpublished improvisations —which charge we have already dealt with—but to the harmonic language of Chabrier's opera Le Roi malgré lui, which Satie assuredly knew and liked. It is possible to stretch such debts too far, however, and there is no suggestion in Chabrier's work of any deliberate prising of chords out of their accustomed harmonic tracks. For that matter it would be just as plausible to invoke the late works of Liszt, some of which—like the Bagatelle sans tonalité—offer a distinct foretaste of things to come.

Indubitably more indigenous to Satie's own aesthetic are the experiments contained in the *Gymnopédies*, which title was evidently taken from the Greek histories in which Herodotus describes the dancing of naked boys at a festival held in honour of the dead of Thyrea. These three pieces are quite different from the *Sarabandes* in virtue of their emphasis upon line rather than harmony. Rhythmically, however, the three-in-a-bar continues to be evident, and is even made more conspicuous by the bass patterns—which remain unchanged throughout—consisting of the single low-placed note on the first beat, followed by the repeated triad further up on the stave. This cliché has the effect of making them sound rather like slow waltzes—a curious effect to confer on pieces so far removed in tone and harmonic framework from the lush *salon* atmosphere we associate with that dance form. The deceptive simplicity of the notation is at first sight equally puzzling. Most accompanying chords, for instance, are found on examination to be in root position. Moreover the melody, if such it can be called, continually turns back on itself, producing something of the sensation we get when seeing a repeat of a film in slow motion. The Aeolian mode in which the set is for the most part located contributes a certain languid charm.

Anyone hearing these pieces when they were originally written in 1889 must have been entirely baffled by their lack of pretension. To try to describe them as evocative of Greek pastoral simplicities, in the manner of Fauré, would result in just as much inaccuracy as any other stereotyped response. One can only say, somewhat helplessly, that they are typically Satiean. To observe the difference between Satie's own utterly unself-conscious inspiration, and the more studied imitation purity sought after by later composers, we have only to compare these *Gymnopédies* with the derivations contained in Ravel's works. The fourth number of *Ma Mère L'Oye*, for example, entitled *Les Entretiens de la belle et de la bête*, has been designated by M. Roland-Manuel as 'a fourth *Gymnopédie*', yet it is obvious by the time we reach the thirtieth bar that we are entering Ravellian territory, with succulent chromatic harmonies, carefully disguised it is true, beginning to intrude upon the landscape. There is absolutely none of Satie's own terrifying willingness to disrobe, shedding all those aids to beauty which the ordinary composer finds indispensable. Even Debussy, who of all his contemporaries might have been thought best fitted to appreciate what Satie was trying to do, showed by his orchestration of two of the *Gymnopédies* in 1897 that he too misunderstood their true significance. The adaptations are more deliberately aimed at special effects than are the originals, having a touch of Debussy's own exoticism about them. They nevertheless continue to be far more often heard than Satie's own piano versions. The programmes of the Hallé Concerts Society for 1966 included at least one performance of them during that season.

It is arguable, of course, that the piano is not the best medium for these pieces. To imagine them as part of a piano recital, as ordinarily interpreted, is very nearly impossible. It is not that they are badly conceived for the keyboard, but rather that they do not seem to have any connection with it. They are all too insubstantial and timeless to find an outlet in any accustomed channel of sound, without seeming to raise the sort of musical issues that they were presumably intended to help disperse. That is, the moment one begins thinking of them in terms of instrumental colour, traditional form and the like, the honesty of response which they were expressly designed to evoke in the listener has gone some way towards being compromised. Indeed the best approach to these works, as to much else belonging to the composer, is to rid oneself of all orthodox musical presuppositions and simply lend them an unprejudiced ear. In this way some of their innocence and candour may succeed in breaking through.

The *Gnossiennes* also involve us in a question of nomenclature. This is partly resolved by the information that they were intended to reflect in some way the composer's interest in the archaeological excavations recently carried out at the palace of Knossos in Crete. The legend of the Minotaur—with its tale of Theseus and Ariadne escaping the clutches of King Minos—hardly seems as expressive of Satie's temperament as the Greek callisthenics theme he had elaborated upon in the previous set of pieces. Nor is there any evidence in the 1890 triptych of a pictorial or other representation of the events set out in the myth. On the contrary, the music is once more slow and solemn, and this time dispenses with bar-lines altogether, a procedure which might have seemed risky in music so obviously sparing of accentuation. The effect is not confusing,

97

however, since the pieces possess a natural flow not unlike that encountered in folk song. The first of the *Gnossiennes* is actually quite similar to the material out of which Ravel fashioned his *Cinq mélodies populaires grecques*, collected at the Greek island of Chios. Beginning firmly in F minor, it moves through a D natural and finally completes its first phrase by emphasizing the tritone, the pedal F in the bass clashing angularly with the B natural of the treble. This capacity for exploiting the dissonant intervals is far more characteristic of the *Gnossiennes* than the *Gymnopédies*, which preserve an unflawed calm. The nearest approach to the *Gnossiennes* among recent piano works is probably the folk song based *Mikrokosmos* of Bartók, where there is a corresponding ruggedness of outline to many of the melodies. In general this set of pieces has had little influence on keyboard forms within the present century. Its impact has been much greater on the mental processes resorted to by contemporary musicians, and as such it has helped to mark yet another stage in the reaction against both Impressionism and Romanticism alike.

Satie and Debussy met in 1891. It was a lasting friendship, and one much prized by both parties. For the most part Debussy acted the role of mentor while Satie was content to listen and admire. Always suspicious of academic musicians and, as he himself once put it, always disposed 'to champion youth against age', he naturally saw in the composer of *L'Après-midi d'un faune* a young Samson ready to attack the Philistines. Although Satie could be highly critical of Impressionism, as we have already had occasion to point out, he tended to exempt his friend from its failings. In his loyalty to Debussy he never at any time wavered. This is remarkable enough at such a time of factionalism, but must be viewed as still more remarkable in the light of Satie's own sharings with that composer. Not many commentators are aware, for instance, that it was Satie who first suggested Maeterlinck as a collaborator for Debussy, and this at a time when he himself was also toying with the idea of writing an opera based on one of the Belgian's plays. Moreover there are indications, from remarks made by Satie to other friends at this time, that he deliberately averted staking any claim to areas of musical experience he had in common with Debussy. To have thought out another and different aesthetic from that of his friend must have imposed a heavy burden on his talents, and it should be seen as part of the man's strength that his touchy pride, so often the opposite of admirable, here served him well, causing him to strike out on his own without looking for that sympathy which is sometimes accorded to the loser. In discovering his own mode of expression Satie also succeeded in doing two worth-while things incidental to his aims: he turned Debussy away from Wagnerism and Ravel away from Debussyism. These were highly significant achievements for so lightweight a figure as he presumed to be, and without them French music would tend to look amazingly different to us today. It could therefore be said without exaggeration that, whatever his defects were, Satie acted as the anchor man for music in France between 1890 and 1910—twenty years in which there was much groping and speculation as well as much solid attainment.

Among the other compositions of the Rose Croix period, special attention might be paid to the Sonneries (or fanfares) written for the ceremonies indulged in by the order, the Préludes to Le Fils des étoiles (one of Péladan's plays) and La Porte héroïque du ciel. These works show the mystical and ritualistic side to Satie's nature. Rollo Myers describes them, in his pioneering study of the composer, as creating effects 'similar to that produced by a piece of rather heavy medieval tapestry'. They are still written for the piano, despite their obviously greater suitability for other instruments, such as the organ or chamber orchestra. Stravinsky has commented in his Conversations that Satie actually knew precious little about instrumentation. Whether this must be taken to apply to the early stages in his career or the later is not clear. Certainly Stravinsky did not himself come into contact with Satie much before about 1913, by which time he had emerged from his second academic baptismal. His work of this period suggests that, on the contrary, he was well enough equipped to carry out his intentions. It is likely that in the eighteen-nineties some of this mastery had still not been acquired, and that he was, moreover, still inclined to see himself as a pianist who composed rather than as a composer who performed at the piano.

The Sonneries and Préludes, for all their organum-like effects and kaleidoscopic shifts of harmony, are not more evocative than the impressive Messe des Pauvres which appeared in 1895. This work embodies in a more systematic manner the vertical techniques of writing. It is deprived of accentuation and lacking abrupt changes of dynamics. As Professor Mellers has commented, this style could easily have led to flaccidity. The fact that Satie managed to escape this fate is due most of all to his careful control of mood and to a certain incipient violence in his harmonic transitions. Harmony was always to remain his strong suit, even after he had mastered the intricacies of counterpoint, as taught him by his Schola teacher Roussel. In the pungency and forcefulness of his discords, he sometimes reminds us of a less colourful Moussorgsky. What also remained with him was his habit of '*dépouillement*', or stripping down of style, a feature of his music which was much later to have a particularly marked appeal for his disciples among '*Les Six*'. Auric and Poulenc were specially drawn to this '*sans* everything' aspect of his art. As Constant Lambert so cleverly put it in his chapter on Satie, contained in the book 'Music Ho!':

> On Satie's chessboard a pawn is always a pawn; it does not become a queen through having travelled to the other side of the board.

This preoccupation with the simple 'thing-in-itself' is the great strength of the composer, and is what serves to put him at the opposite remove from those who deliberately seek to incorporate impurities into their music.

In 1892 Satie's father died and he inherited a small sum of money, enough to launch him on a second career as a musical journalist and polemical writer. The paper, Le Cartulaire—ostensibly a product of the church of Jesus the Conductor—actually became an organ expressive of Satie's musical foibles, and was issued from his lodgings in Montmartre. In it the composer excoriated his enemies, among whom was the tyrannical Henri Gauthier-Villars, better known as 'Willy', who employed a variety of ghost writers to pronounce his music criticism for him. His wife was the indestructible Colette, later to become one of France's leading novelists and the author of Ravel's opera-libretto L'Enfant et les sortilèges. Satie's quarrel with this unpleasant gentleman centred upon the vicious attacks he had published against Wagner. As with Duparc, Satie immediately adopted the role of anti-Wagnerian apologist for Wagner, heaping vilifications on 'Willy' for his arrogance and presumption in seeking to criticize his betters. This was typical of the composer of the *Gymnopédies*. He never renounced his belief in the vision of greatness, and to his way of thinking any composer who deserved to be called great also deserved to be protected from the calumnies of his inferiors. The fact that the object of derision might be Wagner in no way altered his convictions.

Was Satie really suffering from religious mania at the time of the Rosicrucian adventure? Despite the cursory assumptions which have led to his being accused of posing and dissimulation, there are no good reasons for doubting the sincerity of much that he wrote and spoke. Not only did he see music as a divine vocation, but he earnestly held that the inspiration to compose could stem only from faith, and could remain pure only as long as it gave expression to the longings of the mass of the people. His later Socialism helped to underline this last conviction. Perhaps another reason why a religious view of music was so compelling to him was that he was of the opinion, deducible from his unselfish relations with Debussy, that vanity was the greatest sin of which a composer might partake. His determination to avoid this sin often drove him to religious expression of what was in reality a moral precept. Even so, the strength of his religious impulse may be gathered from the fact that, many years later, after his break with the Rosicrucians, he was still willing and eager to discuss theology with the philosopher Jacques Maritain, who had a high regard for the composer's integrity. And he was never heard to utter a single blasphemous phrase.

These unexceptionable sentiments are difficult to equate with Satie's curious behaviour in proposing himself for election to the Academy, which course he took several times between 1892 and 1895. Also, when Debussy's old master Guiraud died Satie petitioned for the vacant place at the Beaux-Arts. It was the Academy seat that he really wanted, since this had been occupied by none other than Gounod himself, and the prospects of any other musician in the running were bound to look good. Satie, though he put in a great deal of effort in canvassing for his cause, was hardly known to any of the eminent men in control of these decisions, so that his candidature from the first appeared inexplicable. Was it that he saw himself following in the footsteps of Baudelaire, whose unsuccessful attempts at election had been the prelude to a long series of factional manœuvres? If so he was doomed to disappointment, since no one in authority had the least intention of dealing with him seriously. It would be more appropriate to invoke a sad parallel—the case of William Blake, whose poor engraver's talents were so ridiculed by Reynolds and his haughty colleagues at the Royal Academy in London.

Another puzzling exhibition which concerned Satie was his behaviour in sending a copy of his ballet *Uspud* to the Director of the Paris Opéra. The chances of this being accepted were clearly non-existent. Yet Satie challenged the Director to a duel after it was declined. That these acts had resulted from vanity can scarcely be credited after the composer's long campaign against this emotion. More probably it was simply the wish to be taken seriously for once that led him to take this apparently conceited step. Knowing full well that he was among the most original composers of his day (perhaps the most original after Debussy), Satie could no longer stomach the consistent championship of mediocrity which existed among the '*pompiers*' ('firemen') residing at the principal institutions, and doubtless felt they should be exposed from within their own ranks. That there may also have been an element of perversity in so blatantly masquerading as a great scholar can hardly be disbelieved. Actually his friends never knew when Satie was going to take in good part a sally directed at his amateurishness, and when he was going to disappear in a fit of deepest dudgeon. Petulance was as much a part of his character, especially in his later days, as was modesty. Whether the very excessive drinking to which he became addicted had anything to do with this is problematical. He was certainly an alcoholic from about this time onwards, a circumstance which it is tempting to attribute in its turn to the failures attendant upon his relations with women. For throughout his life he was unable to rely on any woman. He neither loved them, nor they him.

At one point in his life Satie was heard to say: 'Je suis un homme que les femmes ne comprennent pas.' This astonishingly perspicacious piece of self-psychologizing is a far more profound comment than it might at first appear. Not merely reflecting the disasters of his love life—of which there was really very little—it goes a long way towards identifying him as a type, which was not so much that of the effeminate man as the thoroughly unworldly man,

indifferent to personal success, to whom all but the most unde-
signing women react with justifiable suspicion. Moreover he was
too good a man for most women, who prefer the kind of man they
can hope to reform. Myers tells a delightful story of Satie once
attempting to dispose of a clinging companion by notifying the
police to set a guard around his house. No man who so advertises
his need for protection from the opposite sex can ever hope to win
their respect, let alone their love. The one great *amour* in Satie's
otherwise chaste career was his affair with the painter, Suzanne
Valadon, mother of Utrillo and alleged mistress of such luminaries
as Renoir and Degas.

Their turbulent relationship began in 1893, when this notorious
lady painted the composer's portrait. It is a particularly striking
portrait, and shows him as the 'velvet gentleman' of legend, bearded
and vividly complexioned, yet still not the comical pedant that
Cocteau's more malicious drawings show him to have been. Satie
was to return the compliment paid him by Mlle Valadon by doing
a sketch of her in his own exquisite calligraphy. It adorns a sheet
of music paper on which there are other indications of his penman-
ship, including a few bars of music under which he has written the
words: 'Bonjour, Biqui!', the last word being his affectionate name
for his new mistress. They eventually set up house together in the
Rue Cortot. His fear of being cuckolded (doubtless a well-grounded
fear, in view of Mlle Valadon's previous lively encounters!)
inevitably led to frequent ruptures, and it was a common sight,
witnessed by their many neighbours, to see Satie returning home
late at night and upbraiding his partner in the most violent terms,
brought on no doubt by the quantities of pernod he had consumed
earlier in the evening. It is scarcely surprising that they found an
early excuse to end the whole unseemly charade.

In case it should be supposed that Satie wrote little else than
religious music during this latter phase of his first period, mention
should be made of the remaining piano pieces, some of which
seem bent on continuing the experiments contained in the *Gymnopédies*. Among these pieces, the bizarre-sounding *Pièces froides* are
easily the most important. Also embodying the composer's
principle of the trinity, they too come in sets. The intention behind
this plan is not difficult to fathom. As with sculpture, which art

partakes of many of the qualities for which Satie was looking, a set of variations on the same pattern (one hesitates to say the same theme) enables the listener to perceive the music in a number of different dimensions. In the words of one critic: 'One can walk around a Satie work, viewing it from a variety of angles.' Such deliberate mobility was what the Cubist painters were trying to achieve, and it can be no accident that Satie was among their friends. Braque and Picasso in particular were known to him from quite an early stage in his life. He unquestionably learnt much from their ideas. It is also arguable that the tripartite principle stemmed from some religious or mystical notion.

The first of the Pièces froides is the set entitled Airs à faire fuir. This brings us into touch with Satie's geniality and good humour. The tunes, one of which recalls a nursery song, are bright and popular. Professor Mellers notes the influence of Chabrier again. If this assumption is justified, then it only remains to add that this is the Chabrier of the songs and the piano pieces rather than the harmonic sensualist of the operas. And there is no trace of the thick texture so often encountered in the music of that joyful extrovert. Satie's themes are spindly and slightly impudent in the way that a child who means no harm can sometimes be. Surely Charles Koechlin must have had this set of pieces in mind when he wrote his own delightfully playful Sonatinas for the piano. The second set, called Danses de travers, is the most ostinato of Satie's piano works. Its continuous broken-chord pattern establishes a strict moto perpetuo. As with the other set, the aim seems to be to vary the same material in as many ways as can be made consistent with the form. For the first time, we are here made aware of a real pianistic idiom attaching to a work of Satie's. The style owes more than a little to Fauré, but is none the worse for that, since it represents the sort of cool, glassy writing that wears very well. Once again the chords of the accompaniment are in root position, and the whole texture is extremely simple and limpid. They are not really 'froides'—and the first set is warm to a degree—but they do have a certain incombustible quality about them, a quality which emanates from their clear outlines and immaterial substance.

Much the same could be asserted about the Trois morceaux en forme de poire for four hands. The wildly idiotic title of this charming work was evidently inspired by a criticism which Guiraud once made of the composer. Complaining that his work did not exhibit enough form, Guiraud exhorted Satie to write something with more of a definite shape to it. Satie replied with this *divertimento* 'in the shape of a pear': the '*poire*' being a snide reference to painters like Cézanne, who were at that time endeavouring to bring back form to the visual arts by elevating the still life, and also an oblique tilt at Guiraud himself, since the word, in addition to describing a species of fruit, is used to signify a 'dupe'. The whole joke is a good example of Satie's rather involved humour, which seems to infuriate as many people as it amuses. The pieces which go to make up this work are anything but over-contrived, however, and show the composer at his very best. A glance at the score will suffice to prove how beautifully laid out the work is for the two soloists. Each part dovetails into the other with the perfection of a geo-metrical theorem, and there is no hint of stodginess. A liberal supply of rests ensures that enough air is let into the music to make it thoroughly buoyant. Like Mozart, Satie was never afraid of silence, which he knew to be one of the supreme effects in music. The real advance this composition marks over its predecessors lies in the sphere of contrapuntal writing. Previously rather inhibited on this score, Satie now begins to emerge as the '*prodigieusement musicien*' that Roussel was later to christen him. Rhythmically too there is a sharpening of the awareness, especially evident in the syncopations of the third section. That the melodic facility of the *Pièces froides* had not deserted him may be ascertained by listening to the second section, in which one of his longest lyrical effusions lies embedded. In all, the *Trois morceaux* lays claim to being Satie's finest piano piece, and a staple work for all duettists.

One cannot pass from a consideration of these piano pieces without remarking on Satie's odd habit of covering his scores with verbal quips, disguised as instructions to the player. Even as early as the *Gnossiennes* he had indulged in this trick, inserting one or two mildly silly phrases, such as 'Ouvrez la tête' and 'Postulez en vous-même'. Whether this habit was what led him, during the Schola period, into the tiresome practice of appending a running commentary to all his music has not been clearly established. That he occupied a position as one of Paris's leading wits—ranking alongside Feydeau and Tristan Bernard—is incontestable. Not everyone could appreciate his mordant gifts, however, and there were—and for that matter still are—many to whom his brand of humour seemed anathema. Some of his sayings are undoubtedly very funny—as when he remarked about a certain well-known critic that 'he must have posed for Rodin's *Le Penseur*'; or his sepulchral opening gambit when visiting friends, at the time of the air raids of the First World War: 'I have come to die with you.' He had a special down on critics, as may be readily imagined, and he once compared another of their breed to a double bassoon. 'Let them swallow their beards, and dance on their own stomachs!' served as one of his typical ripostes. Self-mockery was also part and parcel of his humour, and this was often undertaken with a curiously ambivalent attitude, so that his hearers were never quite sure if he really was the butt of his own jokes. 'My humour', he would say, 'resembles that of Cromwell.' The important question is whether or not his sallies are subtractable from his music. Some commentators dismiss them as appendages, better removed from scrutiny. Others insist that the music can only be satisfactorily accounted for in terms that include the verbal adjuncts. The instructions accompanying the *Trois morceaux* are fairly innocuous, and it is only with the works of the following decade that the habit hardens into a mannerism. We shall move on to consider these works presently.

Meanwhile Satie's difficulties in consolidating his reputation as a composer were beginning to come to a head. By 1898 it had become painfully apparent that no one was taking him very seriously. His religious leanings had also begun to lose momentum. Possibly the most insistent pressure forcing him away from his true vocation came from his continued exposure to popular music and the slow attrition which resulted from his over-absorption in the café-concert *milieu*. This stultifying world had seemed a diversion during the palmy days of his youth, but now that he was approaching middle age it came to assume the character of a treadmill from which there was no release. One of the few decisive moves of his life was the retreat to the suburb of Arcueil which he undertook at this time. A tawdry enough district, it nevertheless offered him a new set of roots, while being at the same time within walking distance of his favourite haunts in Montmartre. Some of Satie's critics have interpreted this move as a rather pathetic attempt to immerse himself in practical Socialism and abandon his musical aspirations. There is possibly some truth in this supposition, for the period from 1898 to 1905 is exceedingly sparse in compositions. Moreover there are indications that Satie did attach himself to a new social ideal. He joined the local Radical party at his township, took the neighbouring children on periodic outings and collected for charity. The people gradually accepted him, and he even gained a civic decoration for his work in 1909. Whatever his intentions were, they enabled others to benefit from his kindness, a quality in which he was never found to be lacking.

The silence of the first few years of Arcueil was not like the ominous cessation of inspiration that overtook Duparc. It was discouragement rather than a drying-up of his talents that had forced Satie to become mute. He needed a few years to adjust to his failure, and to make up his mind what to do next. The decision, when it came, could not have been more surprising, for, rather than attempt to circumvent his critics by some novel or original musical stratagem, he placed his faith in a return to the academic discipline. Feeling that his lack of solid training was partly to blame for his failure to secure recognition, he took the extremely courageous step of enrolling, in 1905, in d'Indy's Schola Cantorum, an institution already somewhat notorious for the harsh regime imposed upon its scholars. Most of Satie's friends were taken aback by the plan, not least among them Debussy, who attempted to counter it with the advice: 'A votre âge on ne change plus de peau.' That this piece of common sense seemed worth pondering was not denied by the would-be student. But it was not enough to dissuade him. So, in a new-found spirit of humility, he embarked on his second, less embattled, musical education.

The teachers among whom he was now thrown were much more inclined to sympathy than had been expected. Having Roussel for counterpoint, for instance, was a stroke of good fortune on which Satie had not counted. This young ex-naval officer—'Cadet Roussel', as his older pupil irreverently began by dubbing him— was in the vanguard of French musicians and was a great composer in the making. His phenomenal technical grasp, later to impress such able minds as Martinů and Dutilleux, was put to valuable use in criticizing Satie's exercises in part-writing and fugue. The forty-year-old apprentice made good progress, though he was to find it very difficult to acquire the art of voice-leading and modulation, something he never truly mastered. It took Poulenc to teach French composers how much of this art had been lost since the days of Schubert. Satie's contrapuntal technique came on by leaps and bounds, however, so that whatever his deficiencies were he very soon ceased to be the amateur he had for so long been labelled. When in 1908 he passed out of the Schola, d'Indy himself signed his diploma with the words 'Très bien'—high praise indeed from so stern an authority. The gamble Satie had staked everything on had actually come off.

If his friends had assumed that this surrender to d'Indyism would result in an immediate sobering up of the composer's style, then they had mistaken their man, since alongside the study of strict counterpoint a less edifying discipline had been receiving a share of his attentions. This was the business of adapting the 'chansonnier' style he had picked up in the cafés to the demands of the informal piano piece. He had of course experimented with this sort of thing before, as the assortment of unpublished works he still retained were there to testify. But the urge he now began to experience went a good deal deeper, and seemed more a product of that off-beat humour which had taken possession of his faculties. Not bothering any more to pursue the ideals proposed in the Gymnopédies, he started in about 1908 composing a series of extravaganzas, far more eccentric than anything he had done up to that time, which seemed to harbour as their aim this linking up of music with a furtively comical text. Following the example of the Trois morceaux, he decided to give each new piece a bizarre title, evidently intended to make people sit up and take notice. In short, he was out to do a little sensation-mongering. Unfortunately the jokes contained in these titles did not invariably percolate to their audience. The upshot was that the composer's reputation, already much tarnished by this foolery, emerged even more heavily stained.

The pieces themselves comprise such a choice collection of imponderables that they cannot simply be dismissed. Indeed, distributed among them are a few gems which distil the essence of

Satie's genius like almost nothing else that he wrote. A selection of typical titles will give us some notion of the fantastic conceits he permitted himself in this so-called middle period, which lasted from about 1908 to about 1915, when he turned his attention to dramatic writing. Among the first to be written were the *Aperçus désagréables*—literally 'disagreeable remarks'—which were scored, like the *Trois morceaux*, for piano duet. Whatever one might have expected from a work with such a title, what emerged was something suspiciously like a traditional Chorale, Fugue and Pastorale. A second work for the duo combination also contained a Fugue, yet this was awarded the cryptic designation *En Habit de Cheval*. Similarly the *Véritables Préludes flasques* (the '*véritables*' being a distinctly Satiean touch!) is a work that begins with the most 'unflabby' sounding Toccata, to which the composer added the title *Sévère Réprimande*, presumably in mockery of his pedagogical superiors. There are also several Latin instructions appended to these pieces, a device which Myers describes as 'an additional touch of monkish scholasticism'. It was evident to those who took the trouble to examine the musical ideas present in such fantasies that what Satie had actually done was to clothe some of his Conservatory exercises in fancy dress, indulging in a modicum of parody in the process.

One set of pieces which deserves to survive this ridiculous objective is the Surrealist miscellany he christened *Embryons desséchés*. In this repellent-sounding work, the composer selects three imaginary crustaceans, which he proceeds to describe both in words and music. The first, inventively termed a 'sea-cucumber', is handicapped in its movements by the negative tropism to which it is biologically condemned. Since it is alleged to inhabit the beaches around St Malo, Satie here intrudes a popular song which might be described as a French equivalent of 'I do like to be beside the seaside'. The *embryons* of the second piece are on the contrary forced to lead a hermetic and joyless existence in the more cavernous habitat away from the sea. The music used to depict this life of renunciation appropriately includes a quotation from Chopin's Funeral March in B flat minor, which Satie acknowledges in the text as 'the well-known mazurka by Schubert'. Finally, the last species to be treated is presented as scouring the seas for prey, its eyes elevated on stalks. If it were not for an element of Satie's own waggishness about the whole concept, it might be regarded as the musico-literary equivalent of a Paul Klee drawing.

Without doubt the best of the tableaux written in the Schola years is that marvellously epigrammatic series of character sketches, *Sports et divertissements*. Completed in 1914, this collection of twenty miniatures for piano represents the *ne plus ultra* of the composer's fancies. Suggested to Satie by the publishing firm of Vogel, the work is a musical counterpart to a set of drawings done by the artist Charles Martin to advertise various sports and amusements which were at that time all the rage. Yachting, bathing, tennis, golf and tango dancing are among those whose attractions are portrayed. There is a curious story attaching to the manner in which Satie was approached to fulfil this commission. At first the firm was inclined to want the work executed by Stravinsky, then at the height of his popularity. When the composer of *Firebird* was invited to submit his score, it transpired that the fee which he was being offered was not high enough to suit him. On the advice of Roland-Manuel the firm then decided to award the commission to Satie who, in all ignorance of what had happened, began by declining on the grounds that the fee was too large! This anecdote illustrates how unpretentious Satie was in his estimate of his own worth as a composer. Never wishing to capitalize on his art, it would not have occurred to him that his music might constitute a marketable commodity. 'Monsieur Pauvre' was the nickname by which he was known at Arcueil, and there was not a trace of avarice in his nature. More unusual than this was the fact that his poverty was not just a form of masochism with him. Once, when he was promised a small sum which he needed, he was overheard to say: 'Monsieur, the words you have just spoken did not fall upon deaf ears.'

The *Sports et divertissements*, once completed, were written down on an enormous sheet of manuscript paper, almost two feet square, upon which the composer proceeded to add his own gloss in coloured inks. So prolific are the emendations that the work might easily be taken for an artist's canvas, and indeed the Preface which stands at the head of the score stresses that the avowed object has been to create a new composite art form, in which the demands of music and calligraphy are allowed to unite. It also refers to the famous *Chorale inappétissante* with which the work opens. This typically square piece of four-part writing—which can once again be seen as reflecting the harmony tutorials he had lately emerged from— is stated by Satie to have been inspired by boredom; indeed it is offered as a kind of musical portrait of ennui, which emotion was in a more profound sense the cornerstone underlying all his efforts at composition. Music, for Satie, was always something in the nature of a reaction to being bored, and the man to whom stagnation is a foreign or reprehensible emotion will never succeed in penetrating to the depths of his art.

After the *Chorale* comes a variety of more lively sketches. The *Water-Chute* begins with one of Satie's typically café-concert waltzes —they still find an echo in works like Lesur's *Le Bal* and in Auric's many film scores—but soon gives way to the descending scales of the slide. Satie characteristically inscribes the score at this point with the word 'Attention!' In the leisurely *La Pêche* there is polytonal writing of the kind that made the reputation of many lesser talents in the nineteen-twenties. The astonishing simplicity of the accompaniment to *La Balançoire* ('The Swing') on the other hand reveals what can be done by traditional means—it consists only of a chromatic line set against the tonic and third of the common chord. The golfing sketch, as one could safely have predicted, brings out all Satie's choice mock-English whimsy, and he describes the colonel and his caddy, the former dressed in a violently green Scotch tweed, setting out for the day's activities. As they settle down to the first swing the clouds look up with eager astonishment and the holes begin to tremble. We are left to infer that the ball never reaches its appointed destination, since the final cadence is compromised by the addition of a second dominant seventh chord, superimposed upon the tonic resolution. Rollo Myers has suggested that in the opening bars of this piece Satie anticipated the refrain from 'Tea for Two'. As a whole, *Sports et divertissements* shows Satie's economy of style at its most skilful. Several critics have compared the sketches to Japanese 'haikai', so deft and accomplished do they appear. Probably they have no equal in modern music of the minuscule variety.[1]

[1] Though he was not a dedicated song-writer like Debussy and one or two of his friends among 'Les Six', Satie nevertheless wrote a number of equally charming miniatures for voice. His 'Trois Mélodies', to words by Léon-Paul Fargue, René Chalupt and Ravel's friend Godebski, show how well his comic talents translated into this medium.

Other oddities dating from this period include the *Heures séculaires et instantanées*, which involve the composer in a continuous text, more like that of a dramatic monologue, with the music added; the set of *Descriptions automatiques*, among which occurs the limpid *Sur un vaisseau*, evoking the child's play with toy boats; and the blood-curdling *Vieux séquins et vieilles cuirasses* (literally 'old doubloons and breastplates') embodying a vivid portrayal of a miser, that would have been worth inclusion in Moussorgsky's famous picture gallery. In all these pieces there is the same clear and incisive handling of the material—usually in not more than two or three parts—with the interest stemming, as in the case of amateur photography, from the rapid establishment of a point of view. This is done by means of an unusual rhythm, an unexpected reversal of the textbook harmony, or some other trick of musical phraseology in which the shutter is made to click on a single scene which can then be pasted away in the album, ready for the moment when it is used to reinvoke the whole complex of associations attendant upon its selection.

In 1910, as a result of concerts being arranged by the S.M.I., Satie began to acquire a measure of that fame which had persistently eluded him throughout his long years on the Butte and at the Schola. Ravel, to whom he had been introduced many years previously, while working as a pianist at the Nouvelle Athénée, now began to hail the composer of the *Gymnopédies* as 'a talented explorer', and even decided that the public must be given an opportunity to hear his work. The result was that in January 1911 a concert was held in which the young 'apache', then busily at work on the music for *Daphnis and Chloë*, played the second *Sarabande*, the prelude to *Le Fils des étoiles* and the third *Gymnopédie*—all to a sympathetic and on the whole discerning audience. But there unfortunately it ended; since, in acclaiming Satie's juvenilia in this way, the public went far towards ensuring that the academic parodies of the middle period would continue to suffer neglect. The gap between these two styles was actually so considerable that it is understandable they should have taken this attitude. By a cruel irony those who now found it possible to praise the freedom of the *Sarabandes* were precisely those to whom the pseudo-scholarly trifling of things like the *Sonatine bureaucratique* (a skit on Clementi rather in the manner of Debussy's Dr Gradus) represented the very opposite of progress. Satie, gratified though he was at the interest shown in his early work, remained sullenly resentful at the incomprehension or dismissal drawn by his more up-to-date work.

Whether because of this disappointingly tepid outcome, or the desire for yet another change of direction, Satie did not wait long before making his next step. Always aiming at change and renewal, he was never a man to rest on his laurels, perhaps for the obvious reason that he had never received many. The phase into which he now began to launch himself was by far the most ambitious that he had attempted. As we have observed, almost all of his work up to the time of the First World War had been scored for piano only, or at best for some relatively small combination. In turning his attentions at last to the stage—it is surprising, with his flair for wit and comedy, that he had not considered it worth greater perseverance before—his talents for the first time demanded large scale means of expression. This meant that he would have to submit his training in orchestration to the testing ground on which his rivals Debussy and Ravel (whom he now took to describing as 'les périmés', or those no longer in the van of progress) had stood their appraisal. Having himself taken a strong line on the 'poussiéreux'—or too clouded— qualities then coming to characterize the impressionist use of the orchestra, his policy was to seek out instruments capable of yielding the sharper tones, going out of his way to avoid calculated dependence on atmospheric appeal.

His chance to prove his mettle came in 1915, when he first encountered Jean Cocteau, that disarming jack-of-all-trades and whirlwind pamphleteer. On leave from the front, Cocteau wanted to do a ballet in which the trends then visible in the arts, stemming from Cubism, the cinema, and the new multidimensional music, would be united in one magnificent entertainment. His sponsor in this venture was the fashionable Diaghilev, a fact which went far towards ensuring the success of whatever ingredients were mixed. The result of the plan was Parade, first performed in Paris in 1917 amid storms of applause and derision, and Satie's one undeniable masterpiece for the theatre. A work of stunning originality, it depicts the scene outside a fairground booth, where a small crowd is gathered to watch the antics of the barkers. The entertainers used to provoke trade include a Chinese conjuror, a part taken at the première by the choreographer Massine, a young American girl who is made to undergo a variety of exciting hazards similar to the 'perils of Pauline', among which is a part in a hold-up and a breathless train-catching sequence; and a number of managers who are encased in a kind of Cubist frame or symbolic costume. These last hawkers presented opportunities for the scenic artist, none other than Picasso, to display his skill. One of them is given a huge painted skyscraper to carry around on his back. The story of the ballet is of the slightest moment, and merely follows the action set by the crowd, who tire of each act in succession and gradually disperse, leaving the managers and their troupe exhausted. The theme, which traces the pathetic plight of the artist caught between the desire for self-expression and the need for upholding the technique of illusion, is very similar to that of Picasso's 'blue period' paintings, where the forlorn 'saltimbanques' sit about in groups amid the humdrum properties of their calling. As may readily be imagined, it was not a theme a war-time public would naturally respond to.

Interspersed with the cries of enthusiasm stemming from the Cocteau clique were shouts of 'Boches!' from the pit. Not all of these had been triggered by the subject matter of the ballet. Many had taken exception to Satie's 'futuristic' orchestral effects, which included the use of xylophones, sirens, typewriters and even aeroplane propellers, though some of these devices had been left out on the night of the performance owing to shortage of space in the auditorium. Even so the noises off were too sensational for this pre-jazz age audience, which reacted with a mixture of shock and stupor. Critics likewise tended to see the whole project as aesthetically, if not politically, seditious, with consequences that were to involve Satie himself in something close to a libel suit. He was even sentenced to several months in jail for his part in answering the charges made against him and his music, and it was only with utmost tact that his friends were able to extricate him from the prospect. It hurt him greatly that Debussy was not among these practical supporters.[1]

The music of Parade is eminently taut and lithe, despite the

---

[1] Stung by his comrade's silence, Satie went so far as to write Debussy an abusive letter over this affair. Louis Laloy has recalled that the composer of Pelléas did not receive it until he was on his deathbed. Not having realized his unkindness, all he could do was to murmur the word 'Pardon', with tears in his eyes.

contrariness of these impressions. Each number moves swiftly and unobtrusively into the next, employing to great advantage that *ostinato* style in the pursuit of which Satie had many times demonstrated himself a master. His Schola training comes out once more in the several fugues and chorales contained in the score. The restraint in which everything is couched makes this one of the most epigrammatic of all ballets, however, and in the way the tiny lyrical fragments are juxtaposed with the quick, racy circus themes we sense what really amounts to a précis of the composer's manner. In its assured handling of popular tunes, exploiting to the full the idiom of the day, it provided other composers with a significant precedent. Among these Poulenc (whose *Les Mamelles de Tirésias* is made up of a riotous hotch-potch of contemporary allusions) and the Stravinsky of the middle, 'Expressionist' period, come soonest to mind. Of all those influenced by Satie's experiments in *Parade* perhaps the most directly affected was his disciple in what was becoming known as 'L'Ecole d'Arcueil', Henri Sauguet, whose own ballet *Les Forains* explores a similar vein with something of his master's gentle and uninhibited attractiveness. It is a work, like *Parade* itself, which well deserves a revival. Diaghilev was reported to have said of Satie's ballet, when asked why it was not given more often: 'It is one of the best bottles in my cellar, and I do not want to see it shaken up.' Now that almost half a century has elapsed since its première, the time would seem to be more than ripe for this and other vintage wines to be uncorked and decanted.

The novelties into which he was goaded by acquaintances among the *Coq et Harlequin* circle did not prevent Satie from accepting more serious responsibilities. He had for a long time wanted to write music which would give expression to his interest in the Greek sage, Socrates, with whom many of his disciples have since compared him. The situation of the two men was in many respects the same. Both were ridiculed and vilified by the authorities, while at the same time being the object of a cult among the young. Satie's position as an ageing eccentric, still something of a gadfly on the rump of society for all his years, must have made him feel he had a lot in common with his law-breaking hero; not least the fact that they had both helped to practise that maieutic art by which the answers they were seeking were elicited from others less intelligent than themselves. In 1918, shortly after the fiasco of *Parade*, Satie accordingly set to work on a vocal interpretation of Plato's *Dialogues*, using the very Gallic translation by Victor Cousin of the *Phaedo*, *Phaedrus* and *Symposium*. The work was conceived in three parts, and scored for four voices and orchestra. In style it is far removed from the blatant audacities of most of his other work since the *Rose Croix* period, and in certain respects could be viewed as returning to the earlier manner. A much better source of comparison is perhaps with the five *Nocturnes* for piano, which date from about the same time as *Socrate*, and which display the most slack and tranquil motion. Both enterprises are full of a calm beauty which could probably have emanated only from a truly religious sensibility. Most present-day listeners—when they get the opportunity to hear it—find *Socrate* too pallid to provoke a strong response in them; and in this sense the work may rightly be described as a companion to Debussy's *Pelléas et Mélisande*. Anyone supposing that it attempted the French-Hellenic manner embodied in Fauré's *Requiem*, for instance, would be puzzled by its absence of lyricism. Like Debussy's work it seeks rather to exert pressure on certain syllables of the text without in any way creating a melodic line of its own, or indulging in a blown-up system of accentuation. One of the instructions to the performers reads: 'Recit. (en lisant).' The orchestra's part is equally unassertive, usually consisting of quiet oscillating movements designed to give just sufficient momentum to lift the work out of the merely spoken context. Roger Shattuck says of these deliberately repetitive patterns:

No modulation gives these movements direction; they are arbitrary transpositions which continue until Satie wipes the slate clean with a scale-wise passage of triads or fourths and starts again. He builds with a few clearly shaped pieces of material which fit close together without the cement of harmonic relationships. . . . There is an analogy to early Cubism, which restricted itself to straight lines and planes and rejected the appeal of colour.

One of the few acrid notes struck by this unemphatic work comes in the final panel, when the hemlock which Socrates has drunk begins to take effect. Here discordant seconds are given prominence and the music takes on, for a fleeting instant, a more dramatic aspect. If the work is not Satie's masterpiece, as Mr Myers has implied, at least it must be seen as the consummation of his pious or supplicative style.

After the war, in which Satie temporarily rejoined the militia and adopted, like Debussy, the role of anguished patriot, he continued the old life at Arcueil, but now far less as the queer Utopian thinker than as the fabulous celebrity. Cranks and *poseurs* looked him up with the object of learning a few tricks by which to hoodwink the public, and he became the sphere of interest of agents and managers intent on promoting a variety of aesthetic spectacles. The painter Picabia was one of the *farceurs* who saw in Satie a possible collaborator of genius, and it was their joint talents which were invoked to produce the Dadaist *Relâche*, which is described as being a '*ballet instantanéiste*', in 1924. This rather contrived spoof is an example of what Satie termed *musique d'ameublement*' (or 'furniture music'), and has the object of providing a background of music of no more importance than the visual appurtenances of a room. The very title—which is the word used in France to denote that a performance has been cancelled—is enough to indicate the flippancy surrounding the work. As may be imagined, the handbills advertising the first performance were the occasion of considerable public confusion and annoyance. Most of the audience did not know until the curtain went up whether they had mistaken the night. Among the idiotic uproar Satie himself was suddenly seen driving on to the stage in a five-horsepower Citroën, an event which brought in its wake a tumult of joy and deprecation. Lacking the serious element of abstraction of his other 'painter's ballet', *Mercure*, which had appeared earlier in the same year, *Relâche* merely throws together a wildly improbable assortment of occurrences— including a débâcle with a revolving door, a male striptease and a scene in which one of the characters dances with a wheelbarrow. The whole setting of the ballet consists of a pile of enlarged gramophone records which reaches up to the proscenium. Its vacuousness may be judged from the following quotation, intended to acquaint the audience with the ballet's meaning:

Relâche has no meaning: it is the pollen of our epoch. A speck of dust on our fingertips and the drawing fades away. . . .

It is scarcely surprising that after this capitulation to imbecility

Satie was shunned by many of his well-wishers, men who had been previously won round to his point of view. His own behaviour, hardly orthodox at the best of times, now took an incomprehensible turn. The feeling was widely expressed that this time the composer had gone too far. Whether he was actually known to relent is not certain: for at the time of his death, only a short while after this disgraceful episode, few had been able to make sufficient contact with him to find out much about his future plans. One work he was known to have been contemplating was an opera on the theme of *Paul et Virginie*, with the libretto adapted by Raymond Radiguet from Saint-Pierre. This project, which he never lived to commence, seems to point, as Oscar Wilde might have said, to 'a more serious frame of mind at the end'. It is a pity we have no indication of how Satie would have approached this work, for otherwise it might have been profitable to have compared his intentions with those of Poulenc, who set the identical text after his death.

Mention of Poulenc leads us to repeat the story of that cruel joke he and Auric played on the composer of *Relâche*. Believing that he had reverted to sheer childishness, the two young wits of *Les Six* bought the old man a baby's rattle they had seen in a shop window in the Rue du Faubourg St Honoré. Sending it to him, complete with etched-in beard, they imagined he would have a good laugh at the jest. Instead, he never forgave them. What they had been unable to perceive was that Satie, unlike them, had spent his entire life repelling the charge of infantilism which, on account of his amateur status and childlike sensibility, he had the utmost difficulty in doing. Without realizing it they had struck the weak spot in his armour, the one area in which his irrepressible humour failed to find a berth. Asked by Raymonde Linossier whether he could not reconcile himself to seeing the unregenerate pair again, he replied: 'What can be the use of seeing them again? Debussy himself died without my seeing him again.'

Satie's last days are utterly in keeping with what we know of the man. Refusing to permit visitors to invade his sanctum at Arcueil, he allowed himself to be transferred to a hotel room at the Place de L'Opéra, where he maintained his privacy by means of a pulley-and-string contraption with which he regulated the entries of his guests. Shortly after, the diagnosis of cirrhosis of the liver was confirmed, and he was moved once again, this time to the Hôpital St Joseph where, to the distress of the Sisters, he died in July 1925.

Once it was all over, Satie's friends opened up the apartment at Arcueil where, to their amazement, they found scores of notebooks, in which the composer had written down everything that had happened to him on his daily outings, including the price of drinks, newspapers and the like, all in his familiar neat calligraphy. They also came across the best part of a hundred umbrellas and innumerable handkerchiefs, which he evidently was in the habit of using once only. Behind his antiquated piano, which Poulenc states was quite unplayable and which Braque later bought as a souvenir, two manuscripts were found—one of his puppet opera *Géneviève de Brabant* and the other of the piece *Jack-in-the-Box*, a musical joke for piano which Milhaud proceeded to orchestrate. Of any other scores or relics there were none. Only on the wall outside was there a further inscription. This read simply: 'This house is haunted by the devil.'

Little remains to be said about Satie and his influence. That he was not a great composer in the accepted sense of the term must be obvious. He was, however, a composer who dared the impossible and to a large extent succeeded. By this we mean that he alone of his contemporaries had the vision and the courage to dispense with the customary trappings of the musical art, and write only the barest essentials. He was impressed neither by the pretensions of Romanticism nor by the tonal and other innovations which replaced it. Going his own way with complete conviction, he possessed unshakeable faith in the power of honesty and plainness as musical ideals. Auric, whose ballet *Les Fâcheux* had been disliked by Satie, once said of him that he made his work 'humbly subservient to that "reality" which stifles the nightingale's song beneath the noise of tramcars'. This statement has always been regarded as baffling by Satie's admirers, many of whom have read into it some acknowledgment of an 'anti-romantic' purpose underlying the composer's life work, some scheming philosophy which, when fully understood, would serve to place him among the more systematic denigrators of the nineteenth-century aesthetic. Constant Lambert has rightly contested this explanation, commenting that Satie was no more against nightingales than he was in favour of tramcars. He simply did not think in such factional categories. Instead he would have regarded each, in keeping with his phenomenological attitude to life, as worthy of man's respect. They would have appeared as objects of artistic scrutiny, not necessarily calling for one kind of treatment any more than another, but demanding to be apprehended without prejudice, complete and in themselves. Curiously, for so elementary an obligation, this was something no other composer was prepared to risk satisfying. It is because he submitted himself to the effort that Erik Satie deserves our respect and gratitude today.

Chapter 5

MAURICE RAVEL
Music's Dr Coppelius

'RAVEL has refused the Legion of Honour, but all his music accepts it.' Thus Erik Satie, in one of his wilful moods, was once known to put the composer of *Daphnis and Chloë* in his place. Probably Ravel himself would have been among the first to applaud the neat paradox. Actually, however, no one knew better than he the vagaries attendant on the judgment of the pundits. His trials and ultimate humiliation over the Prix de Rome have already been chronicled. If this rebuff to the French Government was intended as a reminder of the martyrdoms he had suffered, it ought not to be too hard for us to forgive him his vengeance.

Satie's little squib was nevertheless more explosive than this explanation might suggest, and it might be as well to begin our account of him by inquiring just how revolutionary he was. Superficially he displayed every sign of wanting to be a consciously *avant-garde* artist. His spirited defence of Schoenberg, at a time when France relapsed into that naïvely chauvinistic attitude typified by the First World War, might well have suggested such a liking for the barricades. Much the same inference is possible from the response his own music evoked. Indeed the savage catcalls which attended the first and anonymously presented performance of his *Valses nobles et sentimentales* in 1911 showed how far his music was capable of baffling the *cognoscenti*. Yet Ravel never considered himself the prophet of a new musical language. He believed, like Britten, in the inevitable return to tonality, and at no time ranged himself alongside the destroyers who were seeking (in Lambert's apt phrase) to 'apply a pneumatic drill to the foundations of music.' What then did Satie mean when he implicitly bracketed Ravel with the reactionaries of art?

Most likely we were intended to grasp the point that Ravel consistently was opposed to the plan of shocking the bourgeois for the sake of witnessing his expressions of outrage. Satie, like his mentor Cocteau, possessed a firm streak of exhibitionism in his nature. He liked the role of *enfant terrible*, probably out of a feeling of spite. His psychology may be explained in part by reference to the old adage about the rejected king who disdained to become a mere duke. If he could not be looked up to without qualification, Satie preferred to don the defensive garb of professional leper or outcast. Ravel's temperament was totally different. A real sophisticate, he had no time for foolery, and he was much too enmeshed in the technology of art to while away his time in its politics. Moreover he was saddled with a classically introverted outlook in which exhibitionism played not the smallest part. The problem with Ravel was always how to get at the man behind the mask. Nothing would have nauseated him more than to be held up as an object of public derision of the sort which Satie and his followers virtually invited. Nor could he ever be imagined as embracing the attitude which Cecil Gray has imputed to the group known as 'Les Six'; and which he described as resembling 'the revolting candour of a Calabrian beggar exhibiting his sores'. If Ravel had any musical sores they were certainly not on public view, nor would he have consented to putting them there. He believed— and this belief is as typical of his race as any other—that art equalled artifice carried to its highest point, and that the composer's weapons in the battle against both public and critics consisted of subterfuge, disingenuousness and a staunchly invincible technique. About the first two of these qualities we shall have much to say that can best be said later. Regarding the legend of Ravel's technique as a composer we should do better to come to grips at once.

For more than any of the other composers we have described, Ravel was a genius as a craftsman. The son of a distinguished Swiss engineer, he never renounced the fastidiousness we tend to associate with that combination of nationality and profession. Seeing nothing debased in the artisan's calling, he even took it as a compliment if a critic should see fit to call him one. In truth, however, he was so much more than this that it is not easy to illustrate the uniqueness of his skill in the mechanics of his art. Poulenc has recently described how he once had the task of accompanying Madeleine Grey—Ravel's favourite vocal interpreter—in a performance of the composer's song cycle, *Don Quichotte à Dulcinée*. One rather inconsequential note was evidently scamped by the singer—who was a fine but somewhat temperamental artist—with the result that both she and her accompanist awaited with some trepidation the comments of Ravel himself, who had been seated at the back of the hall. Thinking they would put him off the scent, the performers began talking about matters of tempo and expression, Poulenc gallantly endeavouring to share any disapprobation the composer might deliver. When Ravel had heard them out—listening with his usual sphinx-like impassivity—he merely walked quietly over to the music rack, reached out a long finger, and pointed unerringly to 'la note', without saying a word. In such matters as this he was utterly infallible, and there was no use in trying to deceive him. Even the great Toscanini received one of the composer's sarcastic reproofs after a performance in which the notorious *Bolero* had been taken too fast.

These anecdotes serve to indicate how much above even the most exceptional professional musician Ravel stood in his feeling for technical exactness. He was a man of scientific detachment in such matters; and not only that, but he also had something of the scientific genius's capacity for hounding down every scant detail until it was made to occupy its appointed place in the scheme of things. Only Bartók among modern composers could be compared with him for this habit, and even he scarcely reached Ravel's level of scrupulousness. Even so it is entirely characteristic of both men that they sought to avoid public opportunities in which to demonstrate their phenomenal powers. In Ravel's case no one ever caught him composing, as Norman Demuth has rightly pointed out. He worked behind the scenes, generally when others were asleep, and in addition to being omniscient he gave the impression of being unfathomable. The toil and tedium of the musician's existence were deliberately removed from sight, in accordance with his evident wish to be credited with that sort of magnanimous amateurism which used to be the hallmark of English rather than French intellectuals. Beneath the dilettante exterior, however, lay a professional among professionals. This is suggested by the fact that, despite his reluctance to discuss the details of his scores, he was immensely bucked if a listener expressed admiration for the manner in which he had handled some knotty problem in orchestration or balance. Praise of this kind meant far more to him than the conventional rhapsodic effusion. The only way to flatter Ravel— who was indeed a man of frightening, cynical intelligence—was to point out some hitherto unnoticed technical triumph he had attained, since it was only by this method that he could be convinced of another's right to bestow judgment. The smiling mask of reserve with which Ravel unfailingly confronted the world is not impossible of penetration, however, as we shall see. Following the method employed with Duparc, it is possible to observe signs in the music (if nowhere else) of emotional conflicts studiously guarded from the composer's acquaintances. Moreover there are distinct hints of the child within the man in the fondness which Ravel displayed for the astonishing collection of mechanical toys, bibelots, glass models, chinoiserie and other bric-à-brac scattered throughout his villa at Montfort-L'Amaury. His beloved clockwork bird Zizi was one of these cherished playthings, and it was while putting this creature through its paces for the benefit of a visitor that Ravel turned and exclaimed with mock seriousness: 'Look—feel its heart beating!'

This tale illustrates more effectively than any series of propositions the dilemma confronting anyone attempting an analysis of Ravel's style. It also contains the key to Ravel as a man. These aspects are important enough to warrant a good deal of preliminary comment. Most listeners are familiar with the charge that Ravel succumbed to artificiality and that he was what is described as an insincere composer. At the root of such a charge lies a basic misunderstanding of the composer's character and musical aims. To begin with— and this is where the anecdote concerning Zizi comes in—Ravel was actually a highly emotional man, and one who possessed a deep love of innocence and childlike curiosity. Like many men of taste, however, he found the world harsh and scoffing in its attitude to such things. Rather than become the butt of more insensitive people, Ravel sought to escape from the dilemma by adopting a protective armour of coolness and detachment. He superimposed, upon what was essentially a little boy's sense of wonder, the sleek and venerable sophistication of the scholar. Not wishing to be thought sentimental, he converted his more passionate feelings into the attributed longings of his toys and puppets, thus resolving his conflicts in a dimension into which no intruder could enter. In short, his preoccupation with mechanical things was not quite what it at first sight seems.

Not purely and simply an expression of his technical expertise, it actually fulfilled a deeper function in sublimating his true emotions, which his pride would never suffer to see trampled. The obsession with non-human figures in Ravel's works—the animals of Histoires naturelles, the story-book incarnations of L'Enfant et les sortilèges and the various fairy-tale inhabitants depicted in Ma Mère L'Oye constitute ready examples—shows how easy it would be to substantiate this claim with reference to the composer's life work. Always at the back of Ravel's thinking was the desire to scale down human passions to the level at which they become bearable before any attempt is made to confront them. Like the poet T. S. Eliot, he knew only too poignantly that mankind cannot bear very much reality. In this case reality too often meant people to whom his own pristine temperament was anathema, and who exhibited in their persons and tastes a crudeness and ungenerosity of spirit of which he was incapable. Those who wish to represent his reactions as precious or evasive are free to do so. They should, however, bear in mind that a more honest attempt to have come to terms with reality on Ravel's part would probably have resulted in his becoming a pathetic misfit, a Prince Myshkin fatally derided by his inferiors. It was a path that a saint might have chosen, but it was no solution for a man with Ravel's brilliant talents. Having created his mechanical façade, probably the only human beings who were ever to reach the real Ravel beneath it were his mother and the unsuspecting children, like the Godebskis, to whom he could safely entrust his heart. The extent of this caution and reserve may be gauged from the fact that, despite a fairly long life, no woman ever tempted him into dependence on her, and there is no evidence that his own desire for romance led him to impose a like dependence upon others. Present-day commentators may wish to concoct something sinister out of this abstinence, and it would not be difficult to invent some sexual neurosis to account for it. But the truth is much simpler, and will be understood best by those to whom sexual deprivation is not the only source of pain. Unhappiness comes in many forms, as Tolstoy knew when he wrote the first sentence of *Anna Karenina*, and for Ravel the unhappiness which might have resulted from insensitiveness was greater than anything which might have arisen out of frustrated desire.

Along with Ravel's temperamental dissimulations must be grouped his extraordinarily complex view of art as a supreme fabrication. This attitude, which his biographer Roland-Manuel calls 'the aesthetics of imposture', requires the closest analysis. Believing always in the alchemist's approach, Ravel invariably sought to transmute rather than conceive *ex nihilo*. He considered that the copy was superior to the original. This meant, from the musical standpoint, that, far from regarding pastiche as a secondary form of creation, he took it as representing the very essence. Put somewhat more philosophically, Ravel's position might be stated thus. Since reality is a nebulous thing, always seen through the prism of a single consciousness, it is entirely logical to proceed by ignoring the principle of verisimilitude and substituting for it an accepted angle of vision. Indeed it may be possible to adopt a succession of points of view in this sense, as the novelist does when he makes use of a 'stream-of-consciousness' technique. Art tries to be deliberately unlike philosophy in that the contours of the imagination are more important to it than any alleged knowledge that man may claim to possess about the external world. To state the whole doctrine thus might seem to be reducing art to the level of a superior game. Ravel's only objection to such criticism would have been to the use of the term 'reducing'. A game was what life appeared to be, and he would have thought it more appropriate to talk about reducing things to nature.

If we may just pursue this argument one stage further—after which we shall faithfully revert to our accustomed task of chronicling the composer's doings—it is axiomatic, if one accepts Ravel's way of looking at art, that it will become in essence solipsistic; that is, it will thrive only on a diet of personal imagery and encapsulation. This is not necessarily the same as saying that it will be decadent. For, unlike the more steadfastly objective vision, the inward-turning mind has the power to make use of free association and is thrown back on inventing its own symbolic vocabulary. In Ravel's case one can observe that the associations are what carry him so easily from one 'period lens' to the next, while the private symbols he adopts become the means of reintroducing previously hackneyed emotions like tenderness. Ravel's philosophy has in fact been appropriated in equal measure by the writers of the period, the obvious instance being in the theatre of Anouilh, whose delicate exploration of a fairy-tale world, brought into being by an eccentric time machine, offers the perfect literary parallel to Ravel's music. Even the hyper-introverted vision and the elevation of tenderness are present to complete the analogy.

Ravel may therefore be seen as an anti-naturalist in art, and in this he may be contrasted with Debussy, who endeavoured to represent nature with complete fidelity. The title which Ravel gave to a set of piano pieces published in 1905 is particularly characteristic of his outlook. He called them *Miroirs*, and the first thing we need to remember about a mirror is that it presents a distorted image. Debussy's titles for his own pieces were significantly *Estampes* and *Images*. Ravel, being essentially a fabricator, aimed not so much at depicting the object as recording its aesthetic reverberations. He was interested in reacting to the suggestions emanating from the object, and not the object itself. At this point the reader may care to be reminded of the comments made in the introduction to this book, where it was argued that art is frequently nothing more than a reaction to its own image, the 'imaginary museum' coming to seem more significant than the outward world which gave rise to it. This is a development in which Ravel not only concurred but actually assisted. Unburdened by metaphysics, Ravel was among those who advanced the doctrine by choosing to regard art as a process of refraction.

The reader who has been patient enough to bear with this long digression may now be wondering when he will be told something of the circumstances of Ravel's life, not to speak of a few more details about the works themselves. Neither the man nor his works would have been easily comprehensible without this kind of preamble, however, and having disposed of some of the more contentious issues we should feel all the better equipped to enjoy attending to the narrative and analytic aspects of the case. In the matter of biography it must be stressed at the beginning that Ravel was not, strictly speaking, French at all. Despite Guido Pannain's claim that he was the most French of all the great composers, he was actually Swiss on his father's side (a fact we have already noted) and Basque on his mother's, a circumstance which might be thought even more significant. This province in the Pyrenees from which his mother's people sprang was actually where Ravel was born, though his parents came to Paris to live as soon as the child was able to travel. The Basques are a diminutive, independent people, rather reserved yet capable of great passion— and this description fits Ravel very well, except that he also harboured some of the cosmopolitanism which we must associate with his father's wide circle of acquaintances. Music was in the family to some extent, since Joseph Ravel had displayed ambitions in this direction before qualifying as an engineer. All his life Ravel's father was to keep up his contacts with the artistic world (it was he who introduced his son Maurice to the eccentric Satie, whom he might otherwise never have met), and there were no obstacles, such as often seem expected, put in the way of the boy's musical aspirations. The Ravels were fairly rich, and at no time in his career was Maurice compelled to undergo the privations suffered by Debussy. During his early years he did not give evidence of particularly striking gifts and, aside from remarking on his very high intelligence and eagerness to learn, his first teachers saw in him nothing astonishing. When he asked to be admitted to the Conservatoire in 1889 at the age of fourteen there seemed no good reasons for abetting or prohibiting the move.

After working for a while in the class of Charles René, Ravel began to assert his talents by winning a premier prix for piano in 1891, and some years later—he was to spend a total of fifteen years at the institution—he was transferred to Fauré's class, where his interest in composition was immediately stimulated. Content to live the Bohemian life in the company of other well-to-do students, Ravel followed a path during his apprentice years that was both calm and uneventful. He loved his parents and they provided him with a pleasant, permissive background from which to look the world in the eye. Not allowing himself to become as vulnerable as

Portrait of Maurice Ravel by Ouvre

Debussy, he engaged in no quarrels or recriminations among his friends, most of whom liked him for his combination of sartorial elegance and ready wit. His companions of these days were usually the pianist Ricardo Viñès, who was to become responsible for the first performances of most of the composer's subsequent piano works; the critic M. D. Calvocoressi, with whom he shared an interest in Russian music; and the aspiring poet Tristan Klingsor, later to act as collaborator in one of the composer's finest song cycles. These eventually became the nucleus of the group known as 'Les Apaches', a half-humorous designation which they took upon themselves rather in the same manner as the group of painters calling themselves 'Les Fauves'. Both names suggested an unruly pack of rebels, fresh upon the scene.

His first steps in music not being at all typical of the prodigy, it is perhaps not surprising that Ravel never showed very much interest in executing his own compositions. For all the fetish he made about the performance of his works, he was to remain only a moderate performer himself. Like Stravinsky, who described one of his teachers as being 'an excellent pianist and complete blockhead', Ravel was bored by the antics of the virtuoso and tended to assume that performers were a lower species requiring constant restraint and guidance. The human hand and, to a much lesser extent, the human voice, were instruments he regarded with some impatience. They existed to do his bidding: it never occurred to him that he might have adapted his compositional processes more favourably to their idiosyncrasies, any more than he thought it wise to relegate any of the rights of interpretation. The performance of his works he regarded as a matter of simple—or rather not so simple—direction. Anyone who has attempted to play the more difficult Ravel piano works, however, will appreciate that there is a certain amount of justice in the complaints of performers about them. They sound magnificent when played by a master like Michelangeli or Rosen, but they do not really lie well under any but the most acrobatic pair of hands. Since Ravel is a composer pre-eminently associated with the piano, it may be worth while to elaborate these suggestions.

Gieseking has stated that Ravel's works are 'the most pianistic ever written, making the most perfect and universal use of the resources of the modern piano'. So that we should perhaps qualify our last remarks by adding that part of the unprecedentedly difficult character of his keyboard writing must be attributed to this ingenious attempt to extend the possibilities of the medium, incorporating among other techniques those of the *clavecinistes*, who of course had two manuals to play upon. That Ravel occasionally seems to be asking for the impossible is inferable from the well-known finger muddle into which players are accustomed to land when trying to insert the fingers of one hand through those of the other. This may have been simple enough to Rameau, but in the context of Lisztian scales and arpeggios it can only be viewed as daunting. The composer's *sang-froid* in such matters is possibly what is most infuriating. Typical of Ravel's indifference to the complexities facing the performer was his attitude to Paul Wittgenstein, the German pianist who lost an arm in the First World War, and who later entreated Ravel to write him a concerto for the left hand. Complying with a work of terrifying difficulty, the composer was mildly indignant when Wittgenstein was unable to perform it adequately, and he did not hesitate to give the work to Février for its first performance. Since then it has been seen to be manageable, but has become part of the standard repertoire only with the utmost persuasion, and even Cortot, probably the best known French pianist of the century, was alleged to have used two hands on it. From the beginning, then, Ravel must be viewed as rather a dictatorial composer. Unwilling to become the slave of natural disabilities, he was music's master and he left it to others to undertake the necessary athletics.

The earliest work Ravel is known to have written dates from some four years before he entered Fauré's class, and was a *Sérénade grotesque* for piano. Remaining unpublished, it was eclipsed by the better known *Menuet antique*, first envisaged for orchestra, but most often heard in the piano version. Neither of these works gives much hint of the pianism alluded to above. They embody the more dainty side of the composer's nature, and could be regarded as model student exercises if it were not for the obtrusive element of pastiche in the latter. Considered as a *menuet* it is a shade long, with the repeats, but it is formally very exact and looks forward to the similarly titled piece in the suite *Le Tombeau de Couperin* which Ravel was to write in 1917. If there are any other features worth commenting upon they are the singular purity of line—Ravel was always to retain a masterly power of etching his melodic lines with the minimum of interruption—and the neat rhythmic touches which gave an element of syncopation to the work. The contrast of registers is also deftly managed, though for a composer who was to be so much associated with the piano it is a trifle odd to see the tune so low down in the treble.

Exhibiting qualities which we may describe, after the composer's own example, as 'plus Ravel', the next important work was the popular *Pavane pour une infante défunte*, dating from 1899. By the time he had written this piece Ravel had come under the spell of Chabrier, that dazzling master of effects. A comparison of the *Pavane* with the charming but neglected *Idylle* from that composer's suite of *Pièces pittoresques* will establish beyond doubt the extent of the new influence. What is Ravel's own is the rich—possibly rather cloying—harmony with which he clothes the main theme. An interesting example of the concern with imitating older instruments, which was to become one of his later pastimes, is the series of detached notes in the accompaniment to the theme, which cleverly suggests a lute or similar stringed instrument typical of the courts of the sixteenth century. Ravel did not care much for this piece in his maturity, and it can easily be sentimentalized. Those inclined to linger over its expressive qualities would do well to be reminded of the composer's own much quoted comment to a pupil that the piece was intended to be a pavane for a dead Infanta, and not a 'dead pavane for an Infanta'. The curious may wish to know that it was admired by Proust.

Between the two piano works we have described there were a number of experiments which did not entirely succeed. The first was a work for two pianos—the strangely titled *Sites auriculaires*, which is extremely suggestive of Satie. This novelty was performed with the two instruments brought together, the convex curve of the one fitting into the concave curve of the other. This was intended to go some way towards securing greater rapport between the respective pianists. Actually the effect was quite the opposite, since at the première the music racks were so placed that neither performer could see the other, and the result was disastrous. In a passage which Ravel had scored for alternating chords, the two performers played together instead of in succession, and the discords which ensued were evidently taken by the audience to have been part of the composer's intent. Needless to say the work did not prove a success, Ravel remaining very incommunicable on the subject, out of loyalty to Viñès, who had been one of the unfortunate pair of offenders.

The other abortive experiment was an overture to illustrate the *Shéhérazade* story with which he had recently become captivated. This work is possibly the only one of Ravel's to make extensive use of the pentatonic or whole-tone scale. Despite the interest in Orientalism which the Exposition Universelle of 1889 sparked off in him, he did not succumb, like Debussy, to the fascination of the Eastern *ragas*. Most of Ravel's melodies are in fact based on orthodox Western scales, with what is a pronounced tendency to omit the leading note. There is also some modal influence at work, traceable in part to the teaching of Fauré, and this shows itself in his frequent penchant for the Dorian and Phrygian modes. Like most composers, Ravel had his favourite intervals, the descending fourth—such as we hear in the closing 'Maman' of *L'Enfant et les sortilèges*—being the most clearly recognizable. After having the *Shéhérazade* overture performed at an S.M.I. concert in 1898 Ravel withdrew the work, and later made use of some of the material it contained in a much more impressive song cycle which was given the same title. This later work remained one of the composer's favourites, and it is undeniably deserving of a very high place in his output.

If we may look ahead briefly to 1903, when this cycle received its *première*, it will be worth our while to attempt a description of the three songs it contains. Choosing three of his friend Klingsor's poems, he set himself the task of matching in music their lavish imagery of the Eastern bazaars, populous with yellow-skinned and seductive girls, silk-turbaned merchants and placidly corpulent mandarins strutting under their umbrellas. The call was for sleek and easeful writing, set in a rich web of strings and woodwind, and Ravel rose to the demands in a way that he sorely envied in his later and more barren years. The verses themselves are blatantly nostalgic and recall those idiosyncratic translations from Li-Po and other Chinese poets for which Ezra Pound has since gained some of his notoriety. They are quite different from the despairing and death-laden poems of the East selected by Mahler to provide the text of *Das Lied von der Erde*. Klingsor's work is gently soporific, happy to allow the reader to sink into a somewhat self-indulgent reverie, in which an occasional pang of unveiled reality is sometimes permitted to break through as a peripheral irritation. The mood lent itself very well to musical realization.

The first of the set, *Asie*, is by far the longest and contains more variety of expression than the others. Beginning with Ravel's characteristic use of low pedal notes, it rises unhurriedly to a more vigorous and declamatory style as the singer begins to relate her longings:

> I should like to sail away with the schooner
> Which is rocking this evening in the port, mysterious and solitary,
> And which at last unfurls its violet sails
> Like an immense night-bird in the golden sky.

Gradually the tension is allowed to build up, giving vent to a superb opulence of orchestration, crowned by resonant cymbal-crashes and arc-like sweeps on the strings. In the last verse, when the panorama of benevolent China is exchanged for that of the sinister executioners and their victims, the music takes on a more menacing tone, only to subside once more when the words 'Et puis m'en revenir plus tard' remind the singer that it is, after all, a dream. *La Flûte enchantée*, the second song, gives us a foretaste of what Ravel was to do with this dulcet instrument in *Daphnis and Chloë*, and is more genuinely melodious than either of the other numbers. It tells the tale of a young servant lying in bed listening to the strains of the lover's flute as they drift though the open casements. The setting shows, as well as any other, the special talent Ravel had for accompanying the voice with a single instrument whose task it is to weave a discreet counterpoint around the vocal line. It is a device he uses many times, always to masterly effect. Finally, in *L'Indifférent* we are given a glimpse of the moment of lost opportunity as a prospective lover is recognized as such too late and passes by. The last few bars are particularly moving, the dejected spirits being perfectly conveyed through the dropping accents of the voice as it delves lower and lower to reach its cadence. Ravel may have written more complex music for voice in the second part of his career, but he never composed anything more brilliant or more typical of powers than this glowing cycle, still his most frequently heard vocal work.

That he went far towards following in the footsteps of the great French song-writers during this first decade of the new century may be deduced from the fact that Ravel returned to song twice more before its close. During 1904 and after, he wrote his *Mélodies populaires grecques*—or rather, since they were actually harmonizations of existing songs, he undertook their resetting. Unlike many twentieth-century musicians, including incidentally his own pupil Vaughan Williams, Ravel was never to become a folk-song enthusiast, but these five Greek songs, which were collected at the island of Chios by his friend Calvocoressi, are extremely charming and graceful. It is doubtful whether they really inflamed the imagination of the composer who had so lately penned the sophisticated '*Shéhérazade*'. Much more probably the challenge of something new appealed to him, as it was to do at regular intervals in his later years. All his life in fact Ravel was drawn to participate in any sort of musical wager. Many of his other compositions were the outcome of some challenge. Works as different as the *Boléro* and the piano suite *Gaspard de la nuit* were to have a common origin in a '*gageure*' which the composer delighted in setting himself. In the field of folk song, it is symptomatic that only a few years after writing the Greek songs he entered a competition, held at the Maison du Lied in Moscow, for the best arrangements of European folk songs of varying styles and countries. Ravel submitted seven songs, four of which won prizes, and the Hebrew melodies are still occasionally to be heard at concerts of the composer's music.

Infinitely more typical of Ravel is the miniature cycle entitled *Histoires naturelles*, which appeared in 1909 and was a setting of animal poems by Jules Renard. The animals chosen were the peacock, the cricket, the swan, the kingfisher and the guinea fowl. They represent the earliest clear examples of Ravel's talent for irony and satire in music. Intended to be a vehicle for sly humour, the poems received a treatment quite unlike most musical carica-tures relating to the animal kindgom. In most cases Ravel strove to betray the standard expectations of the audience by making each animal display characteristics not normally thought appropriate.

The peacock's strutting is presented laughably, since his lady bird has deserted him on the eve of their wedding, and each time he flaunts his tail feathers it is to the accompaniment of a hilarious upward glissando on the keyboard. The portrait of the cricket is more predictable, though the appoggiaturas by which he is depicted as winding up his watch represent a thoroughly Ravellian stroke. The elegance of the swan is seriously undermined as a result of the inopportune manner in which he is obliged to dart under the water in search of his infinitesimal prey, the gorging of which has long contributed to making him as fat as a farmhouse goose. This song is obviously to be interpreted as a skit on the romantic portrayals of Tchaikovsky and Saint-Saëns. The kingfisher is by far the most lyrical song in the cycle, with its gently sliding sevenths and statuesque pauses. The contrast between this song and the final one, picturing the guinea fowl, where the sevenths are bare and harsh and the cacophony of the cries is searingly vivid, could not have been more marked.

Given a public performance in 1907, the Histoires naturelles were badly received, most of the audience failing to grasp that they were not intended as a series of jocose chansons. The seemingly awkward pauses and jolting harmonies were too much for the average concert-goer's taste, and the more discerning were appalled by Ravel's unscholarly habit of eliding the final vowels of many of the words. To those nurtured on the suavities of Ravel's teacher Fauré the songs certainly seemed puzzling and mildly barbaric. They are still not especially popular, despite the rare testimonial given them by Ravel's biographer, Professor Demuth, who has described them as 'among the most significant works in music, and not only French music'. This is high praise indeed, and perhaps owes its extravagance to the fact that Ravel appears to have succeeded in the very unusual task of giving us a convincing musical setting of what are obviously very unmusical poems. That is, he introduced into French song, by choosing Renard as his unpropitious collaborator, the notion of textual fidelity. This ideal he advanced over older and more stock criteria of suitability such as euphony, romantic appeal and the like.

It can only be thought a pity, in view of Ravel's pioneering outlook in this matter, that he relinquished the task of establishing more firmly the new standards which were to attach to French song. It was left to Debussy to do this work, with Poulenc as his legatee. Curiously Ravel disengaged his attentions at precisely the moment when he might have achieved an important breakthrough. Was it because he had too careless a regard for the niceties of prosody to make it worth while for him to embark on such a career? There is certainly a paradox here, since although he seemed well aware of the direction in which French song was moving, and was instrumental through his own Renard settings in assisting in the movement, his respect for poetry itself seems to have been too scanty to have sustained a more persistent policy. It would not be true to say that Ravel had no tastes in literature, for there is ample evidence that in his student days, at any rate, he warmed to Baudelaire, Edgar Poe and Mallarmé—much the same constellation of writers as appealed to Debussy in fact. Nevertheless words were not the most satisfactory medium through which Ravel could express his personality which, as we have already noted, tended to such a depth of reserve that nothing so direct and meaningful as language was suited to projecting it. In his later years he made a point of withdrawing his books from their all too visible shelves at Montfort-L'Amaury, and it is virtually impossible to judge how far literature continued to mean anything to him. Suffice to say that literature was in all probability much too literal an art for him.

The *parlando* vocal style of the *Histoires naturelles* reached its climax in Ravel's *opera-buffa*, based on Franc-Nohain's comedy, entitled *L'Heure espagnole*, which was written as early as 1907, but did not receive its *première* until 1911. This fifty-six minute 'conversation in music' doubtless appealed to Ravel on account of the marionette-like behaviour of the characters, as presented in the dramatic version. It is a rather risqué comedy, set in a clockmaker's shop in Toledo, Spain, and concerns the amorous adventures of the proprietor's wife Concepcion. Making the most of her husband's day off, the little minx has invited her lover, the poet Gonzalo, to meet her at the shop. Their plans are thwarted by the presence of a customer, one Ramiro, a muleteer who has come to have his watch repaired, and has decided to await the return of Torquemada, the owner. As a ruse to get him out of the shop, Concepcion asks him if he will be good enough to put his strength to some use by carrying upstairs a number of the heavier clocks. This task he performs with such striking ease that the admiring wife is finally tempted to change her intentions, eventually inviting him to undertake one last trip upstairs. When he asks which clock it is to be this time she replies: 'Without a clock.' In the denouement Torquemada returns to find Gonzalo and another unbidden visitor, the portly Don Inigo, hidden in two of the clocks, which he promply forces them to buy, while Ramiro and Concepcion descend to help in the ticklish business of extricating the latter guest, who has found it easier to squeeze his bulk into the hiding-place than to lever himself out again. The opera ends with a joyful quintet at his release, almost in parody of the finale of Don Giovanni.

The whole work has been described by one critic as 'a miniature pornographic vaudeville', and it is rather a surprising theme for Ravel to have embarked upon, for he was always 'très correct' in his moral behaviour and tastes. The combination of puppet-like actions and powerful emotions clearly constituted an irresistible pull, while the opportunities to write music for the endless variety of clocks which, like those in Dylan Thomas's Under Milk Wood, continue to 'whizz, tock, whirr and chime' throughout, were far too tempting to pass up. The work was presented at the Opéra-Comique under Carré, and was successfully revived at Glyndebourne during the 1966 season.

A retrospective glance at Ravel's output for the stage leads us to point to the interesting contrast his works in this medium display. For if Daphnis and Chloë is seen as reaching the summit of purity in Ravel's art then L'Heure espagnole can be regarded as his testament of lasciviousness. Still far removed from the sphere of moral judgment, it nevertheless contains, in its treatment of the hypocrisy and absurdity of the baser human passions, the nearest approach the composer was to make to the world of living people. It is ironical that his age found the work as unacceptable as it did the more fairy-tale evocations from his pen. For his contemporaries, if not for ours, passion meant Wagnerian passion, uplifted by sacrifice and cleansed by the romantic afflatus. Today, when sexual morals are more frank, and the demands of the flesh seem to be more pressing, Ravel's opera might expect to meet with a more appreciative public. In its satirical treatment of human foibles, it should also fit in well with the present mood of Hogarthian disenchantment. The work should not be seen as too overtly didactic for all that. It is no Dreigroschenoper or Rake's

Progress. Ravel's spirit was far too uncommitted ever to be invoked in support of any sociological-cum-moral revolution.

In our account of the development of Ravel's vocal writing we have allowed ourselves to move ahead of chronology by a few years, and must now retrace our steps so as to take proper cognizance of the instrumental music written during this first phase of his career. The piano, as we have seen, was the main focus of his interest, and it was in 1901, only two years after the immature *Pavane*, that he wrote what is the first of his revolutionary works for this instrument—the liquescent *Jeux d'eau*. Owing something to Liszt's study, *Les Jeux d'eau à la villa d'Este*, it nevertheless goes far beyond that work in devising new and striking forms of passage work for the keyboard. The rapid succession of dissonant seconds—an interval which both Debussy and Ravel enjoyed using—seemed unplayable at the time, but have since opened up a rich vein of figuration for piano composers. The poised and floating fourths and fifths in the treble also suggested fresh methods of treating thematic material. What is perhaps most novel is that the themes themselves are not presented in the customary form of melodic phrases, but are conceived more as textural fragments. To describe this method as impressionistic would only be partially accurate, since although *Jeux d'eau* undoubtedly influenced Debussy, to say nothing of his numerous followers, the unique contribution of Ravel lay in his power to retain a certain firmness of line, while at the same time capturing that fluidity we have come to associate with Impressionism. A good example of this power is the opening theme of *Jeux d'eau*, which is really only an arpeggio set off by a series of underlying open fifths and sixths. Yet it sounds distinctly more thematic than the written notation would suggest. Another supreme instance is, of course, the return of the *Ondine* theme in the first of the *Gaspard de la nuit* triptych. Just the bare arpeggio is enough to re-evoke the poignant siren's song with which the work began, perhaps Ravel's most beautiful melody. It is precisely this almost magical economy of means which really goes to strengthen Ravel's stature as one of the great composers of the century; it should be borne in mind by those sceptical critics who lump the composer along with the more glittering Russians as a mere master confectioner.

Following the success of *Jeux d'eau*, Ravel produced his ingratiating

Sonatine in 1905, and the same year was to witness the publication of his suite *Miroirs*. These two ventures were widely different in style. The *Sonatine*, as its title suggests, is a classical work, moderate in technique as befits a composition of limited dimensions. It is none the less a very interesting contribution to the *genre*, partly because it is so perfectly realized and also because it raised the sonatina from its lowly status as a tinkling exercise for juvenile performers to a medium with distinct pretensions of its own. Ever since Ravel's charming little work appeared on the scene, composers from all countries have tried their hands at this kind of miniature perfection with utmost seriousness, and it is proof of Ravel's abilities that none has managed to supersede the prototype. Perhaps the delightful Noël-Gallon work comes closest to it in quality, though the style of that composition owes as much to Fauré as to Ravel. In more recent times both York Bowen and Beryl Rubinstein have produced worthy sonatinas on the Ravel model, so that the tradition continues to be upheld, perhaps because there are more tasteful young players with limited technique than is often alleged.

Ravel's *Sonatine* shows the finger dilemma, to which we have previously referred, in the very first measures. Looking at these on the printed page, it might seem that the distribution of the music between the hands has been made unnecessarily awkward. Closer inspection reveals that the effects Ravel is striving for in the passage cannot be attained as well by any other 'handing' of the music. The natural pressures of the fingers exert their influence, and in time it can be appreciated that Ravel's notation is exactly the one that fits best. Otherwise the accents are bound to appear a trifle forced. The pianist Clifford Curzon has made the same point in relation to the concerto for the left hand, where the roll of the hand upwards enables the thumb to give strong accentuation to the top notes of the melody in a manner which would be impossible if the passage were rescored for two hands. Aside from this and one or two other posers concerning the fingering of the music, the *Sonatine* is without great technical difficulties, and the limpid *Menuet* forming the second movement—which Alfred Cortot has aptly described as a 'colloque sentimentale'—is an admirable introduction to the pianistic world of Ravel.

The *Miroirs* are not quite up to the standard set by most of Ravel's other piano works. Rather uneven in merit, the collection begins with another insect portrayal—*Noctuelles*—which continues the composer's exploration of pianistic patterns, and like the longer *Une Barque sur l'océan* seems over-complicated for the amount of real music it contains. Both pieces veer in the direction of pure Impressionism and represent a style to which Ravel had no further recourse. *Oiseaux tristes* was the composer's own favourite from among these pieces, and the plaintiveness of the principal theme is indeed very fetching, recalling without quite the same eeriness Schumann's prophet bird from the *Waldscenen*. *La Vallée des cloches*, on the other hand, is redolent of Liszt, and might have fitted in well as part of the Swiss book of that composer's *Années de pèlerinage*. The open fourths forming part of the accompanying triplet figures in this piece lend buoyancy to the texture, and the same interval occurs high up in the treble to imitate the cow-bells heard across the valley. More detached from the remainder is the Spanish number *Alborada del Gracioso*, which Ravel saw fit to orchestrate. In both versions it is a splendidly vibrating piece of music, with pungent accents and an exciting climax in which, in the piano score, there are some awesome *glissandi* in thirds and fourths which are fiendishly difficult to play at the proper speed. Ravel was a real 'aficionado' as far as Spanish music was concerned, and he would probably have enjoyed orchestrating Albeniz's suite *Iberia* had not the rights been previously accorded to the Spanish composer Arbos.

By far Ravel's greatest work for the piano is the set of pieces entitled *Gaspard de la nuit*, undertaken in 1908 to illustrate the very Hoffmanesque poems of the minor French romantic Aloysius Bertrand. The three poems chosen are *Ondine*, *Le Gibet* and *Scarbo*, the last being a fantastic piece of *diablerie* which would surely have appealed strongly to the composer of the Faust Symphony. Again exceptionally virtuosic in layout, the first of the triptych is a shimmering evocation of the water sprite of marine mythology whom we have encountered before in Debussy's Preludes. Here the writing is much more brilliant, the arpeggios being lacily spread out over several octaves and demanding the most feathery touch for their execution. Towards the middle of the piece the cascades of falling thirds present the player with much the same hurdle as he has to face in Balakirev's dismayingly difficult *Islamey*, the attempt to outdo which provided Ravel with his motive for writing. Another hazard is the enormous 'splash' near the end of the movement, which signifies the return of the sprite to the depths from which she emerged. By comparison *Le Gibet* seems easier, though the use of the intermittent B flat pedal complicates the rhythmical notation in a way that becomes more obvious to the player than the listener, and for all its slow tempo it is not simple to perform. The grisly theme of the dangling man and the creaking gallows might have been taken from Baudelaire's poem *L'Embarquement pour Cythère*, and is presented through a series of macabre chords moving slowly in strict time. It is in the sketch of the demon Scarbo that we feel the full terror of the impression, however, Ravel underlining the octave leap which begins his theme by writing the words 'Quel horreur!' in his copy of the score. The music of this last movement bristles with fast repeated note patterns and similar pianistic tricks. The diminutive *codettas* which are made to follow each phrase in the theme, in the form of scurrying chords near the top of the keyboard, make the work a veritable nightmare for the performer. As Charles Rosen has suggested, Ravel might easily have called the whole suite *Le Tombeau de Liszt*, so completely does it exhaust all the conventions of piano writing as they had been laid down by the late Romantic school. The ending is particularly expertly managed in relation to the text, as with *Ondine*. This time the final manifestation of the demon is characterized by a highly tentative moment when the poet is not sure whether he still apprehends the creature or whether it has begun to vanish into thin air:

And if I expected him to disappear, the little dwarf would grow taller and taller and stand towering between me and the moon like a cathedral spire, with a golden bell jingling at the top of his pointed cap! But soon his body would turn blue and translucent like the wax in a candle, and his face grow pale—then suddenly he would vanish.

This last disappearing trick is depicted in the music by a rapidly spread chord in which the B natural of the left hand is made to clash inconclusively with an A sharp in the right hand, almost as if to hint that yet another hallucination is to supervene.

Readers interested in the literary background to *Gaspard*—which name is of course a synonym of Mephistofeles—may be fascinated by the dry-points of the erotic artist Felicien Rops, which offer a graphic account of Bertrand's poems. They reveal all of Rops's talent for spidery and lecherous figure drawing and would have made a magnificent cover design for Ravel's suite. A lesser known item of information relating to this work is Ravel's intention to follow it with what he described as a 'pendant', also consisting of three pieces, this time based on the novel *Le Grand Mealnes* by Alain-Fournier. Why the composer should have associated this tender book by a young Frenchman killed in the First World War with the devilry of *Gaspard* is hard to fathom. Possibly he was merely thinking in terms of a second series of mood pictures, and to this aim the novel would certainly have lent itself. Indeed the numinous calm and suffused innocence of Alain-Fournier's writing would surely have found a very sympathetic echo in Ravel's music. As it is it must be put down, along with Debussy's *Chute de la maison Usher*, as one of the maddeningly uncompleted masterpieces of which the history of music is so sadly full.

No account of this period when Ravel's lyrical gifts were at their most spontaneous could be called complete without mention of the fine String Quartet and its more sensuous companion work, the Introduction and Allegro for Harp, Flute, Clarinet and Strings. The quartet ranks with that of Debussy as one of the best in the literature of modern music, and is beautifully laid out for the instruments. The main impression, as with so much of Ravel's music, is one of smoothness and precision. Melodically it is a particularly profuse work, as the first two themes of the initial movements help to testify. Ravel himself had a few doubts about the work at the point of writing, though Debussy, with whom he was still on good terms at the time, urged him not to alter a note of it. Much later in life, Ravel was to say that he would willingly exchange the 'savoir' which enabled him to write his Piano Trio for the 'pouvoir' by which he had come to write this quartet. One can see clearly the distinction he was trying to make.

More deliberately aimed at enchantment, the Harp Septet is actually a puzzling work to describe. To call it a septet is in a way a misnomer, since it would be more accurate to have labelled it a miniature concerto, so important a part does the harp have to play.

Its peculiar charm resides in the fact that it successfully combines the excitement of a work for soloist with some of that intimacy normally reserved for chamber music proper. One could wish for no better introduction to French music than this unassuming divertissement, which the composer did not even list among his principal compositions, having evidently forgotten its existence. Even so the writing is a lot happier than in many more pretentious works, the woodwind parts standing out as clearly as colours on a lithographic plate. Several later French composers have attempted to emulate Ravel in writing for this seductive combination, including Roussel and the neglected Guy Ropartz, whose placid *Prélude, marine et chanson* deserves to be far better known.

The year 1912 was something of an *annus mirabilis* for Ravel, since it was in this year that he launched into the genre for which he has still retained the bulk of his popular acclaim. The reference is, of course, to his music for the ballet, and especially that which he wrote for the Diaghilev company. A lifelong devotee of the cult of French Hellenism, Ravel had long been looking for a subject which would enable him to enlarge on the Greek pastoral themes which his music was so suited to depicting. Having left the Conservatoire and established himself as a composer of substance, Ravel had been approached as early as 1909 to do a ballet for the Russian troupe which at that time was about to create a sensation in London as well as Paris. Stravinsky's *Firebird* had been the *pièce de resistance* of the 1910 season, and *Petrouchka* and the scandal-provoking *Rite of Spring* were in the immediate offing. The choreographer Fokine was the first to suggest to Ravel the idea of using Longus's fable as the basis for a new set of tableaux, and after a succession of production difficulties the final arrangements for the ballet were drawn up, with Bakst engaged to do the *décor* and Nijinsky and Karsavina in the leading roles.

On 8th June 1912 at the Chatelet Theatre the world first heard Ravel's luminous music for *Daphnis and Chloë*, incontrovertibly the composer's principal masterpiece. It had taken him three years to write—the final *Bacchanale* alone having occupied a full twelve months—the task of orchestration requiring to be approached slowly and painstakingly, so that all the myriad problems of balance and texture might not suffer. To help him in achieving his solution,

Ravel imported a number of special effects, including a wind-machine to create atmosphere and a set of *crotales*, or castanet-like instruments. For all the care lavished on the work, however, the resulting ballet was not an unqualified success. Squabbling among the principal personalities involved had reached disturbing dimensions prior to the first performance, and the sources of contention were unfortunately not properly resolved. In particular there was considerable disagreement about the kind of locale in which the ballet was to be set. Ravel's concept of the Greek scene was distinctly tinged with French coloration, notably with the hues we associate with the court painters of the eighteenth century. Diaghilev, on the contrary, wanted a more truly classical setting. To cap it all the stage-artist, Leon Bakst, saw fit to design a too-sumptuous backcloth which could scarcely be said to have fitted in with either conception. Added to these difficulties were certain purely choreographic perplexities for which Fokine was partly to blame. The rhythms of Ravel's score were no help to the members of the *corps de ballet*, however, and in the final *danse* the only way they could latch on to the music was by mumbling to themselves the syllables of the impresario's name—'Ser-gei-Dia-ghi-lev'.

The subject of the ballet, which is in two tableaux, concerns the trial of the shepherd Daphnis, whose pure love for Chloë is successively imperilled by a number of typical misadventures—the lustful ruses of his rival Dorcon, an attempt to seduce him by the temptress Lycenion, and ultimately the capture of Chloë by a band of marauding pirates, who carry her off to their camp in the mountains. Taking pity on the plight of Daphnis, the great god Pan, moved by recollection of his own love for Syrinx, decides to intervene and drive away the kidnappers, restoring the two lovers to their original state of primeval bliss. Perhaps the most striking scenes are those in which Daphnis awakes to the dawn breaking outside the nymphs' grotto, after having previously collapsed with exhaustion in his search for the missing Chloë; and the final general *danse* in which there is a tumult of rejoicing at the reunion of the happy pair. Both of these scenes effectively illustrate the composer's flair for clear, sharp-edged woodwind writing, the brilliant weaving of the flutes in the former helping to create a bird-song background through which the magnificent cello theme cleaves passionately. In the general *danse* it is the brass writing, agile and electrifying, which stands out, rounding off the work with stunning effect.

Ravel's orchestral technique, though no more remarkable perhaps than that of Debussy, is actually quite different in aim. Debussy's most characteristic music displays a vaporous quality, enhanced by the grey, silky colours of his orchestral palette. Moreover the instrumentation aims to create an illusion of movement, generally sluggish and lazy. Ravel's writing for the orchestra usually succeeds in being more linear, in which the colours are picked out with sharp brightness, and in which the sense of movement seems more automatic. Like that of Prokoviev (whom he admired), Ravel's music spins and hums with all the mechanical exactitude of his beloved toys, the finale of *Daphnis* possessing something of the excitement of a clockwork motor ripping away at full tilt. How he learnt the skills necessary to secure such effects remains a mystery, though we do know that Widor was his bible for a number of years, and he was often to be observed asking orchestral players about the potentialities of their various instruments. His composing, as far as can be ascertained, seems to have been done at the piano, however, a trait he shared with his friend Stravinsky and which, according to the Russian composer Rimsky-Korsakov, tends to become established as a habit very early on in the careers of some composers. His delight in the process of orchestration may be inferred from the remark he once made in answer to a question about this aspect of his art. 'C'est un amusement pour moi plutôt qu'un travail,' he is alleged to have said, thus indicating the heuristic basis of his activities. The most obvious influences on Ravel's handling of orchestral problems seem to be Richard Strauss, from whom he must have acquired some of his extraordinary sense of virtuosity; and Saint-Saëns, whose feeling for clarity of texture is occasionally evident. Neither Ravel nor Debussy consciously sought to imitate the orchestral writing of Wagner, whom Ravel once described as 'le grand cauchemar harmonique'. By comparison the Romantic elements in his own scoring—and they do undeniably exist—could be best thought of as temperate and prescriptive of a deliberately lunar coolness.

If the *première* of *Daphnis* was not quite the sensation hoped for, at least it brought the composer further international acclaim. It is unfortunate that the Great War of 1914–18 supervened so soon afterwards that Ravel had little time in which to enjoy his new-found status. Not moved to the excess of patriotism exhibited by Debussy, he was nevertheless anxious to serve his country in a military capacity. Making every effort to enlist in an active branch of service life, he could not convince the authorities that he would not be better off sticking to his musical vocation. His exceptionally short stature—which Poulenc described later as making the composer easily mistakable for 'un petit jockey'—was also against him, and in the end he had to be content with a job as an ambulance driver. This was no picnic, however, and many of his friends were aghast at the miserable conditions he chose to endure rather than take the easier course of opting out. Part of his zeal is attributable to the indignation he felt at the sad fate of his fellow composer, Albéric Magnard, who was shot by the invading armies as a reprisal for having refused to allow his house to be occupied. Throughout the war Ravel wrote eager letters to other composers, hungry for any scrap of musical fare which would help to distract his imagination from the hideous spectacle it was forced to encounter. That this show of horror had its deleterious effect on the composer is certain. He was never the same man after the cessation of hostilities, being thereafter plagued by a persistent lassitude and enervating nervous distractability that dogged him right up to his death twenty years later. Whether the death of his mother, which occurred during 1917, contributed to this rapid ageing of the composer is more problematic. His love for her was unquestionably the strongest he felt towards any person in his life. Whatever prompted the tenacity of their relationship, her passing and the impact of the war were two events which combined to mark an end to Ravel as the sprightly young 'apache' of popular reminiscence. Thenceforward began the gradual combat with failing powers which all artists have learnt to fear.

The only significant work to emerge from the war years was the justly celebrated piano suite Le Tombeau de Couperin, which Ravel dedicated to the memory of various friends who had been killed in action, among them the husband of Mme Long. Consisting of six movements, the composition recalls Couperin chiefly through the subtle punctiliousness of the ornamentation which, as Rosen has noted, almost succeeds in duplicating the 'ping' of the harpsichord.

Otherwise the writing is gratifyingly Ravellian—a fact which caused one unsympathetic critic to lament that the work had not been *Le Tombeau de Ravel* by Couperin! Of the various dance numbers contained in the suite, the *Forlane*—which is oddly enough an Italian form—comes off best. This lilting 6–8 tune is presented with elegance and sobriety, and must be accounted one of the composer's happiest inspirations. Its coda has a neatness which suggests de Séverac's musical box. The forceful *Rigaudon* which follows is as good an example of Ravel's pianism as any, especially the nonchalant middle section where the sonorities are beautifully laid out. These elements are also pinpointed in the *Menuet*—the only composition found on Ravel's music rack at his death—while the *Toccata* is a brilliantly exhibitionist piece which treats the piano very much as a *Hammerklavier*.

Immediately after the war Ravel endeavoured to repeat his triumph with the Russian ballet by writing the Viennese pastiche *La Valse*—which many have described as his most meretricious work. It is not exactly the 'weariness to the flesh' which Cecil Gray termed it, if only because it was envisaged partly to induce this feeling in the listener, the aim of the composition being to describe in musical terms the disintegration of the waltz, from its palmy days as the symbol of courtly munificence to its ultimate ruin amid the bombed palaces and overcrowded ballrooms of a collapsed Europe. Those critics who continue to view it as a mere *tour de force*, in which Ravel was once again intent on ravishing our senses, entirely mistake the composer's purposes. As it turned out, however, the determination to persevere with Diaghilev brought no further rewards. Taking the score of *La Valse* with him to the impresario's apartment, Ravel played the work through on the piano, only to meet with a tepid reception. It offers such a fascinating sidelight on Diaghilev's own astonishing perspicacity as a critic that it is worth relating his objections to mounting the proposed ballet. After listening to the complete score played in this way the ebullient Russian turned around and said:

> Ravel, c'est un chef-d'œuvre . . . mais ce n'est pas un ballet. . . . C'est le portrait d'un ballet . . . c'est la peinture d'un ballet.

Such insight, expressed in so unforgettable a series of phrases, goes far to explain the magnetic power Diaghilev appeared to exercise over the many artists and musicians of genius with whom he worked, and should serve to rebut those sceptics who are inclined to think of the man as nothing more than a colossal mountebank.

That Ravel was deeply upset by Diaghilev's decision goes without saying. Retreating into his defensive reserve, he said nothing at the time, merely packing away his music and bowing out with as much grace as he could muster. But underneath his feelings were raw, and the knowledge that his work had been admitted as a masterpiece of its kind did little to smooth them over. Never again to associate himself with the Ballet Russe, Ravel lapsed into one of those lengthy fallow periods which he had noted in other composers but which up to that time he had successfully managed to evade in his own person. Keeping his hand in with hack work and transcription—which he never did less than superlatively well—he bided his time before embarking on another major venture. By that time critics had got into the habit of openly charging him with insincerity, and the dubious fame attaching to the earlier ballets *Ma Mère L'Oye* and *Adelaïde*, which he had also written in the immediately pre-war period, was such that the epithet 'pasticheur' was in danger of hanging round his neck like an albatross. For some curious reason— probably temperamental antipathy—the public refused to invest Ravel's neo-classicism with the same seriousness as was attached to Stravinsky's more flamboyant dressing up. Feeling that there was an element of chicanery in what he did, they began by expecting him to perform unprecedented feats of legerdemain, only to end by complaining that he had deceived them. It was as if a class of children, spellbound by the tales with which they were being regaled, were suddenly to turn on the brothers Grimm for having perpetuated a succession of untruths. Sensing that the proliferation of period guises was becoming over subtle, his listeners eventually tired of the game and cried out for an end to equivocation. Like Dr Coppelius, the composer was surrounded by hesitant watchers who were never sure of what was real and what an annoying fabrication.

As some of his more astute critics have observed, Ravel so rarely made use in his descriptive music of the actual or historical sources.

Vladimir Jankélévitch has put it so well that one cannot do better than quote him in full:

The period Ravel chose for his prism was usually the eighteenth century: he had always preferred it to the Renaissance, the Empire, the Louis-Philippe period and the Second Empire, and it had been made fashionable by Verlaine and Henri de Regnier. When Ravel looks in the direction of Madagascar he sees it through the prose writing of Evariste Parny, and if he had written an opera on *Shéhérazade* he would have used Galland's translation of the *Thousand and One Nights*. The Chinese element in *Ma Mère L'Oye* is reminiscent of Boucher's pictures, just as Mozart's Turkish effects are reminiscent of the *Lettres Persanes* and the whole 'alla turca' exoticism which belongs very much to the time of Louis Quatorze.

Looking at Ravel's music in more detail, it is remarkable how consistent it is in following this principle of pastiche. M. Jankélévitch is not alone in having pointed out the various lenses through which the composer permitted himself to view his subjects. Rollo Myers, in his gracefully written and intelligent study of Ravel, has noted that the *Tzigane* for violin is really not so much an evocation of a gipsy peasant fiddler as a composition dictated by the Lisztian *Zigeuner* tradition. It is customary nowadays to belittle the so-called romantic folk music tradition for its tendency to embellishment, and the prevailing mood favours a more ethnographic approach, such as Bartók and Kodály have attempted to adopt. Our present attitude is mistaken, however, if we assume that Ravel in particular was not conscious of his habit of elaborating folk harmonies with the sophisticated ninths and elevenths of twentieth-century textbooks. On the contrary he saw his aim as eschewing authenticity in favour of adding something new. Putting it bluntly: he would probably have thought peasant music very suitable for peasants but scarcely so for anyone else. The awful self-consciousness of certain contemporary composers who delight in parading their collection of genuine English or Central European folk melodies—absolutely without adulteration—would have caused Ravel considerable merriment. He would have put them in the same category as the unimaginative productions of 'Sir Stanford' and 'Sir Parry', as he mischievously called them.

It would be tedious to go on providing other examples from Ravel's œuvre to prove the points at stake. It is perhaps more interesting to evoke evidence from the composer's own peculiar connoisseurship of '*objets d'art*' at 'Le Belvédère'. Myers recalls how his passion for the unauthentic extended to the habit of collecting artistic forgeries, and his delight in the '*trompe l'œil*', a taste for which the modern age may be more inclined to forgive him, was frequently so bizarre as to startle his guests out of their critical self-confidence. On one well-known occasion he invited them to inspect what he claimed to be a fascinating piece of rare porcelain, belonging to one of the more coveted dynasties; only to explode with laughter at their faces when he turned the exhibit upside-down to reveal a burnt-out electric light bowl. Another of his pranks was to pass off a fake Monticelli on his more gullible friends in the painting world. Such hoaxes are perhaps not very endearing, but they were not undertaken cruelly or with malice. For the most part they simply serve to illustrate Ravel's unshakeable belief in illusionism of all kinds. To him this quality was the very life-blood of art, which in his view could be correctly described as a '*divertissement de luxe*'.

Using our long perspective to re-examine the foundations of Ravel's aesthetic, it must be admitted that many of the current objections to his position lose force in the light of what we have unearthed. Replying to one of his more unthinking critics, the composer was once heard to exclaim: 'Has it not occurred to him that I might be artificial by nature?' Whether or not such endowments are feasible, it can scarcely be denied that Ravel was artificial by design, and that an approach to his work based on the usual concepts of sincerity and realism must end by foundering in a welter of misapprehensions. A more profitable line of approach to the young of today would be to regard Ravel's music much as one would the art of montage in the cinema. Indeed the cinema offers a variety of interesting parallels to his work. Its power of swiftly locating the spectator in time and of dissolving one scene rapidly into another present unmistakable analogies. Above all there is the common acceptance of a set of conventions through which art may be communicated, the decision to lift it out of the clutches of 'period' and 'style' and confer upon it the freedom to oscillate between the concepts which normally go to make up such categories. What the composer sought was a measure of freedom similar to that enjoyed by the film to create a deliberately unlocalized art form. It is not without significance that Ravel was an addict of the cinema, his favourite actor being the inimitable Chaplin. Charlot's audacity, and the ease with which his humour transcended class and national barriers, left the composer rapt with admiration. Never particularly anxious to write directly for the films, Ravel had more feeling for the medium than for its typical products. Doubtless he felt his music too autonomous to be invoked in support of any concrete scenario or action sequence. On the one occasion when he did write a commissioned score—it was the Don Quixote cycle we have already alluded to—the producers rejected the music, reputedly in deference to Chaliapin's opinion that it was not sufficiently dramatic. As Ravel's brother Edouard was to point out many years after the composer's death, there is undoubtedly much in his stage works that could be adapted to cinematic purposes, and they may yet find expression in this medium. Pre-eminent among those which suggest themselves for this kind of adaptation must be L'Enfant et les sortilèges, for it is hard to stage, but would have made a marvellous film if directed by a more astringent and less sentimental Walt Disney.

The years of waiting came to an end in 1925, when Ravel completed his last work for the stage. The project had lain on the stocks for some while previously, a discussion having taken place between the composer and his collaborator, the legendary Colette, as far back as the final year of the war. Embodying both child and animal fantasy, the story relates the adventures of an unruly and impenitent miscreant whose delinquencies have included the pulling of cats' tails, the tearing up of his school books and the breaking of china. Forbidden by his mother to go to bed until he has made amends for these wrongs by learning his sums, the little boy is left alone in the great Normandy stone house to do as he has been told. As darkness approaches he encounters one by one the dream figures associated with his nursery world. There is Father Arithmetic, a horrible old curmudgeon who prattles away tiresomely at his figures; the beautiful princess who has arisen from the story book the child has torn up, and who pleads with him in passionate and lyrical vein; and finally even the fire, upon whom the kettle had been upset, which rises up in wrath to upbraid the little vandal. Amid this crazy jamboree the child stands stunned and enchanted. A Wedgwood teapot and Chinese cup become partners in a typical jazz-age foxtrot, supplemented by trombone effects in the New Orleans style. Their ridiculous conversation is conducted in a mixture of languages. 'How's your mug?' asks the teapot. 'Rotten,' replies the other in a mock County accent. Still other visitants include the grandfather clock the child has helped to smash, and a delightful procession of shepherds and shepherdesses who formed part of the wallpaper torn down in a fit of rage. In the second scene the child finds himself alone in the garden, gradually becoming aware of the ominous presence of the animals whom he has ill-treated. The bullfrogs growl and the chorus of tree animals threatens. Out for a night on the tiles, two cats perform a stilted duet which eventually culminates in a raucous crescendo in which the singers are instructed to keep their mouths closed. Ravel was particularly vehemently slated in the press for this unmusical intrusion. More melodious are the lovely waltzes for moths and dragonflies which follow, in which Ravel the prestidigitator performs miracles of orchestration. When the terrified child finally hurts himself and cries out for his mother the animals rally round in sympathy, made aware that humans too can feel pain. They console the child with a tender madrigal—utterly French as it is Ravellian—and the magical score closes with the repeated, but now less tremulous, cry of 'Maman'.

Professor Demuth is surely perverse in consigning this enticing work to the lower reaches of Ravel's canon. On any count it demands a higher appraisal. Apart from the ravishing music in which it abounds, its philosophy so perfectly exemplifies Ravel's message that we can only remain grateful that he did not abandon the work along with the other projects that failed to materialize. Full of the mystery of life, the opera is more pantheistic than anything else the composer wrote, and in its portrayal of the unregeneracy of childhood it seeks to underline the by now banal conclusions of the psychoanalysts. Unlike that stolid and literal faction, however, Ravel also emphasizes the child's poetic pre-rogatives, his sole power of commanding the creatures of his imag-ination until, by conquering reality, he is able to make them transfigure the world in which both he and we reside. And in proclaiming the redeeming character of tenderness—the emotion which can succeed, far more even than love, in overcoming evil—

the opera stands as a definitive gesture embodying its creator's only affirmative teaching.

David Drew has said of the ultimate phase into which Ravel now passed:

The last ten years of Ravel's composing career make an interesting study, for his activities during that time are directly symptomatic of the plight of contemporary French music, a plight that becomes almost tragic when it engulfs an artist of Ravel's stature.

The activities alluded to in this sadly brief commentary are too various to be circumscribed in a single phrase. Unlike Debussy, who was mercifully spared survival into the age of blaring saxophones and flat-footed rhythms, Ravel became a part of this makeshift culture, and even acquiesced in certain respects to its demands. Its frivolousness appealed to his by that time painfully disillusioned mood, and his previously withdrawn personality underwent something of a change. Giving up the solitary life for that of the fashionable 'noctambule', he threw himself into the whirl of metropolitan pleasures, refusing to vacate his seat in the cafés until well into the early hours of each new day. Partly an attempt to cure his racking insomnia, this radical treatment did little more than accentuate the purposelessness which was coming to characterize his existence. The Violin and Piano Sonata which he finished in 1927 emanated from what he regarded as yet another challenge in combining 'two essentially incompatible instruments'. Its 'blues' finale was a concession to the tastes of the new age. More expressive of his yearnings for distant places were the Madagascan songs, with their equally topical theme of revolt against the slavery of the black peoples in thrall to the white. They are the most savage and paradisal of Ravel's works, far removed from his accustomed refinement of sentiment. Meanwhile he continued to hanker after new experiences, restless and unwilling to settle down to prolonged work.

A visit to America at this time shows he was still very much of a dandy in appearance and outlook. He took with him twenty pairs of pyjamas, dozens of suits and shirts and fifty-seven ties, most of which he claimed were half an inch too long to be worn. Mme Long, who accompanied him on the trip, has testified that it was a nightmare of mislaid articles and unpunctual engagements. He smoked his beloved *Caporals* incessantly, pronounced vilifications upon American cooking, and lost his heart to California. Musically, America fascinated him by its forward-looking streams of popular art, and he was genuinely impressed by the playing and composition of George Gershwin, who very nearly became the last of his pupils. Back in France he set to work with some of the old zest on two new piano concertos, one for the left hand and the other for the more conventional combination. Both these works were completed only with the maximum of laboriousness, though in the outcome they are indistinguishable from the best of Ravel. Indeed the concerto for the left hand, for all its oddities of construction, is a master work. In place of the brittle charm of the G major, which Ravel frankly conceded to be a *divertissement*, this sombre composition is based on powerful themes, some of them Basque in origin, and reminds us forcibly of one of Bach's Brandenburg Concertos. The many climaxes it contains build up slowly, like that in the overpublicized *Boléro*, and demand playing of an unhurried steadiness. Thus approached, they attain an almost hypnotic compulsion and controlled frenzy. The soloist's lightning dashes from one end of the keyboard to the other also require the right kind of *panache*, without which the work's continuous power to thrill is forfeited. Set out on two staves, the part deliberately seeks to imitate the sounds associated with the double register, so that it is perhaps the supreme instance of illusionism in the catalogue of dissimulations perpetrated by the composer. By common consent, the two-handed concerto is not quite its equal, though the slow movement possesses a sculptural majesty hardly suggestive of any decline in powers. Commentators have ascribed the style of this movement variously to Mozart and to Fauré, whose *Ballade* it somewhat resembles. Actually the contours of the melody are firmly indicative of the composer, and can be traced back to 1918 and the middle section of the *Rigaudon* from *Le Tombeau de Couperin*. Despite some over-elaborate *bravura* writing in the finale, the concerto sustains its place in the repertory, though it has served as the model for rather too many self-conscious young Conservatoire prizewinners in recent years.

Towards the middle of the nineteen-thirties Ravel suddenly began to lose all capacity for further work. Discovering that he could no longer rely on complete movement of his limbs, he gradually relapsed into helplessness, sitting around all day as if expecting some signal to presage his return to normality. Eventually it became obvious that none would arrive. Coming upon him in a particularly despondent pose one day, his friend Hélène Jourdan-Morhange said to him:

'Que faites vous là, cher Ravel?'

'J'attends,' he replied without hysteria.

A more emotional man would probably have broken under the strain of this blank and pointless running out of the sands of his talent. Ravel remained impassive, undemonstrative to the end. Friends who had followed his activities attributed the sudden worsening of his condition to a blow on the head he had received in a taxi accident some while previously. The similarity of Ravel's illness to that of his father, who had died in almost identical circumstances, on the contrary suggests a possible hereditary basis for the disorder. By 1936 the situation had become critical. Still able to think with complete clarity, Ravel's body was less and less able to perform the actions which he commanded it to undertake. Partial paralysis and defectiveness of speech eventually made it imperative that more drastic measures be sought. Surgeons were consulted, and in the following year Ravel entered a clinic in the Rue Boileau, where the distinguished neurologist Dr Clovis Vincent performed a brain operation. Unable to receive anaesthetic, the composer is alleged to have felt the incision. But he was long past caring. One of his last pleas was that he might be spared the terrible ordeal of his poor Chabrier, who lived to sit through a performance of *Gwendoline* without recognizing it as his own music. Ravel's wish was granted, for although his brother Edouard came and placed a toy pelota player on his pillow in the hope of enlivening his waking moments, consciousness was never restored to him, and death claimed its victory on 28th December 1937. A post-mortem revealed that his condition had been due to a shrinking of the brain, causing multiple apraxia and dysphasia.

'He suffers, he is wounded, he bleeds'—thus went the refrain by which the creatures of *L'Enfant et les sortilèges* lamented the afflictions of the child they had come to love. That child was Ravel himself, irreverent and undisciplined, but always mindful of the marvels spawned by the imagination and invoking none but his mother to protect him from the world's darkness. His example serves to remind us that innocence does not need naïvety, nor tenderness passion. In an epitaph written on the death of this exceptional individual, Léon-Paul Fargue said of him:

He liked to do, and to do well: everything that came from his brain carries the mark of perfection. . . . His passion was to offer to the public finished works polished to a supreme degree.

The artist can harbour no worthier ambition than that expressed in these inclinations, and if the perfection sought by Ravel seems too studied an ideal to meet with our approval it cannot be denied that he furnished us with new standards of beauty and proportion. He provided an aim which extends beyond the unpredictable fumblings of nature, and thereby helps to postpone the chaos into which our lives continually threaten to dissolve.

Chapter 6   FRANCIS POULENC
Jongleur de Notre Dame

EVEN though it was the eighteenth-century Buffon who wrote 'Le style, c'est l'homme même', there can be few present-day Frenchmen willing to doubt the signal ease with which this maxim could be made to fit the career of Francis Poulenc. For no composer has ever projected more of his own personality into his work than this droll and roguish petitioner of the Muses. A Parisian with his roots in the Touraine, a vulgarian with a connoisseur's sense of the exquisite, an innocent commuting to and from the infernal regions of art, a practical joker let loose in the temple of the immortals— these and many other paradoxes could be used to describe the man who more than anything else remains quintessentially Poulenc. Indeed the more we learn of the contradictions which beset his character the harder it becomes to visualize any set of polarities which cannot in the last resort be accommodated to his bony shade. His deliberate impiety and childlike candour begin by marking him out as one of those 'revolutionary simpletons' against whom the late Wyndham Lewis led his intellectual tirades; yet we have only to turn the first page of his biography to discover also in him a man of sensibility, and even a devout preceptor of the spirit. His writings reveal with unmistakable certainty the cosmopolitan accents of his race. As the man, so his music. Since if it is habitual to deride the clownish ineptitudes of Le Bal masqué and the Rapsodie nègre, it is also becoming obligatory to salute the sublime lyricism of the Stabat Mater and the Eluard settings. It stands to reason that if musical criticism has one worth-while task to perform in relation to French composers it should be to divert attention from the 'bon enfant' aspects of Poulenc's personality and music, so overpublicized in the nineteen-twenties, and concentrate instead on the admirable body of song of which this composer has become the most important contemporary exponent. When the American Virgil Thomson remarked some years ago that 'Poulenc is incontestably the greatest writer of melodies in our time', comparatively few listeners had heard more than a fraction of his music for voice. The *Mouvements perpétuels* were in the repertory of every aspiring pianist, but not every aspiring singer had come across *Nous avons fait la nuit* or *Montparnasse*. Fashions have changed, but our philistinism continues. It is high time we put both to flight.

Let us therefore avoid further stereotyping, and go straight to the facts of Poulenc's career, which is more revelatory of his true interests than might be supposed. Born in 1899, he could not very well escape being a product of the new century, though even this seems to have been held against him by some of his more reactionary adversaries. It does not mean, however, that he possessed no musical ancestors, and it is not difficult, now that we can view his entire career in retrospect, to place both the man and his music in the context of their time and *milieu*. Being from a well-to-do family, Poulenc grew up amid musical and theatrical influences, some of which were to be decisive for his future development. He was an extremely precocious child, not simply in regard to music but in the eagerness he showed to absorb the aesthetic currents which went to make the capital such a hive of civilized pleasure at the turn of the century. The names and photographs of actresses like Bernhardt and Réjane, the poems of Mallarmé, some of which he knew by heart at the age of ten, the latest 'bon mot' of Lucien Guitry, Debussy's *Danse sacrée et danse profane* for harp and strings—these were all appurtenances of culture with which young Poulenc had a childhood familiarity.

Of all the influences that were to converge on him at this time, it was his mother (whom he adored) who was to exert the greatest pull. An excellent pianist who had been trained by a pupil of Liszt, it was she who gave the boy his first taste of the classics. She played Mozart, Schubert and Chopin with enviable skill, and these composers were to enchant her son from the outset. Nor was he ever to lose his admiration for them. Their influence can be detected time and time again in the texture and feeling of his own music. The variation of Diane from his choreographic concerto *Aubade*, scored for piano, eighteen instruments and solo dancer, is the perfect pastiche of Mozart, without being in any way an offence to his memory. In the composer's Twelfth Improvisation for piano we hear distinct echoes of Schubert. Chopin is perhaps most clearly prefigured in the 'lento subito' section of the first movement of his Concerto for Two Pianos, written in 1932. But there are so many other instances of Poulenc's obligations to these chosen few—each of them be it noted a superb melodist—that it would serve no useful purpose to be reminded of them. What is harder to grasp is the notion that Poulenc's stylistic borrowings are more a matter of naïve homage and effusiveness than conscious plagiarism. When he was not engaged in outright parody he was usually intent simply on paying his debts publicly and to the full. For this he is at least to be preferred to those who display less honesty concerning their musical antecedents.

Although it was from his mother that Poulenc inherited the better part of his musical tastes, his father and his uncle Marcel Royer were also formative influences. Emile Poulenc was a serious man and a pious Catholic. His preferences were for Beethoven, Berlioz, Franck and Massenet, the last being a concession to the inclinations of the typical bourgeois household of the period. His son was to retain something close to an aversion to these composers, or perhaps it would be more correct to say that they never inspired in him the same degree of affection as his mother's favourites. His mother's high spirits and permissiveness completely captivated the boy. He was much later to admit that he wrote what he used to describe as his 'adorable mauvaise musique' out of the sense of freedom she nurtured in him. His uncle Royer, on his mother's side, was also a source of delight to him; 'Uncle Papoum', as he was better known (the name clung to the old-style Parisian man about town), was to be the agent of Poulenc's early infatuation with the theatre. At the focus of these two extraordinarily liberalizing influences it is scarcely surprising that a young man of immediate promise should have emerged.

Poulenc's earliest wish was to be allowed to study at the Conservatoire, but his father, with characteristic firmness and prudence, insisted that he finish his education at the Lycée Condorcet, where he might be expected to acquire greater breadth of outlook, not to speak of better professional prospects. The boy accepted his father's advice, much as he was later to accept the advice of those who warned him not to depend too much on facility and early fame. It says a good deal for Poulenc's common sense that he listened patiently to Ravel when that composer urged him to drop out of the *avant-garde* stakes for a while, and take time off to polish his technique and further his acquaintance with other music. In the meantime he was given every encouragement as a youngster to study the piano, and in 1915 he was lucky in attaching himself to the Spanish pianist Ricardo Viñès, who was to succeed in making a first-rate pianist out of the boy. This colourful extrovert was a person after Poulenc's heart, as well as being one of the few executants capable of sparking off interest in composers like Debussy, Ravel and Stravinsky. In fact it was Debussy's prelude *Minstrels* that Poulenc played to him at their first meeting. It was a good portent concerning their relationship. In his memoirs, *Moi et mes amis*, Poulenc relates what sort of an impression the indomitable Viñès made upon him:

Viñès was a delightful character—some kind of strange Hidalgo with an enormous moustache, a brown sombrero in true Barcelona style, and button boots with which he used to kick me in the shins whenever I was clumsy at the pedals.

Evidently his performance of Stravinsky's *Petrouchka* was in a class on its own, and he had inexhaustible stamina at the piano, making it understandable why it was that Debussy and Ravel came to entrust so many of their *premières* to him. He and Poulenc became boon companions. It remains more than likely that the hard-hitting style of piano writing which Poulenc exhibits in works like the Toccata from the *Trois Pièces*, and in the powerful opening of the Ninth Improvisation, owes something to the Viñès manner. In fact it was Viñès who gave the first performance of the *Mouvements perpétuels* in 1919, and it was this absurdly captivating little work that won Poulenc his first round of applause.

These three miniatures have retained their immense popularity up to the present day, and they illustrate very well some of the notorious Poulenc mannerisms. The ambulatory bass of the first number is comically undermined by the deliberate 'wrong-note' harmony of the upper part, making it one of the most memorable of all Poulenc's pieces. In the second of the set, the simplicity of the opening scales,

Francis Poulenc

in contrary motion, gives us a clue to another of the composer's traits—namely his willingness to commit to paper the most banal thoughts as long as these possess spontaneity and a kind of appealing naturalism. This habit has led many critics to introduce the charge of infantilism. David Drew for instance has spoken for these in suggesting that:

Poulenc is the most frank, if not the most reticent of composers. When he has nothing to say, he says it.

However that may be, there is no denying that the composer who can summon up enough self-irony to name one of his better song-cycles Banalités, after the manner of Apollinaire, is also sophisticated enough to take the measure of most of his critics. French newspapers did not invent the monstrous pun, 'Le leg-Poulenc', for nothing. That the composer could be charming as well as simple is evidenced in the final number of the Mouvements, in which bars 13–16 form an ingratiating contrast to the surrounding ostinato figuration. The piano writing in this suite is usually traced to the influence of Erik Satie, composer of the Aperçus désagréables and Montmartre crank, with whom Poulenc had lately become friendly. These two musicians certainly had a lot in common, and one of Poulenc's last public acts was to record some of Satie's pieces in his own inimitable style of playing. It is equally possible, however, to detect other influences at work. The detached seconds in the right-hand part of the second mouvement are reminiscent of similar devices in Ravel's Jeux d'eau; while bars 4–5 of the finale recall very clearly the passage marked 'expressif' towards the end of Debussy's Minstrels. Tempting though it may be to regard Poulenc as a primitive, like Satie or Rousseau, there is in truth more artifice in his work than this supposition will allow.

After the acclaim following the Mouvements perpétuels, Poulenc trod a cautious path, sticking to the smaller forms and refusing to branch out into the exhibitionist medium of his idol Stravinsky. Two years earlier he had written his first significant vocal work, the Rapsodie nègre for baritone, piano, string quartet, flute and clarinet. This work reflected the cult of Negro art set in motion by Apollinaire in 1912. The poems later became revealed as part of a hoax, and the first performance of the work was very nearly capsized as a result of the baritone's sudden attack of nerves. In the event, Poulenc himself took on the role, carrying it off with splendid *panache*. Far more interesting and important than this work, however, was another cycle, written in 1919, this time on Apollinaire's own poems. The composer was still serving in the army at the time of its publication. This cycle was *Le Bestiaire*, a series of six animal songs, providing thumb-nail sketches of the dromedary, the Tibetan goat, the grasshopper, the dolphin, the crab and finally the carp. The whole set occupies only a few minutes in performance. It comprises a most deft and subtle composition. Apollinaire was to be a constant stimulus to the composer's imagination over the following decades, and this remarkable little diversion was the first in a string of masterpieces to issue from their collaboration. Originally Poulenc had set twelve of the animal verses to music, but acting on the advice of Auric he published only six of them. Scored for piano and voice, there are also arrangements for wind instruments and string quartet as the accompanying forces. It is hard to realize that Poulenc was only twenty when they were published.

One of the striking features of the Apollinaire originals is their utter seriousness. Unlike the animal poems of Edward Lear or Jules Renard, they do not poke fun or engage in irony. While they are not altogether successful in avoiding human comparisons, these are done with the maximum simplicity and ingenuousness. The following translation of the carp's verse by Percy Pinkerton will give some idea of the style:

> Within your tranquil shining pools
> Carp, what a long life is yours!
> Can it be that death pass'd you by
> O carp with melancholy eye?

Poulenc's setting of this particular poem has a lazy accompaniment figure which scarcely changes at all throughout the entire length of the song. It is marked 'Très triste, très lent . . .', and the mood is deliciously languid. Incidentally the dynamic marking 'avec les deux pédales' is one that occurs frequently in Poulenc's piano scores. It is designed to convey a soft haze of sound which he has managed to make all his own. A marvellous example of this is to be found in the closing bars of *Les Soirées de Nazelles*.

Among the other pieces in the bestiary, *Le Chèvre du Thibet* is notable for its nonchalant, swinging accompaniment; while in *Le Dromadaire* the piano amusingly imitates the patient plodding of the creature by doubling the step-wise melody of the voice. The last four bars of this song are taken up with a piano postlude, which seems almost to constitute a little piece of self-congratulation which the animal indulges in on the completion of its journey. This passage too bears one of Poulenc's characteristic instructions—'sans ralentir'—which must be taken to signify the composer's fear of the more sentimental performer, who might ruin his music by the habit of slowing down at the cadences, or else intruding an excessive *rubato*. The typical Poulenc melody—which is more often than not rather short in duration—is given maximum point by being sung or played without any self-consciousness. Sometimes the composer seems to expect his music to be played at a hurricane rate. Like Ravel, he abominated the practice of pausing to admire the view, and in general held to the belief that quick music should be given plenty of impetus. That he was not above injecting a more popular style into his music may be inferred from *La Sauterelle*, from this set, where a hint of the *chanteuse* can be detected at the words 'Puissent mes vers être comme elle'.

The next landmark in Poulenc's career was to be his association with the group, 'Les Six'. In many ways this conjunction was quite fortuitous. It was the critic Henri Collet who brought these young composers together, and his dubbing of them had resulted from nothing more in common than their combined appearance at the popular Delgrange concerts. The analogy, of course, was with the more famous Russian five. It was a link that proved fortunate for Poulenc, despite his occasional irritation with the misunderstandings it was to engender, since it united him with a number of kindred spirits, most of whom were keenly sophisticated in literature and painting as well as music. Indeed the unacknowledged eminence presiding over the group was none other than Jean Cocteau, whose fascinating artistic sleight-of-hand appealed enormously to Poulenc, as did the more enigmatic of his verses, some of which were soon set to music. The three songs, *Cocardes*, were among these early products of the alliance. They display some of the features of the 'new aesthetic' proposed by Cocteau. This philosophy sought to reject the supercharged romanticism of Wagner and the relaxed hedonism of the Debussy camp, turning instead to that purity being revived by Satie and his followers. Such a point of view fitted in well with Poulenc's inclinations at that time, and he and Cocteau became the firmest of friends.

An interesting sidelight on the concept of 'Les Six' was provided by Poulenc himself in a conversation held shortly before his death with Stéphane Audel. It seems that a group of painters was originally envisaged to act as a counterpart to the musicians, and to take their place under a joint venture known as 'Lyre et Palette'. The painters— who were only four in number—were named as Picasso, Braque, Modigliani and Juan Gris. It is particularly fascinating to observe that all of these, with the exception of Modigliani, were later to figure in a song cycle called Le Travail du peintre which Poulenc was to write on poems by Eluard, each poem being devoted to a single representative of the visual arts. This cycle did not appear until 1956, by which time of course Modigliani had been long dead. Whether Poulenc rejected the idea of a poem on this painter or whether he could not persuade Eluard to contribute one remains a matter for conjecture. We do know that Poulenc tried to cajole the poet into writing some verses in celebration of Matisse but, as he was not a painter for whom they shared a common admiration, the project never materialized. It is worth noting that Poulenc always harboured this acute and alive taste for pictures, and we must assume that it was given a considerable fillip as a result of his association with these fellow artists.

In the meantime the musical group—which by the way comprised Poulenc, Milhaud, Honegger, Durey, Tailleferre and Auric—met with great regularity, either at one another's houses, or else at restaurants like Le Petit Bessonneau. At other times they went together to the Cirque de Médrano to see the Fratellinis perform, sharing Picasso's well-known predilection for the tumblers and acrobats of circus and music hall. Milhaud, in his autobiography, describes some of the acts they witnessed as being worthy of the Commedia dell'Arte. It is easy to see how these experiences helped to give Poulenc his sympathy for low life and his ability to mimic some of its preoccupations through the medium of song and opera. A song like Voyage à Paris from the Banalités, with its echoes of the style of Maurice Chevalier, is a prime example of the manner in which he loved to revel in vulgarity. Jazz was an influence at this time too, though its impact on Auric was much more marked. Popular music rather than the elaborations of the jazz band was to be Poulenc's great weakness. The 'blues' style was too downhearted for his unquenchable sauciness of spirit, and he did not possess the technical mastery of a Ravel by which to make use of it.

Despite these riotous excursions into the public domain, it would not be true to say that Poulenc's tastes had failed to progress during the immediate post-war years. In the first place the members of 'Les Six' were themselves so divided in their musical sympathies that he had every opportunity of hearing his assumptions challenged even within his circle. Honegger (to take one example) had likes and dislikes which often ran quite contrary to Poulenc's own. He admired Florent Schmitt's music and had little or no time for Satie. There is a very moving letter which Honegger wrote near the end of his life, in May 1954, in which he confesses to Poulenc that although their tastes have been so different over the long years of their close relationship, they have not allowed this to interfere with their friendship. As he put it: 'Nous sommes deux honnêtes hommes!'

Honegger admires Fauré for his wealth of knowledge and high integrity; Poulenc finds him lacking the sharp edge of feeling required to give wit and pungency to his music. In painting, Poulenc prefers Lautrec to Van Gogh; with Honegger it is the other way around. They discover common ground, however, in their mutual admiration for Strauss, and in their unashamed championship of Charpentier's *Louise*. Setting aside their differences in truly cosmopolitan fashion, Honegger concludes by remarking with absolute sincerity:

We are, I think, of very different temperaments, but I suspect we have this in common: that we both put the love of music before the love of success.

This is well said, and does not in the least reflect any priggishness. It reminds us, as far as Poulenc is concerned, of how much his allegedly *gauche* experiments have stemmed, not from a desire to shock or indulge in self-advertisement, but from a real willingness to expose his musical thinking, without fear of derision. To this extent it remains impossible to impugn his honesty; and we must be grateful to him that he lived to the age of sixty without acquiring the solemnity of those imitation composers who are afraid to quit the safety of their select societies and academies. At no time in his career did Poulenc decline to admit that his path had led up several embarrassing blind alleys. The Ronsard settings, for example, and the piano works *Napoli* and *Les Soireés de Nazelles*, though they have often been admired by others, were treated with contumely by the composer himself: he felt he had failed in these works, and was not constrained to disguise the fact from his contemporaries.

Forthright in his condemnation of what he believed shoddy, Poulenc was very generous in his praise of what he considered outstanding. His early admiration for Schoenberg—a rather unexpected *penchant*, perhaps, in view of Poulenc's own commitment to diatonic music—was enhanced by a visit which he paid to that composer in Vienna in 1921. A similar trip to Italy the following year, in company with Milhaud, enabled him to meet Casella—another embattled protagonist of modern music. These intrepid composers assisted in developing in Poulenc a harder streak. He had always been torn by a rude 'nostalgie de la boue', and there was another side to his nature which looked back wistfully to the unabashed emotionalism of Gounod and Chabrier, whom he often addressed as his 'spiritual grandfather'. These concessions to popular feeling were sometimes in danger of leading him towards the position that music was nothing more than good entertainment. His friendships with Schoenberg and Casella, as much later his attachment to Wanda Landowska, provided him with just the kind of serious stimulus he needed to rise out of this complacency. Unkind critics have more than once deplored Poulenc's tendency to repeat himself, musically speaking, but it should be remembered that he never went for very long in his career without delivering himself up to some new mentor, usually a person who had braved the storms of unpopularity and could testify to the discipline of prolonged study. In his later years Stravinsky came more and more to fulfil this role. Moreover a close scrutiny of Poulenc's scores will reveal that his technical development never ceased.

Up to the time at which we have been portraying him, Poulenc had not been able to complete any really large scale musical enterprise. A suite in C major for piano attempted to repeat his miniature success of the *Mouvements perpétuels*, while a sonata for two pianos gained the plaudits of Ernst Ansermet. Further sonatas for wind instruments—later transcribed for piano solo—show him testing out the timbres of unfamiliar instruments and preparing the ground for his later mastery, especially of the oboe, for which he was always to write particularly happily. None of these ventures ever suggested that he might turn out to be anything more than a brilliant *petit maître*. As it happened destiny was to throw in his path a golden opportunity to succeed on a much more extended scale. In 1923 he was commissioned by Diaghilev to do a ballet in collaboration with the painter Marie Laurencin. The great Russian impresario had fixed notions about how ballet should be created, and one of his obsessions was match *décor* with music. He had already been clever enough to manage this in his bringing together of Satie and Picasso for *Parade*; and again in uniting Braque with Auric for *Les Fâcheux*. What he was now proposing was that Laurencin and Poulenc should attempt something on the lines of a modern *Les Sylphides*—in other words a ballet in which atmosphere was to be more important than story, and which would emphasize elegance and shades of colour.

The composer was only too eager to fall in with these suggestions. He had long admired Marie Laurencin's painting, which exhibited the kind of fashionable meretriciousness he delighted in. Moreover she had been Apollinaire's mistress. Since the poet himself had died (partly as a result of a head wound incurred in the First World War) before Poulenc had been given the opportunity to know him, this living reminder of his past life exuded a certain glamour for the composer. Accordingly they soon set to work and produced a ballet which, in its unique blend of wit and fantasy, of sensuality and tenderness, succeeds in being almost an incarnation of that period we know as 'the twenties'. Poulenc himself wanted to depart a little from Diaghilev's prescriptions by introducing some reference to the '*fêtes galantes*'—that persistent symbol haunting the imagination of sensitive Frenchmen. In the end they decided to dispense with a scenario, and set the ballet in a large drawing-room in which the only item of furniture was to be an enormous couch. Around this single provocative article were grouped a number of young men and women—the 'biches' who were to give their name to the ballet's title. This word was chosen for its deliberate ambiguity. It suggests the English 'darlings', but also refers to the hind, or female deer. The work, then, came to be called *Les Biches*, and its theme is the equivocal behaviour of the sexes. There are more women characters than men, and the whole action includes some subtle sexual innuendo. Throughout the ballet the emphasis is on pleasure rather than love, and to this extent it can be regarded as mildly erotic. There are scenes of covert lesbianism, as in the *pas de deux* between two *danseuses* which, as Poulenc's biographer Henri Hell rightly comments, might have been conceived 'in illustration of the scene between Albertine and a girl friend at Balbec in Proust'. Even so the ballet remains a kind of apostrophe to innocence, and it is precisely in the sense of paradox arising out of these seemingly irreconcilable attitudes that the unique charm of the work resides. What Poulenc seems to be suggesting is that the gratification of pleasure is the most natural of impulses, and in a sense the most uncorrupted, since the pleasure principle is the disposition upon which childhood is founded, and a force in rejecting the compromises of the dissembling intellect. This Freudian moral, when related to the sophisticated goals of pleasure proposed by the world of Cocteau, can be seen to result in an artificial but poetically viable construction. It had its adumbration at Versailles.

In fact it is impossible to arrive at any sort of appraisal of the early work of Poulenc without holding up to scrutiny those ideals of surrealism which had their roots in France before and after the First World War, and which included the notion of art as a hyper-civilized charade, spurning all contact with reality, and attributing holiness only to the twin gods of sex and poetic illusion. Some critics continue to view this notion as a contemptible regression, having its origins in anti-intellectualism and social pessimism. In a sense they are right, but the aesthetic we are describing was far from being a simple reversion to primitivism, and it should not be confused with the crude manifestations of Dada and other marginal cults. It did in fact have a respectable lineage, going back to the eighteenth century, and not simply to that element in eighteenth-century thinking which exalted the motive of naturalism. On the contrary, what this aesthetic sought to do was to combine the innocence advocated by Rousseau and his followers with the more civilized pursuits for which France had long been famous. Arnold Hauser has put the matter very lucidly in saying:

It was a kind of sport to imagine oneself in a situation which held the promise of liberation from the fetters of civilization while retaining its advantages. The attractions of the painted and perfumed ladies were intensified by attempting to represent them, painted and perfumed as they were, in the guise of fresh, healthy and innocent peasant maidens, and by enhancing the charms of art with those of nature. The fiction contained from the outset the pre-conditions which allowed it to become the symbol of freedom in every complicated and sophisticated culture.

This passage was written about the society of Fragonard and Boucher, but, with the proper transposition into modern psychological terms, it might easily stand as a description of the ideals of Cocteau and his disciples in the nineteen-twenties. Such ideals are clearly factitious, but in this they were not so different from the social and political ideals of the period, and they did embody a standard of aesthetic craftsmanship far in advance of that clung to in the following decade.

Les Biches was produced in Monte Carlo in 1924 and was a triumph for all concerned. Poulenc himself acquired a degree of fame befitting a composer associated with the Russian ballet, whose vogue continued to grow throughout Europe. Critics were almost unanimous in their praise, Emile Vuillermoz (Fauré's pupil and apologist) being the only important exception. The extent to which the musical syntax of Les Biches could be described as original became a problem for the more tidy-minded critics. Some saw the work as entirely sui generis, while others fretted over the debts to Scarlatti and even Tchaikovsky which they discovered. Diaghilev himself had not worried too much about this aspect. His own musical tastes were far from irreproachable, as even his friends were later to testify, Stravinsky going as far as to relate, with pardonable exaggeration, that the great showman actually died singing La Bohème. Poulenc shrugged off these discussions of his musical 'time-travelling' with customary imperturbability. After all it was an accepted gambit in the post-war era to flaunt one's indifference to the convention which forbade musical larceny. Grave-robbers were beginning to appear on all sides, smilingly exhibiting their trophies with the same self-consciously scholarly air as their archaeological colleagues. Stravinsky's *Pulcinella* had almost succeeded in making the whole process quite acceptable. The slogan of neo-classicism had come to supplant all others, and the practice of galvanizing the untroubled skeletons of minor eighteenth-century masters, and forcing them to caper to a more jazzed-up refrain, was all too sadly in evidence. Poulenc deserves his fair share of the blame for this vandalism, though, as some of his detractors have pointed out, he did not really come alive to the possibilities of this form of plagiarism until much later.

Those who are intent on unearthing evidence of Poulenc's several peccadilloes in relation to composers of the past would do better to concentrate on the music which he wrote in the nineteen-thirties. In certain respects this was a fallow period for the composer since, although he had by that time a number of undoubted successes to his credit, he had still not been able to acquire that mastery of technical resources which would eventually enable him to tackle a work like *Les Carmélites*. The result was a slight feeling of impotence which shook his confidence in his abilities. At this time, rather curiously in view of his previous reputation for being at the spearhead of advances, he reverted to tricking out older scores, like the dances of Claude Gervaise which went to form his *Suite française*. These tamperings do not represent him at his best, and do much to substantiate the charge that his understanding of ancient music was feeble, and had not been helped by a desire to emulate his friends Auric and Stravinsky. Notwithstanding such indications, it cannot be too strongly emphasized that *Les Biches* was a real achievement. Whatever is alleged about the preciosity of some of the numbers from the ballet, there can be no doubt that Poulenc's own full-throated song runs right the way through its length. The *Adagietto* is surely one of the most affecting and original pieces in his entire œuvre. Rollo Myers, writing after the composer's death in 1963, describes the overwhelming impression that this number made on him when it was played on the piano by Poulenc

during one of the backstage rehearsals leading up to the performance. Its melancholy beauty is without parallel in Poulenc's work,
though it is only one of many instances which serve to make us
wish that the composer had more effectively subjugated the imp
of the perverse in himself, and given us instead a greater taste of
that heartfelt lyricism which lay so near to the surface of his
genius.

The success with larger forms which Les Biches brought to Poulenc
encouraged him to try his hand at writing extended music of a more
abstract kind. Before entering into this phase of his career, however,
he made one significant attempt to combine his obvious talent for
ballet with the more academic demands of the concerto form.
The 'amphibious' work which was to result from this amalgam of
genres was the Aubade, written at the behest of the Vicomtesse de
Noailles in 1929. The object was to provide incidental music for
a fête she was proposing to hold at her home near Paris. Poulenc
complied with her request by producing one of his most translucent
scores. Unusually set out for piano solo, eighteen instruments and
solo dancer, it has movements corresponding to the aria and
recitative pattern, and really fulfils the same function as the old
opera-ballets of Rameau and Lully. The subject is the chastity of
Diana, who is presented as a woman of spirit, made fractious by the
chatter of her ladies in waiting, and enlivened only by the sublima-
tions of the chase, with its prospect of unexpected encounters. The
ballet itself does not achieve a dramatic denouement, its purpose
being merely to portray the frustrated mood of the goddess. The
music is amorous and tempestuous by turn, without ever attempting
to resolve the conflict posed on the human plane. At the conclusion
of the work Diana deserts her distraught companions, leaving the
shimmering forest at dawn as the only remaining bearer of tran-
quillity. One can imagine that it made the perfect divertissement by
which to idle away the time of the resplendent guests invited to
the occasion. The original choreography was done by Nijinska, and
the composer himself performed at the piano.

In the year previous to writing the Aubade Poulenc had made the
acquaintance of a woman who was to have a marked influence on
his musical development. This was the harpsichordist Wanda
Landowska. This tiny bird-like lady also happened to be one of the

most dedicated musicologists of the century—though she would doubtless have hated the word. A real contrapuntal scholar and enthusiast for Baroque music, her playing and general approach to art were an inspiration to Poulenc. Every performance was an act of piety with her. Harold Schoenberg has described the manner in which she appeared to New York audiences towards the end of her astonishing career:

> It seemed to take her a good five minutes to walk the twenty or so feet to the instrument. Her palms were pressed together in prayer à la Dürer, her eyes were cast to the heavens, and everybody realized she was in communion with J. S. Bach, getting some last-minute coaching and encouragement. She looked like the keeper of the flame as, dressed in some kind of shapeless black covering, her feet shod in what appeared to be carpet slippers (they were really velvet ballet slippers), she levitated to the harpsichord. It was one of the great entrances of all time.

To the impressionable Poulenc she appeared as a veritable Jeanne d'Arc of the keyboard, fighting to reclaim those qualities—'clair et lumineux'—which had marked out the music of the *clavecinistes*, those almost forgotten architects of France's heritage. Fortunately this great lady had never been a pedant, as anyone who has heard the outrageous liberties she sometimes took with the classics can testify. So that however incompatible the two friends might have appeared—the moon-faced youth of giant stature consorting oddly with his wizened and diminutive counsellor—they actually got on famously together, each respecting the other's unflinching convictions. More important than any community of tastes was their shared volatility of character. They were both willing combatants in the war against musical pretension and fiddle-faddle.

Proof of contempt for mere chronology is contained in their decision to co-operate on a harpsichord concerto. Aside from the one existing modern concerto for this instrument, nothing had been composed for it since the heyday of the 'style galant'. The agreement was that Poulenc should produce the score and Landowska should perform it at her house at Saint Leu-la-Forêt. The work became known as the *Concert champêtre*, and it possesses some of the airy vivacity of the *Aubade*, coupled with the spikiness only a harpsichord can provide. Along with Manuel de Falla's concerto it is the most remarkable work of its kind written during the present century. It begins with a slow introduction, in which there are some choice discords, and seems to have an affinity with the Hymne which Poulenc wrote at about this time for his Trois Pièces. The ensuing Allegro bounds off jauntily, however, and before long we are in the midst of some brilliant dialogue between the harpsichord and various orchestral instruments. To this end the work is a true concerto, having both concertino and ripieno elements alternately to the fore, and exploiting their opposition in masterly fashion. The horn and trumpet parts are especially vivid, and so are the woodwind solos—in particular a delightfully lazy clarinet solo nearer the end of the movement. An interesting intrusion is the military tattoo music with which Poulenc cheerfully surprises us both here and in the last movement. This was probably intended as a reminder of the Landowska home at Saint Leu-la-Forêt which, though surpassingly beautiful in its situation, had an army barracks for its neighbour. The first movement of the work ends with a lively coda, before which there are some exquisite pastoral sounds rather in the manner of the farmyard noises in his later ballet, Les Animaux modèles. Following this movement is an enchanting Sicilienne, ravishingly scored for strings and woodwind, with pizzicato bass support. A little later there is a fanfare on the harpsichord which endeavours to make the struck keys imitate a consort of brass instruments, much as Scarlatti himself used to do in sonatas like the famous 'pomposo' Cortège in E major. The finale of the Concert champêtre seems more reminiscent of Handel, its opening theme exhibiting some of the vigour and alacrity associated with that composer's suites. Throughout the work Poulenc uses the harpsichord in many different disguises, sometimes even writing arpeggiated ostinato figures to accompany the orchestral tuttis; a habit which might seem less surprising in a Prokoviev piano concerto. The greater obtrusiveness of tone of the harpsichord, however, avoids any clotting of texture, and as long as the figuration remains of musical interest, which it invariably does in this charming work, the upshot is a success.

During the next few years Poulenc was to write many more works for keyboard, most of them for piano solo, but occasionally branching out, as he was to do in the Concerto for Two Pianos, into something larger. The double concerto appeared in 1932 and was frankly conceived as a light work. It would be foolish on that account to dismiss it, for it cannot help striking us as one of the composer's most inspired efforts. Inimitably written for the soloists —perhaps on account of Poulenc's habit of practising in partnership with his friend Jacques Février—the work captures something of the effervescence of the Ravel Concerto, which had appeared only a year earlier in 1931. Poulenc was never able to aspire to the fantastic flair for orchestration shown by Ravel, but it is surprising how audacious he could sometimes be; this concerto shows him at his most consummate. The Balinese pastiche with which the first movement closes is a case in point. Its mysterious cello theme and delicate *pointilliste* scoring make it a small triumph of imagination. The second movement is a Larghetto, very Mozartean in its symmetrical phrasing and rococo ornament. It is broken up by a fast and rakish waltz, too Gershwinesque to form a particularly tactful contrast, and we are forced to acknowledge the justice of Constant Lambert's complaint that Poulenc's:

. . . changes of style are executed with such abruptness that not the most lynx-eared of the fashionable *cheka* who are the self-appointed arbiters of vogue has the time to exclaim: 'A bit dated, don't you think?'

The finale of this eclectic work relies heavily on the composer's *blague*, the rather plebeian tune in B flat getting a rousing send-up towards the end.

Of the numerous piano works Poulenc was to write in the following decade the most attractive are the *Huit nocturnes*, which recall Chopin rather than Fauré; the *Douze improvisations*, to which he later added three more, one of them dedicated to his favourite Edith Piaf; and *Les Soirées de Nazelles*. The suite *Napoli*, which was a relic of his former trip to Italy, had already been published in 1925. It can, however, be conveniently grouped with these other works as far as its style is concerned. Together these pieces form an impressive treasury of music for an instrument which, in the twentieth century, has been too often forced to occupy a subordinate role. Despite this, Poulenc's own judgment on this aspect of his production is very curious, not to say perverse. A most versatile performer himself, he tended to minimize the significance of his piano works, arguing that the accompaniments to his songs showed his gifts in this direction to far better advantage. In itself that is a verdict with which it would be churlish to quarrel. It does, however, overlook the real contribution which Poulenc has made to the literature of the instrument itself. It is difficult to think of any other composer of his generation who has written so much that pleases the amateur performer.

Napoli is a suite in three movements, the first of which is a barcarolle. Quite unlike the works of this type for which the Romantics are famous, Poulenc's piece avoids thick harmony and texture. Instead he makes do with two parts only, engaging in some quite unseductive clashes, chiefly between the oscillating open ninths of the accompanying triplets and the high-pitched song of the treble. Despite this instance of the denuded pianism so sought after by the more austere composers of our age— Bartók's Suite Op. 14 seems to be the example that everyone strives to emulate—there is much charm in Poulenc's treatment. The nocturne comprising the second movement is more lyrical, though this too is shattered by the intrusion of some inexplicable and hideous discords. It is in the finale that the composer's gift for melody is allowed untrammelled expression. In the passage marked 'très chanté' in 3–8 time Poulenc gives us a magnificently Italian chanson, which is none the worse for having a marked resemblance to the prelude to Act I of La Traviata. This at least is richly pianistic in its figuration, and when heard from the fingers of an Artur Rubinstein succeeds in restoring confidence in the power of the instrument to thrill modern audiences.

Les Soirées de Nazelles is an even finer work, and puts the listener on the same ground as Chabrier's Pièces pittoresques. It is a long work— unusual for Poulenc—and consists of a Preamble, Eight Variations, a Cadence and a Finale. The work was evidently improvised on successive evenings at a house in Nazelles in 1930, though not published in complete form until 1936. The variations are not thematic metamorphoses, but are meant to be interpreted in the ballet sense: that is, they are separate numbers each having some independent colour or narrative significance to impart. In this case they are portraits in music of various friends of the composer, having something in common with Elgar's imponderable gallery.

Poulenc's low opinion of this work seems utterly incomprehensible. Professor Demuth, not notable for his admiration of the composer's work, states:

> It is vastly superior to anything else which Poulenc has written, except the famous *Pastourelle* which was his contribution to *L'Eventail de Jeanne*. Here Poulenc seems to have taken more trouble than usual, in spite of the improvisatory nature of the material.

The length of time which elapsed between commencing and finishing the work may of course be adduced to account for the paradox noted by the professor. Otherwise one cannot but agree with his evaluation. Symptomatically performers have responded with admiration—when they have troubled to acquaint themselves with the work. Terence Beckles, who has played it at the Wigmore Hall on more than one occasion, has described himself as being 'devoted to the suite', though his performances of it have omitted a section of the finale present in the first edition of the work put out by the firm of Durand. The cut was authorized by Poulenc himself, whose dissatisfaction led him to attempt a shortening of the work. Perhaps it would be presumptuous to claim that the discarded section contains some of the finest piano writing in the suite; it certainly includes some attractive material, very effective when well performed.

What led the composer to disavow it so completely? One can only speculate that Poulenc felt constantly on his guard against relapsing into the more romantic style of piano writing, and that his feeling was that both here and in *Napoli* he occasionally let himself go, giving free rein to his lyrical powers. If this is the case we can content ourselves by adding that, at least to those who do not share the composer's preference for using the piano as a percussive instrument, these two works are a gratifying concession to more poetic tastes. The members of 'Les Six' have been notoriously unwilling to abandon their original predilection for what can only be termed a superior kind of high jinks, and there are many listeners who recollect only too well what John Warrack meant when he described the group as that 'black French frivolous flock'. Poulenc has not disdained to bare his emotions in many other spheres of his art—the religious works and the songs come first to mind—but for some reason he continued to regard the piano as a refined substitute for the atavistic instruments favoured by more distant cultures. In the *Soirées* he suspended this belief to the extent of writing some of the most limpid music the instrument has inspired since Schumann. The preamble and first variation contain evidence of how finely Poulenc was able to judge the sonorities of chordal writing for the piano: something he could do as succinctly as Debussy when the occasion demanded it. The second variation, *Le Cœur sur la main*, gives rise to another of the composer's nostalgic waltzes, this time much more indicative of his own felicitous gifts. Similarly *Le Charme enjôleur* is a particularly happy *trouvaille*, its second section having all the lilt and gaiety of a discreet cabaret tune. A more turbulent expression of the *demi-monde* occurs in the middle of the sixth variation; while the seventh, with its forlorn title of *Le Goût du malheur*, pours out its melancholy in the epicurean accents of Ravel. The finale is marked 'follement vite, mais très precise', and is intended to go at breakneck speed. It is one of those exercises in combining verve with scrupulousness; just the sort of opposites, in fact, which Poulenc delighted in bringing together to test the player's mettle. The closing pages of the work are more affecting, however, and constitute a kind of *résumé* of the themes of the other movements. Taken in all, it is probably the composer's best piano work and a worthy successor to the great keyboard suites of Debussy and Ravel.

The *Nocturnes* and *Improvisations* are all quite short pieces, not too difficult to play and full of the composer's wit and technical effrontery. The first and second of the *Nocturnes* are probably the finest of the set; the former being a perfectly sincere and lyrical piece, without a trace of affectation, while the latter is an animated 'bal de jeunes filles', placing rather a different connotation on the generic name attaching to the group. The fourth is accompanied by an epigraph from a book by Julien Green, and its rhythm is similar to that of the famous A major Prelude of Chopin. There are more *Improvisations*, a good title to use in describing them since they have a refreshing off-the-record quality about them, which is perhaps why the composer tended to value them above those other piano works into which he wrote too much detail. Like much of Poulenc, they are packed with jibes and salutations in the direction of other composers, past and present. It is interesting to observe how effects previously considered outworn—like the eighteenth-century Alberti bass—are deployed in a thoroughly modern manner. The seventh and tenth of these pieces serve to illustrate this. Snatches of Offenbach are occasionally allowed to burst through the fabric of the music (as in bars 38–44 of the ninth of the series) reminding us that not even the composer's beloved comedians of music are exempt from being guyed. Prokoviev, Schumann and Chopin are other composers whose styles are assumed and discarded with an abruptness recalling the changes of costume at a children's pantomime. Some of Poulenc's liveliest piano music has in fact been written for children: his L'Histoire de Babar, completed in 1945, constitutes an irresistible musical enactment of the fairy-tale world of Jean de Brunhoff, and continues the now extensive tradition which includes Ravel's Ma Mère L'Oye, Fauré's Dolly suite and Debussy's Children's Corner. Works for piano continued to flow from Poulenc's pen right up to within a few years of his death, but few of these compare in interest with those already described. An exception might be made for the richly flowing Intermezzo in A flat, and the sprightly Humoresque, written for the pianist Gieseking. A longer work, the Thème varié of 1951, scarcely justifies its position of status.

During 1935 another event took place which came to have far-reaching effects upon Poulenc's interests. This was his decision to appear regularly as accompanist to the baritone Pierre Bernac. The two musicians had met on one occasion some years previously, but the possibility that they might form a fruitful partnership had not occurred to them at that time. Poulenc certainly admired this singer's interpretation of his work, especially the superb diction for which he had gained considerable praise. Yet they did not seem to have so much in common, Bernac being at first more interested in Lieder. After a very successful joint recital at the Ecole Normale in April 1935, however, the two artists began to plan what was to result in an altogether new career for Poulenc, a career lasting well into the late nineteen-forties, when Bernac decided to retire from the concert platform. The importance of this switch of interest on Poulenc's part was revealed in the much greater attention he began to pay, from this time onwards, to the art of song writing. That he was a born song composer cannot be doubted. Le Bestiaire, as we have seen, was an extremely imaginative work for any young man to have written. What distinguishes the songs of the middle and later periods is their immense professionalism, both with regard to the technique of combining piano with voice and the scrupulous attention to prosody they prefigure. Much of this new-found skill owed its existence to the secret trials and revisions of the rehearsal room. Poulenc had not stopped writing songs since his early days, but like Fauré before him he had not always found it easy to light upon the precise poet who could stimulate his fancy. The initial poets he set were principally Apollinaire and Max Jacob, both renowned for their powers of wit and parody. These subtle humorists brilliantly reflected the moods which the composer experienced in his youth, as well, it must be admitted, as appealing to certain basic proclivities of Poulenc's temperament. Neither, however, could succeed in matching the growing spirituality and need for deeper human identification that were to arise out of the experiences of middle age. The serious tone of public events in the nineteen-thirties came as a chill wind after the tireless posturing of the previous decade. Though never swept up by any ideology, Poulenc could not but respond to the more reflective currents then beginning to penetrate every corner of artistic life. His search for a poet to express his expanding philosophy came to a halt when it reached the verses of Paul Eluard.

As with Bernac, this Surrealist poet had been known personally to the composer for many years prior to their closer relationship. Poulenc and Eluard had met in 1916, long before the poet was recognizable as one of France's greatest lyric writers since Baudelaire. At that time, however, Poulenc was probably not ready to react sympathetically to his poetry. It does seem from his memoirs that his normally very acute judgment in matters relating to poetry had been put temporarily in abeyance during their first meeting. Contrasting the relatively sudden conversion to Eluard with his more confident awareness of the abilities of many of his other collaborators, Poulenc wryly admits:

Au premier abord, Eluard était un homme comme les autres, et rien dans son comportement ne le signalait spécialement à l'attention. Il fallait bien le connaître pour deviner le poète chez lui. Il n'avait ni plaid sur le dos, comme Mallarmé, ni l'allure bohème d'un Verlaine ou d'un Rimbaud, ni le gilet rouge de Théophile Gautier, ni même cette lourde silhouette asymétrique et si spéciale d'Apollinaire.

He goes on to add, before allowing his self-disparagement to go too far, that he had always found Eluard's poetry very beautiful, but there was a calmness about it which he did not understand. It was not until much later that he discovered its hidden energy, and could appreciate both 'la fraîcheur' et 'le feu' as these qualities came to be designated.

The very first of the Eluard settings, the Cinq poèmes, date from 1935, and were not regarded by the composer as anything more than experimental—'the key began to creak in the lock', as he explained it. It was with the cycle Tel jour, telle nuit in 1937 that the partnership came into its own. There are nine songs in this incomparable work, which not only remains Poulenc's finest vocal achievement, but is probably the finest to be found in French music since Debussy's Trois poèmes de Mallarmé, if not earlier. In its fervour and emotional eloquence it marks an altogether new dimension in its composer's aesthetic development, and one which critics who had already written him off as a brash Captain Spalding of music had never suspected him of entering. He and Auric had been lampooned in the French press as 'les sportifs de la musique', a smart enough cliché as far as it went; but it did not go far enough. This great Eluard cycle was to establish Poulenc's claim to serious stature, much as his Dialogue des Carmélites was in later years to advance his right to be regarded as a master of the larger as well as the smaller forms. If he had not occasionally reverted to his former cap and bells after this time, he would scarcely have been Poulenc; but from now on his compositions were generally much more expressive of his quest for enlightenment, using that term in its broadest sense. About this time too his friend Férroud—also a composer of great promise—was killed in a car accident. The impact of his death was sobering, and Poulenc for some time sought solace at the shrine of Rocamadour, where a carving of the Virgin inspired him to write his litanies for women's voices and organ. All things considered, the years from 1935 to 1937 may be seen as a watershed in the career of the composer. It was Blake who said: 'If only the fool were to persist in his folly, he would become wise.' Poulenc's persistence had been rewarded, in the form of that self-understanding which was to transform him from an uninstructed and irreverent *farceur* into what his father would have recognized as a good Catholic and a humble seeker after truth.

Tel jour, telle nuit represents one step in this new and more spiritual direction in that, although the poems on which it is based are concerned with earthly love, Eluard's peculiar gift for generalizing the emotions he describes—a talent he shared with the more overtly romantic Shelley—lifts the work on to a more metaphysical plane. The songs themselves reveal different moods of the poet as he glimpses, one after another, a variety of natural scenes—a sorry patch of grass, a deserted shell, a covered wagon—and reach a climax in the heartfelt affirmation with which he turns to his unknown lover at nightfall. The cycle begins with a quiet salutation, *Bonne Journée*, which was suggested to Poulenc by the sight one Sunday morning of a locomotive appearing to glide mysteriously through a grove of trees near the outskirts of Paris. This optical illusion, highly in keeping with the Surrealist ethos in which the poems were conceived, brought to mind the extract from *Jeux fertiles* which forms the first poem in the series; and later, on the evening of the same day, the music for it slowly began to take shape. The style embodied is very much 'très lié', and there is some high *tessitura* for the voice reaching up to a top A flat, the range covered by the song extending over an octave and a sixth. The second *mélodie* is also calm and smooth, with a poignantly unadorned accompaniment. The third, dedicated to the poet's wife, is more animated, while the fourth has in it something of the same ominous cacophony as the *Suite dans les idées* for piano. *A toutes brides* goes, as we should expect, with a rush, propelled along by its scurrying semiquaver movement. The sixth of the set, *Une Herbe pauvre*, is a miracle of pathos, only twenty-four bars long, having a dynamic range which extends from *piano* to *pianissimo*. The succeeding two poems presuppose greater movement, the second resulting in the most agitated and brutal music. Finally, in *Nous avons fait la nuit*, Poulenc attains the pinnacle of sublimity, the voice's passionate outburst at the words '. . . et dans ma tête qui se met doucement d'accord avec la tienne avec la nuit' striking the listener as a searingly vivid climax to the whole cycle.

The success of these nine *mélodies* inspired Poulenc to embark on further settings of Eluard. It was not until 1950, however, that he attempted a second complete cycle in 'La Fraîcheur et le feu'—a somewhat shorter work, containing only seven poems. The result fails perhaps to attain quite the high level reached by the former cycle, though it is without any doubt a fine work. Unlike its predecessor, it begins violently in a series of fortissimo chords, beneath which runs an undulating and powerful arpeggio accompaniment. Indeed it is the piano writing that begins by capturing the attention in this work, both on account of its subtlety and its complexity. We have only to examine the second song, Le Matin les branches attisent, to test the strength of this attestation. Its easy expertness is evident in the brevity of the whole design, the last four bars of which achieve new standards in combining maximum effectiveness with absolute economy of means. Tout disparut, which follows it, quotes a few bars from Stravinsky's Serenade for piano. It also exhibits a beautiful vocal climax at the words '. . . vivaient d'un univers sans bornes', the leap of a fifth being cushioned by the soft spread-out chords of the piano, all undertaken pianissimo. There is a very similar ascent in the sixth song, which is possibly the best in the cycle, and which is entitled Homme au sourire tendre. Here the deceptively simple sounds disguise some of Poulenc's most brilliant modulations, so that by the time the denouement is reached in 'Il n'est rien qui vous retient' it exudes a freshness that only the greatest song writers are capable of. How right Henri Hell was when he stated that Poulenc has 'kept alive the beautiful and almost forgotten art of modulation'. His mastery of this art is demonstrated over and over again in the songs, where it is clearly shown to best effect.

In 1940, with the German occupation descending on France, Poulenc returned to his first love, Apollinaire, for what is his most popular if not his greatest song cycle. Choosing five markedly contrasting poems, he grouped them together under the ironical title, Banalités. He had come across the verses among some old scrap-albums at his country house, Le Grand Coteau, near Noizay in the Touraine. Wanting something with a good clear rhythm to begin the cycle, he hit upon the Chanson d'Orkenise, a brisk folk song, with a certain resemblance to the Flemish Chevaux de bois which Debussy included among his Ariettes oubliées. To follow, Poulenc chose a poem with the city background so dear to his heart—the deservedly popular *Hôtel*. This is a mood piece which evokes the morose disenchantment of the metropolitan dweller, imprisoned in his hotel room by the forces of ennui and loneliness, wishing only to idle away the day in smoking and memories. It is perfectly realized through the tired *legato* of the voice and the bitter-sweet harmonies of the supporting chords. By contrast *Voyage à Paris* celebrates the promises of the city, its call to pleasure and freedom from care. Poulenc himself referred to it as a 'deliciously stupid' song. The jewel of the collection is the last and longest of them—the unforgettable *Sanglots*. This poem reveals a more committed side to Apollinaire's nature, and is amply worth its place as one of the best half-dozen songs in the composer's output. The last page is particularly wonderful in its compassionate and declamatory accents, made almost unbearably sad by the piano's tenuous harp-like *appoggiaturas*. No one listening to it can fail to be moved by the veracity of its emotions and its revelation of the unspoken misery that lies at the heart of the human condition.

It would be remiss to conclude this account of the protracted partnership with Apollinaire without mentioning one or two of the individual songs not attached to any of the cycles. The early *La Grenouillère* is certainly one of the finest of these, evoking as it does that favourite haunt of Renoir, where the full-busted *filles de service* flirted rowdily with their striped-vested escorts. A slightly wistful little poem, it visualizes the river when long past its most attractive, a landscape without figures, lacking even a Maupassant to chronicle its legendary past. Poulenc's setting is touchingly disconsolate, mirroring the mood of *Hôtel* and using almost the same harmonic vocabulary. A much longer song is the celebrated *Montparnasse*, described by Professor Mellers as 'quintessential Poulenc'. Its subject is the idyllic Bohemian existence lived at the edge of the great city, and its method purely phenomenological. In its unpretentious images it recalls those lyrics of Rainer Maria Rilke, written while he roamed the Luxembourg gardens in the intervals from his duties as Rodin's secretary. Curiously enough, the Apollinaire poem also includes among its *personae* a 'bearded German poet', a blond vagabond who at first appears to the author in the guise of an angel, only to revert to his role as a penurious walker in the city, who dreams of spending his Sundays at Garches. Spontaneous though the song sounds, it cost Poulenc many an anxious hour, and in fact had to be written in a number of separate fragments, the whole being reassembled, in the manner of a jigsaw puzzle, some four years after it was begun. Such labour over detail came to seem characteristic of the composer during this period, when the war interfered with so many of his other interests. A breathtaking instance of his newly acquired skill in modulation occurs just before the words '. . . vous connaissez de son pave', where the previous phrase comes to rest on the dominant of E minor, and then goes down to the B flat which forms the seventh of the chord of C minor. The transition is as natural as it is unexpected. The preponderance of such artful devices came to constitute the signs by which the master was about to be proclaimed.

Many other tributes to Apollinaire may be found scattered through the breadth of Poulenc's large output, not least of which are the songs entitled *Calligrammes*. These were specially liked by the composer himself, who was amused by the typographical absurdities in which the poet indulged. These eccentricities have since become part of literary history and time prohibits our devoting more space to additional explanatory commentaries. Instead we may just take brief cognizance of two final cycles which the composer wrote on verses by poets with whom he had no established relationship. The first of these was also a product of the war years, and was in fact inspired by the conditions they imposed. The composer, long a devout admirer of the novelist and poet Louise de Vilmorin, discovered that she was being held at a castle in Hungary, a consequence of her marriage to a foreign nobleman. Without any apparent prospect of release, she was given light sustenance by the song cycle, *Fiançailles pour rire*, which Poulenc wrote for her. Intended as a kind of feminine counterpart of *Tel jour, telle nuit*, it fell short of the standard set by the Eluard work, but is nevertheless full of interest for its grace, humour and litheness, qualities which had for some little time not been apparent in Poulenc's songs, as opposed to his instrumental compositions. This fact is not surprising perhaps when we reflect on the poems which comprise the cycle. They describe a comic betrothal in which some of the incidents are full of a characteristic mixture of irony and sentimentality immediately

recognizable to those who have read the author's novel *Madame De* . . .
The fifth song is called *Violon* and induces the voice to imitate the
long-drawn-out *portamento* accents of a stringed instrument. Other
numbers in the cycle, like the third, cleverly catch the sense of
exaggerated flurry common to all events of the kind depicted.

The last of Poulenc's song cycles—written as late as 1960—is the
uproarious *La Courte Paille*, based on verses by Maurice Carême. In the
very short time since its publication this work has come to occupy
a special niche in the composer's list. The dedication is to the
singer Denise Duval, chosen by Poulenc some years earlier to sing
the lead in his opera-bouffe, *Les Mamelles de Tirésias*. The cycle takes its
name from the saying, 'tirer à la courte paille', which might be
translated as 'to draw lots by the method of a short straw'. A more
idiomatic English title for the work might be 'At Random'. The
seven songs it comprises are a curious ragbag of whimsy and mock
alarm. The repeated shrieks of 'Mon Dieu!' emanating from the
second sufficiently explain the hilarity with which it is generally
received in the concert hall. The fourth song is scarcely less risible,
with its ridiculous designation, *Ba, Be, Bi, Bo, Bu, Be*. This is a
chatter song which requires the words to be articulated at a speed
designed to defeat all but the most loquacious of singers. The cycle
is not without its unaffected moments, however, as the initial song,
Le Sommeil, proves. It is a remarkably lovely setting, the phrasing and
modulations perfectly judged. The whole cycle was meant by Poulenc
to be sung for Denise Duval's son, then six years old.

Otherwise than in this enforced preoccupation with technical
development, the war was to affect Poulenc in a number of ways.
His pride in France's cultural glory was to suffer a hurt under Nazi
rule, yet at no time did he forgo hopes for the restoration of his
country's rights. He abhorred Fascism, and one of the musical acts
by which he betokened his resistance to it was in dedicating the
Violin Sonata of 1942 to the memory of the great Spanish poet,
Federico Garcia Lorca, murdered by the Nationalists in the Civil
War. Another deliberate piece of defiance was his setting of Louis
Aragon's poem entitled 'C'. The odd designation refers to a contraction of the name, Les Ponts-de-Cé, which denotes a town near
Angers. Aragon was the acknowledged poet of the French Resistance,
and his poem lamented the capture of 'C' by Nazi troops as they

passed over the Loire. The actual words of the poem recall the town's legend in which a mad duke was reputed to have made quixotic forays from the local château. At its première, given by the composer in the company of Pierre Bernac, the Germans present were at a loss to account for the storm of applause it obtained.

A venture calculated to give the composer great pleasure, since it enabled him to adapt his talent for ballet to the need he felt for asserting his pride in France and her achievements, was the writing of the stage work, Les Animaux modèles, the title of which had been suggested by Eluard. The ballet brings together a selection of La Fontaine's fables—The Ant and the Grasshopper, The Amorous Lion and Death and the Woodcutter among them. These are made to fit into a series of tableaux in which the allegorical aspects are subordinated to a plot in which a penniless danseuse, a young libertine and a beautiful society lady form some of the chief characters. In other words the work is a drama involving real personages, while at the same time suggesting certain archetypal themes. It is a genre which has appealed greatly to the French in recent years, both in films and on the stage, as the scenarios and plays of writers like Anouilh and Giraudoux indicate. Poulenc's ballet did not repeat the triumph of Les Biches, though the work itself was thought by several of the composer's friends to be the best thing he had done. Auric in particular was extravagant in his praise.

The ballet opens by showing a group of peasants seated around their board, partaking of a humble meal before embarking on their day's work in the fields. It is an occasion for some calmly transparent chordal writing in Poulenc's most immaculate manner. The costumes for this and the concluding scene, which reveals the same figures at supper after having completed their labours, were designed in imitation of the paintings of Le Nain. Indeed the whole work has considerable pictorial interest, since when the actual fables themselves come to be represented the characters are dressed in clothes redolent of the epoch of Louis XIV. The charm with which they are addressed, musically speaking, is almost worthy of Domenico Scarlatti, the divertimento between the two cocks, also resplendently attired, being specially brilliant. It is the tableau depicting Le Lion amoureux which contains the most passionate and melodious music, however, and the flirtatious Java with which it ends has some distinctly tongue-in-cheek references to nineteenth-century ballet music of the kind written by Messager and Delibes. Notwithstanding this episode, the work as a whole is serious to the point of gravity; the *adagio* which marks the entrance of Death, got up as a beautiful masked woman, impresses as having the severest dignity. It is perhaps the most profound page Poulenc ever wrote. The first production took place at the Opéra in Paris in 1942, with choreography by Serge Lifar, who also played the part of the Lion.

In complete contrast is Poulenc's other theatrical enterprise of this period. The opera-bouffe *Les Mamelles de Tirésias* is a salacious fantasy which is at the same time a skit on the feminist movement. Though it too has a classical ancestry, the play on which it was based was actually a Surrealist drama written by Apollinaire in 1903. As may be imagined, Poulenc's propensity for the more sedulous forms of horseplay is given ample scope in this farcical entertainment. The abrupt changes of rhythm, mood and tempo are such that he has also an unrivalled opportunity to display his gift for parody and stylistic transformation. The score abounds in dance numbers of all kinds—waltzes, polkas, gavottes and pavanes. Set in a small town on the Riviera, the action depicts an ardent devotee of the cause of women's rights. Thérèse, who is paid out for her presumption by suffering a change of sex, finds her breasts floating skywards to the accompaniment of cloying entreaties on the strings. In the next scene her husband, who has experienced a corresponding mishap, is courted by a lascivious gendarme in true French farce tradition. The upshot is a situation in which pregnancies begin to proliferate thick and fast, and the stage becomes so cluttered with cots and cribs that the characters have no room to move. The capacity of the French nation to rehabilitate its members is fully vindicated once more, and order is restored. The opera had to wait until after the war for its *première*, but has since been revived many times, and is one of the few of Poulenc's stage works to score something of a success abroad. Aldeburgh launched a production of it some years ago, and this limited and discerning type of audience is likely to be more appreciative of the work than the public at large, who will probably continue to react to it with the same shock and embarrassment as it greets experimental plays of the type of *Ubu Roi*.

Though he was to have a final fling at fantasy in his lyric monologue *La Dame de Monte Carlo* in 1961, Poulenc devoted the ultimate
phase of his career to more serious concerns. The awakening of his
religious impulses, upon which we have already commented, led to
a determination in the years after the Second World War to build up
a body of sacred works which would establish his reputation as a
choral composer. He had always had capabilities in this direction,
as his early teacher Koechlin had discovered. One of the singular
facts of his association with this learned and benevolent man was
the tacit agreement which the two musicians reached about the
nature of Poulenc's training. Realizing that the youngster had no
aptitude for counterpoint, Koechlin had encouraged him to
concentrate on learning the *a cappella* style as an alternative. This
meant endless exercises in harmonizing Bach chorales and the like.
Pointless as this procedure may have seemed at the time, it was to
pay handsome dividends towards the end of Poulenc's career, when
this urge to write straightforward choral works was to take possession of the composer. 'J'ai la foi d'un curé de campagne,' confessed
Poulenc one day to one of his friends; and there is a studied
unpretentiousness about these last religious works. They possess
neither the grand gestures of genuflection to be found in his
admired Gounod, nor the emotional disengagement of Fauré. It is
quite characteristic that, when it was suggested to Poulenc that he
should write a Requiem, he demurred at what he considered to be
too ostentatious a title, saying that he would prefer to call his
composition a *Stabat Mater*, which course he did in fact adopt.

This work, which appeared in 1950 and is written for soprano
solo, mixed choir and orchestra, is generally considered near the
summit of Poulenc's religious compositions. Jean Roy has described
it as attaining a perfect equilibrium between voices and instruments.
Other critics have pointed to the tender soprano writing of the
Vidit suum. Not all have agreed that the work lacks weaknesses, however, and at least one commentator has objected to the topheaviness
of the vocal ensemble. Certainly Poulenc's basses have not the
rock-like solidity of Fauré's, or even those of Duparc. Yet his
religious works do sometimes succeed in possessing a lightness of
texture which imparts a suitably ethereal atmosphere, often lacking
in the music of more turgid upholders of the tradition. For even in

his church music Poulenc sought to avoid mournfulness, of which there is hardly a trace in this work. His willingness to write an opera on religious themes—*Les Dialogues des Carmélites*—is another proof of this attitude. At the head of this score—which was written around a drama of Bernanos, describing the protest and execution of a group of Carmelite nuns during the French Revolution—Poulenc inscribed the words: 'God preserve me from the drearier saintly figures of history.' Nothing could be more typical of the composer's unidolatrous beliefs. Again, his *Gloria* sounds so light-hearted that critics have not hesitated to label it sacrilegious. Poulenc himself has answered these critics in saying:

J'ai pensé, simplement, en l'écrivant, à ces fresques de Gozzoli ou les anges tirent la langue; et aussi à ces graves bénédictins que j'ai vus un jour jouer au football. . . .

So the sportsman and the devout Catholic refused to be separated. Only the lord of misrule was finally exorcized.

In the last year of his life Poulenc returned to the chamber music with which he began his career. In two final works written for the British publishing firm of Chester he distilled the essence of his skill at the duo combination of clarinet and piano, and then oboe and piano. These sonatas, which are reminiscent of Debussy's final chamber music in their marvellous craftsmanship and appearance of late-flowering genius, are dedicated to Honegger and Prokoviev respectively, both loyal friends who had predeceased him. They stand out in Poulenc's œuvre by virtue of their extraordinary richness of melody and fluency of inspiration. To listen to Pierlot play the *Déploration* with which the Oboe Sonata ends is to be reminded of the almost Schubertian gifts lost to the world at Poulenc's passing. The work remains a swan-song of which the mightiest composers could well have been proud.

Within a few years of his death it has become possible to see Poulenc as certain of his place in that tradition of French music which exalts the human voice above all other instruments. Looking back on the pioneer achievement of Fauré, on Duparc's magnificent spurt of inspiration, and finally on the unique and poetic world created by Debussy, few Frenchmen could have had the temerity to suppose that the gods would favour their race with yet another singer of genius, able to pursue a stage further the grand design set in motion by these artists. The cry of 'Le Roi est mort!' which must have escaped their lips on the death of Debussy had the effect of posing in the same breath the problem of who, if anyone, was fitted to carry on the succession. Little could they have imagined that, when the various claimants had all been disposed of, the dynastic features they were seeking would emerge plainest on the countenance of none other than the court jester, that obscure changeling whose inconsequential airs they had permitted to enliven their solemn deliberations. For the truth is that, within this kingdom of the voice, Poulenc, for all his moonstruck folly, was of the royal line and his summons will not be denied.

ENVOI

HISTORY is an indifferent guide to prophecy, and the reader whose diligence has borne him unexhausted through these pages may still find that he lacks the key to what the future holds for French music. A rapid glance at the contemporary scene must suffice to lend credibility to his prognostications.

The modern movement which began with Debussy, and which for convenience we may term impressionist, took shape appreciably later in music than in the rival arts of painting and sculpture. The final exhibition mounted under that joyful banner was held as early as 1886, almost a decade before the completion of the *Prélude à l'après-midi d'un faune*. This time lag, which has its counterpart when we come to consider the impact made by more recent revolutions in the arts, is scarcely long enough to provide us with a really enlightening parallel; yet there remain compelling reasons why a comparative study of this kind should make a rewarding starting point from which to embark on our summary.

In the main, the impressionists were interested in light and colour. Their concern with form was marginal and oftentimes non-existent. Thus, through their drift towards looseness and fluidity, they unconsciously paved the way for the more formalized art of the twentieth century. It is important to emphasize that this transition was not achieved without strain. Had it not been for the outstanding abilities of certain artists of the flanking intermediate generation it is doubtful whether the success of modern art would have been assured. A bridge had to be flung between the two styles which might otherwise have given the appearance of standing at the opposite poles of immediacy and planned design. The work of linking up, in the visual arts, was carried out by the post-impressionists, and most of all by Cézanne. Those well-known revolutionaries Picasso and Braque were in effect only pursuing to its logical conclusion, in their cubist and constructivist phases, a set of principles first enunciated by Cézanne, which centred upon a belief in the 'reductiveness' of nature, its tendency to revert, in the eye of the painter, to a series of geometrical planes.

A not quite parallel development attended French musical life once the Debussyistes had been given the *coup de grâce*. Having baulked at further explorations in tone-painting and the use of static harmony, the composers of the intermediate generation conceived their role as a matter of reasserting the claims of architecture and form, leaving it to the musicians of the present day to formulate that extremism which has resulted in the severing of music from all representational intent. Looked at in this way, we can observe a somewhat unsteady line of development from, say, *La Mer* through the work of the latter-day Schola pupils to the serialism of the sixties.

The immediate reaction to Debussy's innovations, however, was to counter them by an appeal to tradition in one or other of its guises. At best this signified a retreat into academicism of the kind implicit in the work of such an otherwise important figure as Roussel. At its worst it resulted in something far less innocuous: that puerile and uninformed neo-classicism practised by *Les Six*, than which there has been no more disreputable philosophy in France's musical history. Short-lived as were its offspring, its tenets contributed to that uncertain climate of speculation amid which composers were becoming accustomed to live.

From our comfortable observation chamber in the present, it is perhaps too easy to see what road should have been taken at this juncture. Unfortunately composers, no less than politicians, are denied the privilege of hindsight. From their own standpoint all they could be sure of was that both romanticism and impressionism appeared played out, and there was no new ideology to invoke. Since the way forward was thus blocked, the only remaining course seemed to be to step backwards. This course, accompanied by lengthy and devious rationalization, was the one most artists elected to take. No doubt they would have responded with greater sense or wisdom had they been exhorted by a prophet, another genius of the stamp of Berlioz or Debussy. Instead they were forced back on their own counsel, and no one from among the assembly showed himself possessed of the necessary charismatic qualities to bring about an advance.

It is worth considering closely the unenviable and false position into which older composers, those who had survived Debussy and the official revolution, were propelled by the course of events. Ravel and Satie, for example, were forced into the role of being embarrassed spectators of their own humiliation, such was the tide of feeling aroused. Having formerly endured a long period of rivalry with their more illustrious colleague, they were now confronted with the task of warding off the post-mortem opprobriums which were being hurled at his ideas.

In this sense, Debussy's death solved nothing. For Ravel the conflict continued between his infatuation with impressionism and his apparently growing conviction that popular music or jazz would eventually supply a much-needed transfusion. Satie, on the other hand, was insufficiently able to efface his eccentricities, with the result that any directive he might have sponsored foundered on the ineluctable fact of his own personality and reputation. Neither man possessed the qualities required to lead a new school of French composers of the younger generation, and neither lived quite long enough to witness the inception of such a school at the hands of other musicians. 'There will never be a school of Satie,' remarked the sage of Arcueil, with more truth than he knew, for the abortive group to whom he gave his blessing, including Henri Sauguet and the conductor Roger Désormière, succeeded in canonizing only the nostalgic Satie of the ballets, the pathetic clown with his touching faith in simplicity. To have created an institution out of this elusive quality was beyond their scope.

Instead French musicians elected to pursue an ideal of intellectualism similar to that which had dictated the obscurities of contemporary literature and metaphysics. Vincent d'Indy had already hammered out the framework for such a philosophy, and it only remained for the more cosmopolitan to look towards Vienna—where Schoenberg and Webern had held court—to observe a practical embodiment of it, neatly parcelled for export. In the work of René Leibowitz, who came to Paris from Poland in 1925, Frenchmen were able to experience a foretaste of the twelve-tone music their countrymen would soon be writing in profusion. The native product, when it arrived, was predictably more than a mere imitation, however, and it owed less to foreign models than to the liberal teaching at Paris's own Conservatoire, especially to the harmony lessons of Olivier Messiaen, a teacher with a large and heterogeneous following. Among his pupils was the implacable young Pierre Boulez, whose cantata *Le Marteau sans Maître* (based on poems by the surrealist poet René Char) was soon to constitute the '*porte étroite*' to the knowledgeable world of present-day serialism. Thus many would argue that dodecaphonic music in France arose out of currents stemming from external and internal sources. What is now undeniable is that the vaunted musical leadership of Europe, once secure in the hands of the new Viennese school, has yet again passed into French keeping.

From the angle of tradition, it is noticeable that none of the composers treated in the later chapters of our book had the formative influence expected of them, and none succeeded in becoming the bridge-figure for music that Cézanne had been for painting. Not only did they lack his stature as artists, but the qualities they did possess turned out to be tragically misunderstood. Satie's very real discoveries were either brutally swept aside or else transmuted into a chic and ephemeral gaiety such as we find in the work of Jean Françaix and his imitators. The position of Ravel became even more ludicrous, miscast as he was as the purveyor of 'Frenchified' Rimsky-Korsakov. These two composers vividly illustrate the truth that at no time in an artist's life is he more likely to be misappraised by the public than at the moment of his death. That Ravel, in particular, was well aware of the ironical fate which was about to overtake him only adds poignancy to the issue.

More surprising than any of these facts is the relatively small influence which seems to have been exerted by Poulenc, despite his almost unchallenged position at the forefront of French music over the past thirty years. As was the case with Satie, there are psychological as well as artistic factors to be adduced in explanation of this. Less plagued by the determination to be original than most other composers, Poulenc was temperamentally seduced into playing a Janus-like role, evidently enjoying its alternate compulsions to be both contemporary and anachronistic. When the demand was for up-to-date idioms he was able to assail his listeners with the harshest of discords; as the call for a more ingratiating style emerged, he proved equally well able to beguile them with recollections of palmier days. In a less eclectic artist this splitting of the personality would have resulted in a troubled conscience at the very least. Poulenc's response was simply to keep on stirring the pot. That it never quite managed to boil over may continue to be pleaded in his favour as a musician of infinite dexterity. It cannot, however, mitigate his sins of omission as a putative leader of his nation's musical life. At his best Poulenc worthily upheld the traditions into which he was born; but it is no use pretending that he was ever able to offer the younger composer a well-built road into the future. Like Britten, whom he much resembles in the figure he presents to his juniors, he somehow managed to say something new and fresh with materials about to be jettisoned; and in so doing he inadvertently stayed the hands of many whose talents were better served by abandoning rather than strengthening their ties with the music of the immediate past.

By a quirk of irony such as can rarely have occurred in the history of any art, the real focus of influence among French composers of the present generation has been none of these figures, but the man against whom was directed the original chorus of protest—Debussy himself. This paradox needs careful elucidation, and we should at once make clear that there were at least two Debussys. On the one hand, we can point to the poet and water-colourist—the exquisite Debussy of the songs and the Nocturnes. Behind him, however, stood an altogether sturdier and less literary or pictorial figure. This was the propagator of that abstract and athletic style we associate more with the sonatas and *études*. Curiously enough, both these musical selves exerted a positive impact on the minds of composers born during this century.

For instance, it is obvious that the mystical ardour which inhabits the early work of Messiaen—and which reappears in pantheistic guise in works like the *Cantéyodjayâ* and the *Catalogue des Oiseaux*—owes as much to middle-period Debussy as to any belief in Franckist transcendentalism. Similarly the pursuit of quasi-magical and incantatory properties which we encounter in the *Danses Rituelles* and other works of André Jolivet, the musical director of the Comédie Française, can without contrivance be traced back to the orientalism of which Debussy and the younger Roussel were the prime cultivators. The later works of these men do not so much continue to draw on this influence, however, as exploit the possibilities of polyrhythm and athematic germination, rather in the form of an extension of the experiments found in Debussy's final compositions. The ballet *Jeux*, as well as the ultimate chamber works, may to that extent be conceived as a point of departure. The enthusiasm Boulez has recently shown for the two-piano suite *En blanc et noir* is a typical expression of that unbidden proclamation of debt which living French composers are in the process of issuing.

Naturally Debussy ought not to be regarded as the sole luminary in this sudden rush of acknowledgment. Hardly less important for music has been the presence among Frenchmen of Igor Stravinsky, at one time a French citizen and a perennial apologist for many of the so-called Gallic qualities in art. During the inter-war years, in particular, when this composer's changeable outlook seemed to fasten upon the neo-classical and symphonic ideals in turn, he was looked up to as a saviour of chastity and grace, a puritan in the Babylon of contemporary sound-making. Since then the barometer on which he records his mysterious apprehensions has wobbled alarmingly, only to point in the end to the twelve-tone ideal. Thus Stravinsky appears to have brought together in his own person, and in the persons of his acolytes, the two most powerful trends to have converged on our own times. Of these the linear emphasis (or perhaps we should say, following Stravinsky's example, the intervallic emphasis) can be seen, in retrospect, to have revealed itself in the later work of both Fauré and Debussy, and is hence not unrelated to the traditions out of which French music has lately evolved. The other trend, of course, is much less indigenous, and is represented by that wide range of atonal composition engaged in by the internationally assorted disciples of Webern. Whether it is really possible to reconcile these two trends as easily as Stravinsky himself appears to have done must continue to remain problematical. Alliances are often dictated more by expediency than by the prospect of a common goal, and perhaps this attempt at unification is only the latest manœuvre in the eighty-year-old Russian composer's lifelong search for a conceptual or other rationalization that would lend sanctity to his inspiration.

If then we are still left with the conviction that no agreed counsel has prevailed in the matter of musical style, might we not do better to turn our attention to other aspects, such as *genre* or instrumentation? These aspects ought, in theory, to yield us several important clues, since it has been maintained throughout this book that French composers have been sharply characterized by their preference for the small as against the large, the sophisticated as opposed to the spiritual, indeed by their studious concentration on a few intimate media through which they have aimed at expressing only the most controlled emotional philosophy. The question we may now wish to ask can be put thus: Is there any evidence that these scruples are being upheld today, and if so what new forms are they seeking to take? How valid, for instance, is the claim that keyboard music continues to remain the focus of a large quantity of inspiration? And what of the much-stressed unity of text and music which went to characterize the great period of French song we have devoted so much time to describing? Answers to these questions are by no means clear-cut, nor can we be absolutely certain that such manifestations of the tradition as we do discover serve to guarantee that a measure of the uniqueness of French musical culture is being perpetuated.

In the first place there can be no doubt that the interest in the keyboard does continue, even into the present phase when electronic and tape sound-sources are being more widely canvassed than the conventional instruments. Indeed it comes as something of a relief to learn that such self-consciously *avant-garde* composers as Jean Barraqué and Yvonne Loriod are actually writing music for the piano, and Messiaen is adding to his already formidable treasury of organ music. The range of styles has now become a more complex phenomenon, however, and it no longer seems sensible to argue in terms of carrying on a Lisztian line, or practising a Debussyan manner. Experiments with extreme sonorities are not in themselves new, but the fresh impetus given to this kind of writing by the aural clusters, rhythmic pedal-points, and generally non-thematic apparatus favoured by composers of the post-Messiaen generation, does much to substantiate the suggestion that such music is really of a kind different from that previously known to western culture.

Works like the Boulez piano sonatas, in which there are novel *sforzando* effects requiring new forearm positions, pursue a percussive technique that makes light of the modest experiments in that direction which we attribute to composers such as Bartók and Prokoviev. Much of the music at present being written comes under the heading of 'aleatory' or 'stochastic' composition, and scarcely any of it seems adapted to the demands of the performer in the way that, say, Chopin's music is so obviously and intelligently adapted.

In so far as there is no overt recognition of the value of a conventional piano technique, it would be true to say that the pianist must forget what he has learnt, or must be prepared to acquire an altogether new set of reflexes. Further inroads tending to break up the pattern of orthodox virtuosity come from the use of a 'prepared' piano similar to that invented by the American John Cage, which consists of inserting metal or wooden objects between the strings of the ordinary piano, thereby producing sounds of indeterminate pitch and uncertain tone-colour. So far French composers have responded to this deliberately shocking device in only a minimal way, seeking to avoid the extremes of exhibitionism.

The plight of vocal music at the present time seems less critical, if only on account of the relatively unmodifiable character of the human voice. Alterations in the technique of breath control or in the approach to *tessitura* are feasible to the extent that they do appear, without evident protest from singers, as a prerequisite of performance in a number of works of the fifties and sixties. But, as was the case with keyboard instruments, there is still a good deal of music being written which can without difficulty be accommodated to the conventional demands, or something very close to them. What is perhaps most significant is that younger musicians are apparently still looking for inspiration from among the most highly valued literary sources.

Aside from the much discussed link between Boulez and Mallarmé —promulgated in the composer's recent set of improvisations, entitled *Pli Selon Pli*—there are many indications that living French musicians are deeply conscious of their obligations towards the literary heritage, which is undeniably one of the world's finest. Yves Baudrier, who is the third member of the group formerly called '*La Jeune France*' (the other and better-known members were Messiaen and Jolivet), has written a song-cycle on poems by

Tristan Corbière; whilst the graceful talent of Daniel Lesur, also admired for his attractive Piano Concerto, has been expended on verses of Cécile Sauvage, who was incidentally Messiaen's mother. Meantime Eluard has continued to find an interpreter in Serge Nigg, and Tristan Klingsor (Ravel's fellow apache) in Georges Migot.

Living composers of the older generation include the prolific Milhaud, now domiciled in America and largely crippled by arthritis, who nevertheless continues to draw his inspiration from the work of his wide-ranging literary acquaintances—witness the setting he made in 1957 of twenty-four poems by Francis Jammes. This makes for an interesting comparison with his much earlier setting of Gide's *Alissa*, still a popular work among connoisseurs of the French *mélodie*. Sauguet is also a song-writer of some repute, his texts having been drawn from among the great names of the symbolist and surrealist movements, in particular from Laforgue and Max Jacob. In all this, one aspect of the tradition remains alive.

Resuming briefly what has been said, we have been able to point to the existence of several distinct elements in the contemporary situation. First of all, there is the new school of exoticism, derived in part from the vestiges of French orientalism, but also receiving much of its stimulus from the process of assimilation of remote cultural forms now so characteristic of our western way of life. This particular tendency may be compared, in the terms of our original analogy, to the recently eclipsed phase during which painting and sculpture came under the combined influence of African and pre-Columbian styles. The effect, in both media, has been to help to liberate occidental thought from the stultifying parochialism under which it has often appeared to labour.

Alongside this development other sources of inspiration continue to be evident. The concept of musical composition according to 'tone rows', whether they take the form of twelve-tone systems or systems based on a less comprehensible range of permutations, seems to have been widely accepted in France as in most other countries in Europe. Even where this method does not assume the form of a preconceived formula—a danger of which younger composers are not always fully aware—there is every sign that it is serving to unite many varied talents and beginning to act as a

'lingua franca' without knowledge of which both critic and composer incline to lack the means of communication. Donald Mitchell
has recently adopted the notion that the serial method is in the
process of exerting the same widespread influence over music that
abstract design has exercised over art during the decades since the
First World War. This makes an illuminating comparison, even if it
remains true that the origins of these respective movements relate to
different countries and refer back to different antecedents. For what
both movements portend is the conviction that art exists in and for
itself, bleakly disdaining all attempt to represent, prefigure or
symbolize anything beyond its own man-made frontiers, and
comprising in essence nothing more or less than a non-referential
language.

To those who continue to cherish the belief that one purpose of
art is to express extra-artistic values, this profession of self-sufficiency
must come as a counsel of defeat. Ortega's famous prophecy that
art would in time become 'dehumanized' has in fact been realized;
though it is not by any means certain that the artist can, by an act
of will, expunge all but the components of his art. Nor is it necessarily the case that art which is 'dehumanized', in the rather limited
sense of not wishing to conflict with other human concerns, is
wholly contemptible. On the contrary it might well be argued that
much of the art of previous epochs has become unendurable
precisely on account of its over-attachment to the kind of concerns
which presented themselves as humanly important.

It is of course quite possible that the current emphasis on con-
tainment—to resort to a military metaphor—is directed less towards
purging art of its ramifications than to expressing a growing dissatisfaction with the materials it has to make use of. To that degree,
the language of art is no different from that of ordinary speech.
They both suffer from the effects of attrition. Whatever emotional
referents have developed alongside a set of artistic principles, it is
accordingly probable that in the end they will cease to be mutually
invigorating. At this point, what becomes postulated is not a new
repertory of emotions—a clearly impossible demand—nor a naïve
determination to eschew emotional connections. It is a different
arousal system, aimed at replacing the old stimuli or investing them
with new significance. The present obsessive scrutiny of materials—

evident in the search for artificially produced sounds and newly designed instruments—may therefore present no greater threat to the integrity of music than is inferable from the situation we have described. It is the natural reaction to confronting a language that has become moribund.

In conclusion we should do well to remember that promise lies neither in the language nor the culture of which the artist partakes, but in the quality of the individual vision. As Bizet long ago expressed it:

The artist has no name, no nationality; he is inspired or he is not; he has genius, talent, or he has none; if he has some, he should be adopted, loved, acclaimed; if he has none, he should be respected, pitied, forgotten.

SELECT BIBLIOGRAPHY

APOLLINAIRE, Guillaume. *Selected Poems*, translated by Oliver Bernard. Penguin Books, 1965

BELL, Clive. *Civilization*. Chatto & Windus, 1928

BRERETON, Geoffrey. *A Short History of French Literature*. Pelican Books, 1954

CAMPOS, Christophe. *The View of France*. Oxford University Press, 1965

COCTEAU, Jean. *Reminiscences*. Peter Owen, 1960

COOPER, Martin. *French Music from the death of Berlioz to the death of Fauré*. Oxford University Press, 1951

COPLAND, Aaron. 'Gabriel Fauré: a neglected master' in *Musical Quarterly*, October 1924

CORTOT, Alfred. *French Piano Music*, translated by Hilda Andrews. Oxford University Press, 1932

COX, David, 'France' in *A History of Song*, edited by Denis Stevens. Hutchinson, 1960

DEBUSSY, Claude. *Monsieur Croche: anti-dilettante*. Dover Books. Constable, 1960

DEMUTH, Norman. *Maurice Ravel*. Dent, 1947
French Piano Music. Museum Press, 1959

DREW, David. 'Modern French Music' in *European Music of the Twentieth Century*, edited by Howard Hartog. Routledge, 1957

ELUARD, Paul. *Choix de Poèmes*. Pasquelle, 1951

GONCOURT, Jules and Edmond. 'Life of Watteau' in *Eighteenth-century Painters*. Phaidon, 1948

GOSS, Madelaine. *Bolero: a life of Maurice Ravel*. Tudor Publishing Company, New York, 1940

GRAY, Cecil. *A Survey of Contemporary Music*. Oxford University Press, 1924

HALL, James Husst. *The Art Song*. Oklahoma University Press, 1953

HANSON, Laurence and Elizabeth. *Verlaine: prince of poets*. Chatto & Windus, 1959

HAUSER, Arnold. *The Social History of Art.* 2 vols. Routledge, 1951

HELL, Henri. *Francis Poulenc.* Calder, 1959

HODEIR, André. *Since Debussy.* Secker & Warburg, 1961

HUTCHESON, Ernest. *The Literature of the Piano.* Hutchinson, 1950

JANKELEVITCH, Vladimir. *Fauré et ses mélodies.* Librarie Plon, Paris, 1938

    Ravel. Calder, 1959

KOECHLIN, Charles. *Gabriel Fauré.* Dobson, 1946

LAMBERT, Constant. *Music, Ho!* Faber, 1944

LANGER, Suzanne K. *Problems of Art.* Routledge, 1959

LOCKSPEISER, Edward. *Claude Debussy,* 3rd ed. Dent, 1951 and 1966

    'French Chamber Music' in *Chamber Music,* edited by Alec Robertson. Pelican, 1958

    The Literary Clef. Calder, 1958

    'The Significance of Debussy' in *Music and Musicians,* vol. 10, no. 12, August 1962

    Claude Debussy: his life and mind. 2 vols. Cassell, 1962 and 1965

LONG, Marguerite. *Au Piano avec Claude Debussy.* Juilliard, 1960

    Au Piano avec Gabriel Fauré. Juilliard, 1965

MACINTYRE, C. F. *One Hundred Poems from 'Les Fleurs du Mal'* (translations from Baudelaire), bilingual ed. California University Press, 1947

    Selections from Verlaine, bilingual ed. California University Press, 1958

    Selections from Mallarmé, bilingual ed. California University Press, 1959

MALRAUX, André. *The Voices of Silence.* Secker & Warburg, 1954

MELLERS, Wilfred. *Studies in Contemporary Music.* Dobson, 1948

    'Romanticism and the Twentieth Century' in *Man and his Music* by Wilfred Mellers and Alec Harman. Barrie & Rockcliff, 1962

MYERS, Rollo. *Maurice Ravel: life and works.* Duckworth, 1960

    Erik Satie. Dobson, 1948

    'Hommage à Poulenc' in *Music and Musicians,* vol. 11, no. 7, March 1963

    'Ravel on Stage' in *Music and Musicians,* vol. 13, no. 8, April 1965

NORTHCOTE, Sydney. *Henri Duparc.* Dobson, 1949

NOSKE, Frits. *La Mélodie française: Berlioz à Duparc.* Presses Universitaire de France, Paris, 1954

    'The Solo Song outside German-speaking Countries' in *Anthology of Song.* Arno Volk Verlag, 1958. Distributed by Oxford University Press

SELECT BIBLIOGRAPHY

ORREY, Leslie. 'Gabriel Fauré, 1845–1924' in Musical Times, May 1945

'The Songs of Gabriel Fauré' in Music Review, May 1945

PANNAIN, Guido. 'Maurice Ravel' in The New Book of Modern Composers ed. by David Ewen, 3rd ed. Knopf, New York, 1961

PERLEMUTER, Vlado and JOURDAN-MORHANGE, Hélène. Ravel d'après Ravel. Editions de Cervin, Lausanne, 1961

POULENC, Francis. Moi et mes amis. La Palatine, Paris-Genève, 1963

QUINN, Patrick. The French Face of Edgar Poe. Southern Illinois University Press, 1954

ROLAND-MANUEL. Maurice Ravel. Dobson, 1947

ROY, Jean. Francis Poulenc. Editions Seghers, 1964

SCHOENBERG, Harold. The Great Pianists. Gollancz, 1965

SHATTUCK, Roger. The Banquet Years. Faber & Faber, 1959

STARKIE, Enid. Baudelaire, 2nd ed. Faber & Faber, 1957

STRAVINSKY, Igor. Conversations with Igor Stravinsky. Faber & Faber, 1959

SUCKLING, Norman. Gabriel Fauré. Dent, 1946

TEMPLIER, P. Erik Satie, Editions Riéder, Paris, 1932

TEYTE, Maggie. 'Memories of Debussy' in Music and Musicians, vol. 10, no. 12, August 1962

VALERY, Paul. 'France' (VII) in History and Politics: collected works of Paul Valéry. Routledge, 1963

VALLAS, Leon. The Life and Work of Claude Debussy. Oxford University Press, 1933

VERLAINE, Paul. Choix de Poèmes. Pasquelle, 1960

VUILLERMOZ, Emile. Gabriel Fauré. Flammarion, Paris, 1960

DISCOGRAPHY

THE usual method of compiling a discography is simply to list, according to artist and label, the records one is intent upon recommending. I have decided to depart from this practice for a number of reasons. In the first place, it tells the reader so little about the actual performances—how idiomatic they are or what special merits they possess—that in the last resort all it seems to do is save him the trouble of thumbing through the latest edition of the long-playing record catalogue. I hope that by commenting on points of style I shall be of some assistance to those whose aim is, on the contrary, to discriminate; and who accordingly wish to be given a few criteria of excellence so that they may bring nearer the day when they can hope to act as their own critical guides.

A further reason for adopting this alternative procedure is that it will, I trust, facilitate the appreciation of many of the suggestions I have made in the book itself, which might appear, without benefit of illustration, to lack cogency. My purpose has been to use this discography to shed light on the distinctive features I have attributed to French music and musicians in the course of the earlier analysis. Limitations of space have naturally led me to take a selective view of this task.

Instead of treating each composer as a separate entity, I have divided the field up into the various *genres*: vocal, pianoforte, orchestral, operatic and chamber music. In this way it has been possible to examine the contributions relating to special composers without having to duplicate the numbers of miscellaneous records. This procedure should also encourage prospective collectors to develop a balanced library in which a wide range of music is represented.

Inevitably the selections I have put forward reflect my own prejudices, but other opinions can be sought in the back numbers of various musical journals such as the *Gramophone*. A no less exasperating shortcoming will doubtless arise out of the present proliferation of new records. Accessions (and deletions) nowadays occur at a rate that no amateur can any longer hope to keep up with. Even granting average durability, it is likely that by the time these words appear in print many of the choices they set out to specify will have been rendered obsolete. The only consolation this situation offers is that such competitiveness must surely lead to higher standards. Technical advances in recording alone serve to ensure that most of the discs we at present cherish will eventually be superseded. Even so, I have resisted the temptation to accelerate this process by eliminating all but those of the most recent vintage. For convenience sake I have also avoided over-reliance on specialist discs, accessible only to the connoisseur. The few imported records I do mention can be ordered from appointed agents in this country. The record numbers refer strictly to the stereo versions, except where a disc has been issued only in mono.

VOCAL MUSIC

Possibly the best known interpreters of French song to have made a rich contribution to the gramophone are the soprano Maggie Teyte and the baritone Pierre Bernac. Both these artists have now retired from concert work, though records of their singing are happily still available. His Master's Voice have reissued two records of Maggie Teyte in their 'Great Recordings of the Century' series. A Debussy programme, which includes the *Fêtes galantes*, *Chansons de Bilitis* and *Trois ballades de François Villon*, is contained on COLH 134. Her performance with orchestral accompaniment may be judged from the companion disc, COLH 138, which features Berlioz's *Les Nuits d'été* and Ravel's *Shéhérazade*. Several of Duparc's songs are also included on this record in their versions for voice and piano. In general these records set a standard of vocal declamation by which other artists have come to be assessed. Particularly inimitable is the way the balance between word and tone is impeccably maintained. Dame Maggie's singing of the recitative-like elements in the Debussy songs presents special claims to authenticity in consequence of her having studied this art with the composer himself.

The art of Pierre Bernac is no less impressive, though records of his singing are harder to obtain in Britain. A good sample of his collaboration with Poulenc may be heard on Vega C30–A293, which couples the Apollinaire song-cycle, *Banalités*, with the other of that composer's masterpieces, the Eluard cycle, *Tel jour, telle nuit*. This historic disc can be ordered through Discurio Ltd, 9 Shepherd Street, London, W.1. Points to notice are the singer's expert diction and cultivated irony of inflection. Equally worth studying is the piano playing of his accompanist, full of that conscious volatility that so characterized the man himself. Other accompanists may be more adept at avoiding wrong notes, but none has conveyed a more zestful or committed impression.

Among present performers Gérard Souzay stands apart. This exquisitely gentle and refined singer has all the qualities required of an interpreter of Fauré and Debussy. Less obviously suited to the music of their successors, he perhaps lacks the wit and pungency of his teacher Bernac to do them full justice. The suppleness and agility of his voice are not in dispute, however, and there are few baritones to equal him in any sector of French music. The voice itself was never particularly rich or ample and it has regrettably darkened in recent years, coming to approximate more to the tones of actual speech. To appreciate how much subtlety and beauty remain it is necessary to hear him alongside other singers in the repertory at which he has gained his distinguished reputation. Many of his favourite groups of songs have been recorded by him on more than one occasion, making the choice of discs a matter of balancing the respective claims of youth and maturity. However, one could do no better than listen to his recent disc of Fauré's Venetian songs (Philips SAL 3505) which has the merit of also giving in full the later cycles *Mirages* and *L'Horizon chimérique*. Superb breath control and a unique feeling for the length of a phrase combine to make these performances as near to definitive as one can imagine. Dalton Baldwin, the pianist, acts as a sensitive partner. The same pair of artists has made a version of *La Bonne Chanson* on an earlier disc, Philips ABL 3371, which is also the authoritative performance, at least as far as the gramophone is concerned. Souzay's recording of the Duparc melodies, Philips SAL 3434, is marred by a rather gritty acoustic for the voice, though once again the actual interpretation has classic status. A splendid disc to begin a collection of French songs would be Souzay's anthology of melodies by Gounod, Chabrier, Bizet, Roussel, Fauré and Ravel (Philips SAL 3480).

A relative newcomer to the lists is the Danish baritone Bernard Kruysen, whose records for the firm of Valois have only lately attracted attention in this country. This singer has a most thrilling voice, lyrical and tender, yet capable of powerful projection. It would be foolish to suggest that he is yet able to stand comparison with Souzay—his inexperience would reveal itself in innumerable small touches of style, especially of phrasing. But there seems no doubt that he is already a considerable artist, possessed of really beautiful French and an immediate awareness of the problems of his art. Many critics would claim that his Debussy recital (Valois MB 929) offers the best available versions of most of the songs it contains. Souzay duplicates fourteen out of the seventeen songs on a Deutsche Grammophon disc made at about the same time. It is of the greatest interest to compare these two records. Kruysen appears to have the larger voice, giving wider dramatic emphasis to the melodic lines, whereas Souzay relies more on the effects of shading and nuance. Both singers present marvellously convincing accounts. Souzay appears on SLPM 138758.

A comprehensive selection of Ravel songs appears on yet another Valois disc (MB 969) and this includes the rarely heard *Chansons Madécasses*, as well as the brilliantly witty *Histoires naturelles*. Kruysen sings the latter cycle with much greater sense of serious identification than is evident in the interpretation of Bernac. His account of the *Don Quixote* settings—also contained on this record—is equally unconventional in that it shows much more restraint than most singers are willing to adopt. Both interpretations are tenable, and listeners must make up their own minds which they prefer. The recording quality of the two Valois discs—which are incidentally more expensive than other discs—is magnificent. Together they would make up an excellent acquisition for the discophile specializing in this sphere.

No survey of French song on records would be complete without mention of Régine Crespin's sumptuous performances of the Berlioz melodies and Ravel settings of Tristan Klingsor, already listed in connection with the Maggie Teyte reissues. Mme Crespin is better known as an operatic singer, and it could be argued that her voice is a trifle monotonous for the more intimate art of song. For all that, she possesses a full, encircling tone that is just what is required of the Ravel *Shéhérazade*, which is deliciously sung. There is precisely the right degree of languor in her interpretation. The Berlioz cycle is also well performed, though the singer (SXL 6081) transposes a number of the songs, including the opening *Villanelle*, which loses a little by being lowered a semitone into the less bright key of A flat. A valuable recital of French songs with orchestral accompaniment (including yet another version of the popular Ravel work) is Victoria de los Angeles's record, made with the Paris Conservatoire Orchestra under Georges Prêtre. This contains Duparc's *L'Invitation au voyage* and *Phidylé*—reprehensibly but most seductively arranged for female voice. The number is H.M.V. ASD 530.

Recent versions of some of Poulenc's music for voice, while doing nothing to outclass the composer's own recordings made with Bernac, do at least have the merit of more up-to-date engineering. Kruysen again triumphs with a varied selection of early and late songs, including *Montparnasse* and the heart-rending *Sanglots*, which are tastefully sung on Era 50.176. The accompanist is Jean-Charles Richard, a player lacking in Poulenc's special *panache*, but who is far from insensitive in other respects. Colette Herzog, a high soprano with a somewhat limited tone colour to her voice, has put on disc the first versions of the Louise de Vilmorin and Maurice Carême cycles; and her record has the added advantage of coupling Debussy's otherwise unavailable *Cinq poèmes de Baudelaire* in their entirety. These sombre works are sung here without much erotic compulsion, however, and the Poulenc songs suit her style much better. The number of this record is DGG-SLPM 138882.

PIANO MUSIC

Pianists are among the most indefatigable recording artists, and it is more difficult to reach a satisfactory selection of material in this sector. The now slightly dated contributions of Gieseking in Debussy and Ravel seem to have maintained their popularity with certain sections of the public, despite the shallow recorded tone— a factor of some importance in music so obviously dependent on richness of sonority. For those who demand his imprimatur, it is still possible to obtain his version of *Jeux d'eau* on Columbia 33CX 1761, though his records of the later Ravel works are fast becoming collectors' items. The special qualities Gieseking brought to the interpretation of French music included a fast light touch, combined with an undisputed mastery of tonal gradation, ranging from his barely audible *pianissimo* upwards. It may be agreed that his technique was of the facile rather than the transcendental variety. Where he particularly excelled was in the expression of those delicate washes of colour to be found in middle-period Debussy—witness his limpid playing of the *Images* on 33CX 1137.

The piano music of Ravel bristles with difficulties of a different kind, and an integral recording (i.e. one which offers the entire works) consequently represents a desirable possession. The Vox Box (VBX 410) by Vlado Perlemuter certainly fulfils this condition, though the playing is short of authoritative. Perlemuter cannot but be regarded as an authentic source—he is the only surviving pupil of Ravel and the author of an erudite monograph on the composer's works—but his treatment of dynamics seems oddly cavalier. Needless to say, indifference to the score was one of the weaknesses concerning which Ravel himself remained notoriously merciless. A more circumspect, and surprisingly enough a more brilliant, reading of those two embattled masterpieces, *Le Tombeau de Couperin* and *Gaspard de la nuit*, is that given by the American pianist and musicologist Charles Rosen. His version appears on 33CX 1888, and it is accompanied by a sleeve note that contains some masterly criticism of the music. The final movement of *Gaspard*—the one which depicts the evil sprite Scarbo—is executed with diabolical menace and fantastic momentum. It is in a class on its own as a performance, even though it is more than the recording can stand in places. By contrast the young Ashkenazy gives an unexpectedly subdued reading on Decca SXL 6215, which may nevertheless bring greater pleasure to those who wish to see the poetry restored to its rightful place.

A first-rate piece of programme planning, as well as playing, characterizes Artur Rubinstein's French recital on RCA-Victor (RB 6603). This offers a wellnigh perfect performance of Ravel's *Valses nobles et sentimentales*—so difficult to phrase and pedal really convincingly—as well as a scintillating selection of Poulenc pieces, including the well-known Mouvements perpétuels and two attractive Intermezzi. I unhesitatingly recommend this disc as a sampler for all who are drawn to French piano music.

Samson François is another player who commands a magnificent technique, and his account of the two Ravel concertos (Columbia SAX 2394) will take a great deal of superseding. The histrionic character of his playing is not likely to please the professors, however, as may be inferred from his Debussy recital on SAX 2469. L'Isle joyeuse is here played with superb élan. Listen also to his iridescent manner of approaching Le Danse de Puck, which is almost too brilliant and certainly too terpsichorean for most to emulate.

The account of Pour le piano, given on the same disc, also has its moments of brilliance, but the sublime Sarabande is ruined by this pianist's wilful distorting of the rhythm and slovenly habit of letting his left hand come down fractionally in advance of his right in what are meant to be unified chords. Possibly the best investment for Debussy collectors at present is the Vox Box (VBX 432) in which Peter Frankl performs the Estampes and Images along with a variety of lesser pieces. Connoisseurs will agree, however, that for the demanding Etudes one has to go to the impressive and probably definitive account by Rosen on Columbia SAX 2492. Monique Haas plays the Préludes on DGG-SLPM 138831 and 138872.

Fauré's piano music, as has already been stated, has come in for a reappraisal in the past two or three years. Evelyne Crochet's fine integral recording on two Vox collections (VBX 423 and 424) gives us the opportunity of hearing it all (except for the Ballade) in what is surely the best version we are likely to have for some time. Indeed the only other version at all easy to obtain is that by Eric Heidsieck—a pupil of Cortot and a very promising young artist— on French H.M.V. His recordings, however, omit the Barcarolles and Impromptus in favour of the Nocturnes and the Theme and Variations. Of the two versions Mlle Crochet's is the more strict and in keeping with Fauré's unassertive style. Heidsieck's approach could be termed more Chopinesque and inclined to brilliance. Both are very fine in their own ways.

It is a pity that, aside from the Rubinstein disc already described, Poulenc's piano music is presently lacking representation in the catalogues. One would have supposed his death might constitute a signal for a number of new recordings. As it is, the works for keyboard and orchestra seem much better represented than the solo works. An altogether outstanding disc, and a richly treasured possession by all who own a copy, is the coupling of the Concerto for Two Pianos with the delightful *Concert champêtre* on H.M.V. ASD 517, the former being played by the composer in company with Jacques Février, while the latter is undertaken by the harpsichordist Aimée van de Wiele. A valuable companion disc to this might be the Nonesuch cheap edition (H 71033) of the *Aubade*, combined with the two late wind sonatas.

After such a harvest of technically exacting music for the instrument, a record of Satie's piano music might come as something of an anticlimax. However, those who admire its pious (and deceptive) simplicities should acquire Aldo Ciccolini's sedate recordings of the *Nocturnes* and *Gymnopédies*, along with other miscellaneous pieces, on FCX 561, a record obtainable on E.M.I.'s Special Order list. A second recording by Ciccolini is about to be issued at the time of writing, and is rumoured to include the *Aperçus désagréables*, among other things. Jean-Joel Barbier has in the meantime made a version of the twenty short sketches, *Sports et divertissements*, but this is not generally available in this country, and would have to be imported specially. Discurio Ltd again accepts orders.

ORCHESTRAL MUSIC

There is such a large quantity of music in this category that once more the recommendations must be limited to a few. Pride of place must, of course, go to the acknowledged masterpieces of the impressionist school. Of these Debussy's *La Mer* and *L'Après-midi d'un faune*, and Ravel's suite *Daphnis and Chloë* No. 2, form the chief works. Conveniently enough, all three are contained on a really outstanding disc by the Berlin Philharmonic Orchestra under Herbert Von Karajan (Deutsche Grammophon SLPM 138923). The playing on this record almost beggars description, so fine is it. The woodwind in the Ravel play at an impossible speed, yet the articulation remains perfect. Similarly the flute in *L'Après-midi* comes nearer to suggesting the drowsy world of Pan than any other I have ever heard.

The Paris Conservatoire Orchestra cannot match the suppleness and precision of these Berlin performances, but there is a good account of Debussy's *Jeux* and orchestral *Images* by this unmistakably Gallic body under its conductor André Cluytens (Columbia SAX 2548). The same orchestra has acquitted itself very creditably in a complete set of the orchestral works of Ravel (SAX 2477–9). Among these three useful discs the second of the set, containing a delicate and poetic performance of the ballet suite *Ma Mère L'Oye*, is specially commended. The hushed and sibilant playing of the final number—*Le Jardin féerique*—admirably expresses the composer's sentiments. The Paris Orchestra plays Roussel on SAX 5251.

Ernst Ansermet is a name to conjure with when it comes to French music. Several of his discs, made with the famous Suisse Romande Orchestra, reveal the taut, animated style he practises as a conductor. The underrated *Petite Suite* of Debussy is presented on Decca SXL 2303, along with Fauré's incidental music for *Masques et Bergamasques* and *Pelléas et Mélisande*. This makes up a delightful record for those wishing to explore the lighter side to the work of these great composers. A record entirely devoted to the music of Chabrier is SXL 6168. It includes the *Suite pastorale*—transcribed from the composer's piano pieces—as well as the more rumbustious favourites. Ravel's choreographic poem, *La Valse*, appears on a miscellaneous programme with Honegger's *Pacific 231* and a symphonic study by Dukas on SXL 6065. All Ansermet's recent discs have the benefit of expert recording, though occasionally the double-basses seem uncomfortably close.

American orchestras excel at producing the opulent sound many people associate with the French repertory. The Philadelphia Orchestra, under Eugene Ormandy, oblige with a glowing account of Ravel's *Rapsodie espagnole* (SBRG 72353), sensibly coupled with Debussy's *Nocturnes*. The ensemble does not have the neatness and precision we should expect from musicians schooled in the Ansermet tradition, but the extra tonal nourishment supplies a dimension too often missing from European performances. Three attractive ballet scores may be heard on a single exciting disc made by the Paris Conservatoire Orchestra, this time under Georges Prêtre once more. These combine to give the listener a clear impression of what French composers have been able to achieve in this livelier sphere. The scores comprise Poulenc's tender *Les Biches*, Milhaud's jazz extravaganza *La Création du Monde*, and Dutilleux's deservedly popular music for Roland Petit's *Le Loup*. All are played with surpassing *éclat* on H.M.V. ASD 496.

Unfortunately there are few other orchestral works by Poulenc currently on record, though the *Stabat Mater* and Penitential Motets are combined on H.M.V. ASD 583, making use of the same performers as in the previous disc, to whom are added the voices of Régine Crespin and the Duclos Choir. This record is not an unqualified success—the chorus is weak in bass and lacks unanimity of chording—but the lyrical moments come over well. By comparison Fauré's major essay in religious music, the submissive *Requiem*, is gloriously realized by the Brasseur Choir strengthened by the services of Dietrich Fischer-Dieskau and Victoria de los Angeles. The number of this desirable issue is H.M.V. SAN 107.

OPERA

Complete opera recordings are a luxury when they run to Wagnerian length, but fortunately for French enthusiasts there are several quite short operas which make for ideal listening through the medium of the gramophone. Foremost among these is surely Ravel's enchanting *L'Enfant et les sortilèges*, which gets as fine a performance as one could reasonably wish from the Paris National Orchestra under Lorin Maazel on DGG-SLPM 138675. The same conductor seems less successful with Ravel's other brief masterpiece, *L'Heure espagnole*, though the actual playing and singing come over without serious fault. The trouble lies rather in the balance, which places the orchestra too distant in relation to the voices (DGG-SLPM 138970).

A purist might level the same complaint at Ansermet's second recording of Debussy's *Pelléas et Mélisande*, a much longer work than either of these, requiring three complete records (Decca SET-227–9). That this set has its own merits goes without saying, but there are some who feel it is less than satisfactory. Aside from the low level of the recording, certain other doubts arise. Erna Spoorenberg does not seem entirely at home in the language (though it must be remembered that Mary Garden, the originator of this part, was English and not French), while George London seems too substantial for Golaud in what, after all, is the most etherealized of all operas. The veteran Maurane is exquisite as Pelléas, however, and listeners will probably have to wait a long time before a superior version turns up.

A most worth-while undertaking was the committing to disc of Poulenc's only large-scale opera, *Les Dialogues des Carmélites*. This moving work contains most of the best qualities we attach to the composer, and represents his strongest bid for major stature. E.M.I.'s Special List offers this opera on FALP 523–5 in what is a first-class performance and recording. Crespin and Denise Duval head a splendid cast.

CHAMBER MUSIC

Though Franck is usually the first name to be advanced in discussions of French chamber music, the claims of Fauré deserve to be taken even more seriously. It is therefore all the more discreditable that he should be so sparsely represented on disc in this capacity. However, the two violin sonatas (the first of which actually preceded Franck's very similar work) are performed with passionate conviction by Christian Ferras and Pierre Barbizet on French H.M.V. ASDF 856. These artists form an irresistible duo, caring more for the spirit of the music than for any pedantries associated with it. Their playing of the *Scherzo* from the first sonata should win over the most sceptical music lover. Similarly lavish praise is invited by the magnificent account Tortelier gives of the two cello sonatas on Erato 50101. No one who cares at all for Fauré should miss either of these two discs. Records of the composer's piano quartets and quintets are much more difficult to come by. The second of the quartets—the one in G minor, Op. 45—has been recorded in stereo by the Festival Quartet, but the record has so far not become available in Britain. Earlier performances of the other works for piano and strings include versions by Thyssens-Valentin (who was Fauré's editor in the piano works) and by Emil Gilels on the Russian MK label. These performances are some years old, however, and what we presently need is a modern recording embracing the whole canon of chamber works, including the still infrequently heard quartet for strings alone which Fauré wrote at the very end of his life.

217

Debussy's chamber music offers the listener a wider range of choice. The 'lunar' Cello Sonata is given a truly great reading by Rostropovitch and Britten on Decca SWL 8503, while the Violin Sonata (a much lesser work) is again catered for by Ferras and Barbizet on H.M.V. Valois valuably groups the three sonatas on MB 938, together with the flute solo, Syrinx.

A Ravel disc by the same firm (MB 969) brings together the rarely heard Sonata for Violin and Cello and the better known work for violin and piano. Once again these records maintain a high standard of recording and performance, though of the two the Debussy disc is possibly the better. Neither quite aspires to the rich elegance discernible in the Melos Ensemble's playing of Ravel's Introduction and Allegro for Harp Septet, Debussy's Sonata for Viola, Flute and Harp, and two pieces in similar vein by Roussel and Guy-Ropartz (Oiseau-Lyre SOL 60048). This last record would undoubtedly be my choice for a stimulating beginning to a collection of French chamber music. The string quartets of Debussy and Ravel—both masterly compositions and very frequently recorded—still await their definitive versions, though the combined performance by the Vlach Quartet on Supraphon SUAST 50040 should afford temporary satisfaction.

Poulenc's chamber works have been eclipsed by his more popular vocal and orchestral compositions; but it would be a pity if the collector were to neglect his late, elegaic Oboe Sonata, included with its more jocular companion work, the Clarinet Sonata, on Nonesuch H 71033. The Wind Sextet is also available in a version featuring the composer himself at the piano on SBRG 72133.

INDEXES

Persons

Works